THE SENATOR
FROM
SLAUGHTER COUNTY

by
HARRY M. CAUDILL

Introduction by
MARGARET RIPLEY WOLFE

The Jesse Stuart Foundation
Ashland, Kentucky
1997

THE SENATOR
FROM
SLAUGHTER COUNTY

Copyright © 1973 by Harry M. Caudill

Library of Congress Cataloging-in-Publication Data

Caudill, Harry M., 1922-
    The Senator from Slaughter County / by Harry Caudill ; edited with an introduction by Margaret Ripley Wolfe.
        p.   cm.
    Originally published: Boston : Little, Brown, 1973.
    ISBN 0-945084-66-8
    I. Wolfe, Margaret Ripley, 1947-   .   II. Title.
PS3553.A9S46   1997
813' .54--dc21   97-31650
                                                                          CIP

Published By:
The Jesse Stuart Foundation
P.O. Box 391   Ashland, KY 41114
(606) 329-5232
1997

THE SENATOR
FROM
SLAUGHTER COUNTY

Illustrated by
Jim Marsh

INTRODUCTION

A decade separated the publication of Harry M. Caudill's *The Senator from Slaughter County*, the second of his three novels, and *Night Comes to the Cumberlands: A Biography of a Depressed Area*, his first and most important work. The release in 1963 of *Night Comes to the Cumberlands* in tandem with Harry's public-relations skills turned his home and office into a clearing house for the region. Although a renewed interest in Appalachia had already begun to develop prior to the publication of *Night Comes to the Cumberlands*, this book served as a catalyst for the parade of political candidates, troops of VISTA volunteers, and waves of photographers and writers that commenced during the early sixties and continued into the early seventies. From around the country and around the globe, curious visitors and investigative journalists poured into eastern Kentucky; and Harry and his wife, Anne Frye Caudill, routinely gave what they themselves eventually termed "the grand poverty tour." In this manner, the Caudills focused national and international attention on the ravages of both underground and strip mining and on the plight of downtrodden mountaineers in Appalachia.

As the Caudills welcomed literally hundreds of visitors to Letcher County, Kentucky, not infrequently providing them with bed and board, they managed somehow to honor their family responsibilities and maintain a successful law practice. If Harry became "Mr. Appalachia," as some observers claimed, Anne surely qualified as the "Mrs." This marriage represented a true partnership, a successful union, and a source of considerable happiness to both husband and wife. Harry would eventually be the author of ten books, but during the most challenging and tumultuous decade of his life, with Anne's assistance and support, he found time to write and publish three new volumes, *Dark Hills to Westward: The Saga of Jenny Wiley* (1969), *My Land Is Dying* (1973), and *The Senator from Slaughter County* (1973).

In the public arena of the 1960s and 1970s, *Night Comes to the Cumberlands* defined Harry M. Caudill, casting him as crusading environmentalist. Although he relished this role and courageously carried the banner, he was at the same time a complex man with many facets of personality. His life began on May 3, 1922, in Letcher County, Kentucky, near Whitesburg, when his parents Cro Carr Caudill and Martha Victoria Blair Caudill, welcomed him into the world; and it abruptly ended by his own hand at his home near Whitesburg on November 29, 1990. He made the decision to halt the suffering of a body wracked by the ravages of a debilitating disease and the pain and discomfort of wounds and illnesses that still haunted him from his days as a World War II infantry soldier in Italy. During his sixty-eight years, Harry M. Caudill lived a full and remarkable life. He was a devoted son to his parents and a loving husband and the father of three children; a successful lawyer, a Kentucky state legislator and public servant, and always a civic-minded citizen engaged in the political fray; a prolific author, a university professor, a much-sought-after lecturer and media figure, and a public intellectual. He was a hero to those who loved and admired him and a pariah to those who did not.

Because of the serious issues he championed, he was sometimes described as "God's Angry Man." Nonetheless, Harry possessed a well honed and highly developed sense of humor. His skills as a keen observer of the human condition combined with his abilities as an orator to render him a magnificent storyteller. Not infrequently his tales revolved around Kentucky politics. Indeed, his first national publication, "How an Election Was Bought and Sold," appeared in Harper's Magazine. He did not use his own byline; the author was identified only as a Kentucky legislator. In the October 1960 article, Caudill described in graphic detail laced with humor what had been required for his recent victory. Just about every major group had to be paid off in one way or another—from the church deacons and PTA ladies to the so-called "vote haulers" and the drunks. In fact, this was the principal reason that Caudill, who served three terms in the Kentucky legislature, decided to cease running for public office and turn instead to writing and speaking about issues that particularly concerned him. As he himself admitted in *Slender Is the Thread: Tales from a Country Law Office* (1987), "Most lawyers come from political families and have heard much talk of elections and political spoils. Thus their professional lives may be extensions and fulfillments of early political ambitions." He acknowledged that "was true to some extent" for him. "By his mid-thirties," however, he "had concluded that politics was too costly a game and should be abandoned so some money could be saved."

Harry could denounce certain politicians in venomous terms and at the same time not despair of the political process. Although he often rejected the practices of the established political order, he did not abandon it. Throughout much of his adult life, he participated in Democratic politics at the local, state, and national level. He was a child of the Great Depression, and it is not surprising that in his politics he resembled a New Deal Democrat. He had no problem with capitalism per se—he himself liked the good life—but he thought capitalists should be accountable for their actions and respectful of the land and natural resources. Whether writing the muckraking nonfiction for which he is best known, telling his tales as a country lawyer, or dabbling in fiction, he never strayed too far from politics.

Caudill actually wrote three novels, *Dark Hills to Westward: The Saga of Jenny Wiley*, based on the real-life story of a pioneer woman who was taken captive by the Indians; *The Senator from Slaughter County*, for which Dr. B. F. Wright of Letcher County served as a model; and *Lester's Progress* (1986), which reflected Caudill's disgust with the welfare system. Although critics and readers never warmed to Caudill the fiction writer as they did to Caudill the master of expose, *The Senator from Slaughter County* nevertheless stands as a powerful statement on rural politics. It is as revealing of county powerbrokers in the twentieth century as Edwin O'Connor's *The Last Hurrah* is of big-city machines. O'Connor's novel drew its inspiration from the career of urban boss James Michael Curley of Boston. It had been released by Little, Brown and Company in 1956, later the publisher of Caudill's

The Senator from Slaughter County. O'Connor claimed that Roosevelt and the New Deal were the undoing of bossism, at least in the case of Frank Skeffington, his fictional Boston mayor. Caudill, however, credited the seemingly bottomless coffers of the New Deal and the political skills of the wily Roosevelt with the rise and success of his principal character, Dr. Thomas Jefferson (Tom) Bonham of Slaughter County. Whether the New Deal destroyed the boss system or strengthened it has been duly considered by urban historians and political scientists alike. More of them seem to be inclined toward Caudill's interpretation than O'Connor's.

With *The Senator from Slaughter County*, Caudill is truly in his element as raconteur par excellence, a diligent student of state politics and human behavior, and a narrator intimately acquainted with the finer points of electioneering in the mountain counties. "I had the good fortune," Harry wrote in *The Mountain, the Miner, and the Lord and Other Tales from a Country Law Office* (1980), "to be born in 1922 in Letcher County, Kentucky . . . The Kentucky hills were a fascinating place in which to grow to manhood." Harry's father demonstrated a great enthusiasm for county and state politics as practiced in the Bluegrass State; and his son, from his earliest years, had more than a passing familiarity with the political process. A 1929 photograph taken in Cro Carr Caudill's office during his tenure as county court clerk shows young Harry clad in overalls and perched on his father's knee.

A coal miner turned elected official, Cro Carr Caudill introduced his son to the world of politics Kentucky style. Having lost his left arm in a mining accident, the elder Caudill managed to win election to the position of county court clerk in 1925 and again in 1929. The candidate's strategy had included a bid for the sympathy vote. He hired a woodcarver to turn out hundreds of wooden bird-like figurines with the right wing outstretched and the left conspicuously missing. The "one-winged crow" later served as local campaign manager in Letcher County for several prominent Kentucky politicians. When still a teenager, Harry accompanied his father on his rounds, sometimes serving as Cro's driver. He listened to the plotting of insiders, witnessed first-hand the rough-and-tumble campaigns, and warmed to the oratory of the likes of Albert B. "Happy" Chandler and Alben Barkley.

Following World War II, Harry M. Caudill completed his law degree at the University of Kentucky and established his practice in Whitesburg. For twenty years he served as personal attorney to "Doc" Wright, Letcher County's political potentate. At Harry's request, Doc shared his winning formula: "I don't pay much attention to the good people among the voters. They will generally split about even between the candidates. I go after the trash vote. The man who gets the trash vote wins the election!" As Caudill explained in *Slender Is the Thread: Tales from a Country Law Office* (1987), Doc recognized that the citizenry was gullible, greedy, and selfish. "The remarkable thing about the common people," he observed, "is that they're so damned common."

It is fitting that the Jesse Stuart Foundation reprint this volume, for it merits further consideration. Harry M. Caudill's insightful fictional account of a coal company doctor turned political powerhouse is as helpful in understanding Kentucky counties as historical works devoted to them, because fiction often contains as much truth as history. For the skeleton and sinew of local politics, look to Robert Ireland's *Aristocrats All: The Politics of County Government in Antebellum Kentucky (1970)*, *The County in Kentucky History* (1976), and *Little Kingdoms: The Counties of Kentucky, 1850-1891* (1977). For the flesh and blood of it all, go to Harry M. Caudill's *The Senator from Slaughter County.*

Harry's use of the salty language of the folk and the straight-forward vernacular of the politicians is not designed to spare tender sensibilities. At the time that he wrote this book, neither Harry nor hardly anyone else in America anticipated the emotion-ridden advent of multiculturalism nor the zeal of the footsoldiers for political correctness. Nonetheless, for those who like a good read as well as a good lesson in nepotism and patronage; for enthusiasts of politics practiced with the chicanery that may not be unique to Kentucky but is so familiar in the Commonwealth; and for serious students of rural politics in the twentieth-century South, *The Senator from Slaughter County* awaits them.

Margaret Ripley Wolfe

Margaret Ripley Wolfe, professor of history and senior research fellow at East Tennessee State University, is an American social historian whose research focuses on the South and Southern Appalachia. Her most recent book, *Daughters of Canaan: A Saga of Southern Women,* was published by the University Press of Kentucky in 1995. Wolfe is currently conducting research for a biography of Harry M. Caudill.

CHAPTER
1

In the beginning, it was all a great swamp.

The dark water of the shallow sea was fringed by a stinking tangle of gigantic ferns and club mosses. Overgrown fungi and soft, shallow-rooted trees grew on saturated hummocks and along the steaming shore. Daily cloudbursts were dissipated by a blazing sun and in endless layers the obscenely rank vegetation sank into the morass. The water boiled with bubbles of gas from the rotting plants. The litter accumulated to great depths, then, as the climate changed, was covered by broad and deep banks of mud washed down from higher ground. The weight of these overriding strata and unthinkable reaches of time turned the organic deposits into coal and, trapped far below the coal beds, huge quantities of petroleum and natural gas. Three hundred million years later, forested mountains covered the mineral riches left by the swamp.

The man who moved so resolutely along the narrow trail bore an air of competence and assurance. His step was brisk and his dark, narrow eyes mirrored alertness and cunning.

He was tall and slender, with long, almost delicate fingers. His feet were shod in homemade boots that fell soundlessly on the forest mold. His hair was black, and his complexion betrayed the Cherokee blood of his grandmother. His nose was thin and imperiously arched.

The slight scowl at the corners of his mouth and eyes betokened impatience and quickness of temper, but caution was apparent in his relentless scouting of the land. Sight, smell, and hearing combined to measure every canebrake and grove and each breeze that blew through them.

He wore a shirt and breeches of gray homespun and a jacket of fringed deerskin that fell almost to his knees and was gathered by a thong at the waist. His head was covered by a broad-brimmed, round hat of black felt. A foot-long butcher knife was sheathed at his side and a powder horn and shot pouch hung under his left arm. The ungainly, .41 caliber silver-mounted rifle in his right hand was five feet long.

John Bonham was of the fourth generation to bear his name in the New World. His great-grandfather had supported Cromwell and the Commonwealth from Edgehill to the Restoration and found England unbearable under James II. He escaped to North Carolina with little more than his life and family and a steadfast distrust of authority. His descendants had crept westward with the painfully advancing frontier, a people of log cabins, endless Indian wars, fiddle tunes and strong opinions.

The year was 1789, and Bonham was thirty-five. As a militiaman, he had fought in half a score of battles and campaigns against the British in the South. At Kings Mountain he had been shot "square through" the abdomen with a .70 caliber musketball. A surgeon wrapped a handkerchief around the end of a ramrod, soaked it with rum and used it as a swab to cleanse the hole. That he survived surprised no one more than himself, and the fledgling republic had rewarded him with fertile western land—provided only that he go and wrest it from the Indians. On long hunts he had scouted many valleys in search of the combination of rich soil, abundant game and remoteness from neighbors which he so strongly cherished.

On the foremost horse sat Sarah Bonham, two years younger than her husband and the mother of five. She was a handsome, diligent woman with a broad, sturdy face and sure, steady hands. She carried a baby in her arms, repeatedly lowering her face over the child to protect him from impeding vines and branches. She had been happy in the valley from whence they came, and her sad eyes mirrored her reluctance to move into the wilderness. She had coveted a little education for her children and was dismayed by the realization that for a generation at least her descendants would know neither books nor teachers.

The second horse was ridden by twenty-year-old Mary Crawford. She and her family had been "cleared" from the Scottish hills by a landlord eager to graze sheep on their farm, and she had reached South Carolina as an indentured servant bound to seven years of labor in the household of a planter. She had fled to the frontier, attaching herself to a band of returning backwoodsmen who had carried bundles of pelts to coastal trading posts. Sarah had taken her into her cabin, and the girl nursed a slender hope that in the West she might someday find escape from the age-old afflictions of drudgery and poverty.

The two Bonham girls rode with her, five-year-old Susan

and six-year-old Elizabeth. The boys were John, who had just turned nine, and Isham, a man-child of twelve. They brought up the rear with Black Adam, a slave. He had been bought with money from the sale of the Bonham farm. He carried a rifle and looked to the western hills to diminish the ever-present threat of the torrid tobacco fields.

It was late in March and a brisk breeze stirred the few remaining dried leaves of the forest and shook the clustered ferns that grew by mossy boulders and fringed the murmuring creeks. Gigantic tulip trees lifted their tufted tops a hundred feet above the trail. Colossal sycamores leaned their silvery branches far out across creeks and rivers. Unblemished and ancient beeches, oaks and hickories mixed with dark green pines and hemlocks, thickets of impenetrable rhododendron and laurel and groves of stately chestnuts. The forest covered the Appalachians like the folds of a mighty carpet, broken only by the bottom lands with their tangled growths of wild cane.

In such a setting and for a people like these, hunger was unthinkable. The hills rustled and fluttered with wildlife. Strings of turkeys and grouse rose from thickets. Squirrels chattered from treetops. Wolves howled along the craggy ridges, and foxes barked inquisitively from behind trees and fallen logs. Buffaloes bellowed in the canebrakes and herds of deer fled at their approach. Ending their hibernation, thousands of black bears crept from their hilltop lairs and hunted for food.

The creeks and rivers teemed with frogs and turtles, bass, perch and catfish, and baskets of mussels could be raked out of the shoals.

But even without flesh or fish there was an abundance of food. The fallen mast of oak, chestnut, hickory, walnut, hazelnut, and beech piled up inches deep. And in the ground there were many varieties of edible roots. Except in spells of wintry storm when the earth and creeks froze deep and hard and snow lay in drifts, even a novice at woodcraft could find abundant fare.

For nine days the little caravan followed the deepening game trace to the west and north, and then for a week they camped and rested under a long, deep cliff. The sandstone shelter was dry and clean, and a spring of cold water bubbled out of the sandy floor. It would be remembered as the "rockhouse," and the wild stream that tumbled below it would come to be called Rockhouse Creek.

Early in April, they left the cliff and moved off down the creek. They ascended a ridge and passed through a low gap into a valley dark with the trunks and branches of huge oaks. Bonham led them along the murmuring stream until he made the discovery that would give a name to the valley. He whistled when he stepped across a mossy log and saw the bones strewn beside the trail. The hunter had been tall and strong and strands of red hair lay by the grinning skull. The rotting jacket had been shredded by scavengers gnawing on the ribs and a rusty buckle lay by the broken rifle. A triangular hole shaped like the cutting edge of a Shawnee tomahawk gashed the upper forehead. Adam dug a shallow grave and covered the bones with a couple of feet of loam. The grisly discovery gave the stream its name, which would one day appear on maps as Dead Man Creek.

That night was an uneasy one. The men slept beside

loaded rifles, and axes lay within easy reach of the two women. But the surly dogs guarded them well and the night passed without incident.

The next day they passed the mouth of a turbulent tributary flowing in from the south. On a little flat lay a heap of firewood and a mound of cold ashes.

Many hunters had camped there and for several days. Bonham turned up the Camp Branch for five miles, following a trail worn by centuries of migrating hooves. Where the stream ended in a windswept gap, they climbed up and crossed into another valley that pointed almost straight south. In this new watershed a little way down from the wellspring of the stream, the smooth trunk of a huge beech bore the old and deep carved initials of a long vanished hunter, "T. Finn 1778." For seven miles Finn's Fork led down through a widening valley until it surged into the gray waters of Indian River. John Bonham had been there twice before, and in the pale spring sunlight, he appraised the land with satisfaction.

To the south and north, the valley floor was walled by long straight ridges 2,000 feet high. Points ran out of them like the teeth of a giant comb, dwindling into gentle flats that gradually faded into rich bottom land. Midway between crest and base, the slopes were marked by a broad bench or flat above which immense limestone crags jutted upward and out like the walls of a titanic fortress. The decaying limestone had sweetened the soil so that the tulip trees or "poplars" that soared up from the hills were gargantuan. They exceeded in girth and height all others he had encountered in his long rambles through the southern mountains. Above the limestone cliffs, the hills rose almost sheer, cloaked with pine and laurel to the base of other immense rock ledges. These were of dark brown sandstone which wind and rain had carved into fantastic shapes—giant towers, gracefully arched bridges, and round, precariously balanced boulders.

The valley floor was three hundred yards wide, and the soil of the level bottom was deep and black and rich with dissolved lime. Ancient game trails led from shallow fords through the canebrakes into the coves between the ridges. A primordial stillness brooded over the empty immensity, broken by an occasional whisper of sound when the wind carried up the gentle murmur of the river.

The ridge to the south was known to hunters and trappers as the Big Laurel Mountain. Thirty years earlier, an explorer named Christopher Gist had discovered "fine sea-coal" near the base of the other, and wanderers had seen black lumps in the turbulent creeks that tumbled out of its hollows. It had come to be known as the Stone Coal Ridge.

Here at the mouth of Finn's Fork, the little caravan ended its journey. The letters patent in Bonham's saddlebag entitled him to "take-up" one thousand acres, to be his land and that of "his heirs and assigns forever." Here he had found his land and his destiny.

A broad, rounded knoll overlooked a sweeping bend of the river in which stalks of corn from an "Indian old field" stood black and rotten amid a growth of new cane. They made a camp under a cliff and throughout the spring cleared the cane from the deep sandy loam and planted rows of corn, beans, squash, potatoes and tobacco. When the crops were in, growing pens were built to protect the livestock against bears and wolves. Then, in midsummer, work was begun on the house. Men, women and children toiled together at whatever task was at hand—clearing out the cane, planting, felling trees, hewing logs, cooking or hunting. There was no room for the shirker or fainthearted, nor for social niceties that treated females as weak or inferior.

The cabin was raised on the knoll above the river, and the first round of logs that rested close to the ground were hewed with broadaxes from the trunks of giant black walnuts. The dark, oily wood was almost imperishable, and John Bonham was building for permanence. The subsequent rounds were of yellow poplar, twenty-four inches wide and eight inches thick. Two rooms joined by an eight-foot "dog-trot" rose sixteen feet to form two stories topped with a snug loft and roofed with smooth chestnut boards. The rooms were square, twenty-two feet on a side, and secured by two immense chimneys laid up out of thin shards of hard limestone. The doorways were low and broad, and the heavy portals were fashioned of white oak hinged and bolted with hickory. Opposite each door, a yard-square window admitted air and light when the massive oaken panels were swung outward. The cavernous fireplaces opened on wide hearths. Six loopholes were cut upstairs and down commanding with rifle fire a hundred yards in every direction.

For more than a year, the house required every moment that could be spared from other tasks. When Fort Bonham, as John called it, was finished and crude beds, chairs and a table had been fashioned, all experienced a little sense of relief and relaxation.

The fields widened as the house grew. The feared red savages attacked the fort only once, on a misty morning of an Indian summer day in 1792. A dozen Shawnees in leather breeches and outlandishly colored trade shirts whooped and shrieked as they poured bullets and flaming arrows against the gray walls. But their assault was disastrous, and two of their number were left behind for Adam to bury. One of the dead carried an ornate pipe tomahawk which John Bonham hung above his fireplace and from which Adam occasionally smoked a handful of tobacco. After that, the place was left in peace, and war whoops never sounded again along Indian River.

As the years passed, John and Adam built a small beehive furnace beneath the limestone cliffs, "churned" iron ore out of the rusty rocks and with the hot fire from hard maple charcoal "drew" iron which they fashioned into plows, axes, nails, hinges, and even rifles. They boiled water from saline licks for the bushels of salt required for dinner table and smokehouse. They obtained sulfur by boiling water from "powder springs" and mixed it with charcoal and saltpeter to form a crude but deadly gunpowder. And always they cleared the land of the dense and oppressive forest, sawed firewood, hunted and fished. Their toil was rewarded as Bonham's became the most impressive farm for a hundred miles in either direction along the Appalachian frontier.

And steadily the frontier withered and died. Four years after the cabin was completed, a new state was admitted into the Union and the upper reaches of Indian River lay within its borders. A county of ten thousand square miles was created with a seat and primitive courthouse a hundred miles from Finn's Fork.

John went back to the old, eastern settlements and brought back a surveyor to define the boundaries of his land and map it for registration under the title laws. Nor was he a moment too soon in acquiring his seal, for crude little mud-daubed cabins were springing up like ugly, oversized fungi. George Day settled with his wife and four children on the Rockhouse Creek and Elijah Brown built a low hovel on Camp Fork. Callihans, Simpsons, Smiths and fifty other families pushed into the valleys within a thirty-mile radius of Fort Bonham. The people bred prodigiously, matured quickly, married early and new waves of settlers washed up the creeks, then into the narrowing forks and their ever-more-constricted branches. The cleared patches widened, the game thinned, and many of the young pushed on toward the West, dragged by a lust to keep up with the savage edge of the frontier.

Like a biblical patriarch, John Bonham begat sons and daughters. First on the body of his patient and fruitful Sarah he sired a round dozen, all of whom survived in a turbulent tangle of male and female boisterousness. Then as Sarah aged and cooled, he turned to Mary Crawford and got her with child at their first coupling. Though his lawfully wedded wife took umbrage at the arrangement, she served as mid-wife when the child was born and helped raise it and the seven that followed. The cabin grew as rooms were added to contain the new humanity, and the Bonham tribe grew up as a close-knit and loyal clan who looked to John, the aging patriarch, for guidance and law.

As they came of age the young found spouses, and though some left for the West, most took their procreative instincts to new cabins on nearby creeks where new families were quickly spawned. When Sarah died of old age in 1829 she left a staggering number of descendants. They brought a Baptist preacher for a proper funeral and ninety-two children, grand-children and great-grandchildren looked at her passive face within the homemade coffin.

John lived eleven years longer. The government pensioned him as an ex-soldier during the last three decades of his life, and he used the gold coins to buy land from settlers who were moving on to Illinois and Missouri. He died of a fever on a spring morning in 1840, fifty-one years after he un-packed his mules and made his camp on Indian River at the mouth of Finn's Fork. The faithful Mary Crawford, still strong and active at seventy-one, was at his side when he gasped his last, and she sounded a blast on a gnarled ram's horn trum-pet to warn his descendants that he was gone.

The sons of Isham and John fashioned a coffin out of an immense hollowed log and he was buried by the side of Sarah, a dozen feet from the final resting place of Black Adam. His issue or "generation" by the two loyal women trooped in across the hills from a score of valleys to mourn his passing. His stamp was on all of them in their long slender hands, slim bodies, brownish complexions and, above all, in their high imperious noses. As Isham remarked, "It seems like no matter who you cross a Bonham with, the young'uns always turn out to be full-blooded Bonhams!"

There were one hundred and thirty-one descendants al-together when the ponderous coffin was lowered into the ground and a rock carved with his name was set up over the grave. They scattered to their various and varying pursuits, but for generations a mystic attachment would bind them and their descendants to Old John's place, to the grim, tall angular cabin in the valley under the beetling cliffs, and he would live on in their common memory as "Old John-of-All," the patriarch and progenitor of the hill Bonhams.

CHAPTER
2

When Isham was twenty, he grew weary of the narrow, twisting valley of Indian River with its gloomy cliffs. He pricked up his ears when he heard men talk of the "open country" to the east and west of the mountains. His discontent was fanned by an encounter with a new settler named Sam Runyon. Isham was hunting deer on the Camp Fork of Rockhouse Creek when he heard the faint, rhythmic strokes of an ax. Following the sound, he found a fresh clearing near the old campfire. The man who hewed and notched the logs he had rolled down from the hill was short and thickset. Isham studied him through the dark curtain of a young hemlock and was impressed by the diminutive newcomer's frank and unpretentious face, his sure, quick steps, and self-assured bearing.

Isham came out of the forest and hailed the stranger and through a long afternoon helped him raise the heavy slabs of wood into place. He and Runyon liked one another from the beginning, and he returned on other days to assist his new friend until the cabin stood neat and tightly roofed. He watched with pleasure as Runyon's small deft fingers hewed and carved and sawed to bring beds, benches, tables and chairs out of logs of hard black walnut and smooth straight poplar. Sam and Esther Runyon and their six children lived amid comforts to be found nowhere else in the valley of Indian River.

Runyon had moved up from Georgia where vast open fields were bordered by immense stands of pine and oak, and the sun blistered the earth and its creatures with a fury unknown in the cool glades of the Appalachian hills. He told of small armies of black men and women who toiled to plant, cultivate, and harvest huge crops of cotton, to clear the forests for new fields and to raise brick mansions for their masters. He frowned with bitter distaste as he remembered the slaves and the horror of their existence and spoke with hatred of a ruling class that would manacle and flog their fellow creatures. He had been a skilled carpenter and brickmaker with a decent market for his skills but had moved hundreds of miles to the north and west to put his children beyond the sights and sounds of human bondage. He taught them to hate and fear slavery as an unsurpassable evil.

But even as he listened to Runyon's denunciation of the South and its slaveholders, Isham's mind formed a different opinion. He felt himself drawn as by a magnet to this glamorous world so very different from his own backwoods. One day he disappeared into the forest and was not seen, nor heard from, by anyone on Indian River for twenty-five years. He shouldered an ax when he left Fort Bonham and told his mother he would fetch wood for the fire that burned always on the hearth. When he did not return, searchers found the ax sunk deep into a stump beside the trail and surmised that he had followed in the footsteps of many others and gone west.

Sarah was an old woman when he returned, as he had gone, without warning. The trail down Finn's Fork had long since lost its covering of black loam, and she heard the clang of iron horseshoes on the naked stones. When she looked up from her rocking chair, she saw a strange cavalcade bearing down upon her. The man in front rode a magnificent brown horse and was dressed with an elegance of cloth and tailoring totally alien to the hills. Sarah had hoped always for the return of her firstborn, and as the man drew near and she studied the face beneath the broad hat brim, a cry escaped her. "O Gracious Lord," she whispered, "it's Isham."

And Isham it was, come back at last to the remote valley beneath the towering walls of rock and their mantles of rhododendron and pine. But he did not return alone and empty-handed as he was when he went forth. The tall, handsome woman who rode down the trail behind him was his wife, and the procession that stretched out to the bend in the trail was their children and their slaves.

Isham had been to Georgia and that he had prospered was apparent. He never talked much about the years of his absence, but in time his parents learned that for a while, at least, he had been an overseer of a large and prosperous plantation. He had driven a multitude of blacks to profitable labor in expanding fields and had risen to become a land-owner himself. The eleven slaves who followed him back to the hills were a part of the wealth his diligence had earned.

Whatever it was that brought Isham back to the hills he kept to himself, but his return was total and wholehearted. He bought land from families who were moving on toward Illinois and Missouri, and patented from the state other boundaries that still lay unclaimed in the public domain. And he bought and bred slaves so that the number of his black chattels increased with his lands. He enclosed his cleared fields with fences of split rails and grew crops of tobacco and corn. The grain was distilled into whiskey which he stored in barrels of charred white oak. In the late autumn his slaves built huge rafts and floated cargoes of tobacco, whiskey, and hides down the river for sale in the growing towns along the Ohio and its tributaries. His slaves built him a spacious L-shaped house of crude red bricks which they fired at the site, and joined with mortar slaked from the limestone cliffs. The house stood near the mouth of Bonham's Branch, a twisting tributary of Indian River and a mile above Fort Bonham.

The confident and competent wife who bore his children had been used to more congenial surroundings, but she accepted the role of a backwoods wife without complaint. She had some education and read books and newspapers that came to her through the uncertain mails. She kept Isham's accounts in order and ran his household with frugality and stern discipline. She scourged dawdling slaves with the whip that hung on her kitchen wall, and her tongue could flay as deftly as her lash. She would be remembered for generations as "Ole Miss," the name by which in their dread they referred to her.

Margaret Strother Bonham loved the land with a passion and caused her husband, and later her sons, to buy huge tracts of it. She spent long hours in solitary wanderings by mossy cliffs and fern-grown streams. She loved, especially, the deep coves and their brooding, giant trees. She told her children again and again, "Take good care of the land and the land will take good care of you!" If she ever yearned for the red hills of Georgia, she suppressed all inclination to speak of it.

The labor of his slaves and his expanding lands gave Isham impressive wealth for his time and place, and the scores of Bonhams and the families into which they married looked to him as their leader and counselor. He used his prestige amongst them astutely so that he became the dominant political power in all the upper reaches of Indian River.

In 1835 the state legislature created a new county embracing 420 square miles of extremely rugged territory, "including the Big Laurel Mountain and Stone Coal Ridge, together with all their foothills, and extending from the prime source of the Indian River with the meanders of same downstream for a distance of sixty miles." Joshua Slaughter was the governor and Slaughter County was named in his honor. The seat was to be called Blacksville in memory of Colonel Nathan Black, a hero of the Indian wars. Of course, nothing approaching a town or hamlet existed anywhere within this new entity of three thousand people, but a commission was appointed by the governor to "locate and lay out" the future town.

Isham was designated as chairman of the commission, and he and two other slaveowners selected a broad bottom where the ridges stood far apart and low spurs faded into gentle knolls. Here a log courthouse was built, a single room thirty-two feet on a side and fitted out with benches for jurors and spectators and an elevated bench for the circuit judge. His Honor would come for court twice a year, in April and October, and the county's first government provided him with a sturdy log jail or "bullpen" for the keeping of such miscreants as might come before him.

Isham used the power of the Bonham votes—and some of his own dollars deftly spent—to elect himself sheriff of the county. Despite the relentless hemorrhage of people to the west, the clannishness of the Bonhams—their abiding affinity for "the blood"—maintained Old John's eldest son in a position of power as long as he chose to exercise it.

But there were some who despised Isham Bonham and anyone who supported him. Sam Runyon, the friend of his youth, spoke to Isham only once after he came home. When the slaveholder visited him and extended his hand in greeting, Runyon spat with distaste and turned his back. "I am not," he said with utter finality, "a friend to any man who keeps other men in bondage!"

As Isham grew old and his lands and influence widened, he was troubled always by the people on the Camp Fork who looked at him and his with contempt in their cool, steady eyes.

CHAPTER
3

Isham and Margaret were a compatible pair, and he was nearly fifty when she bore him the last of a dozen children. The older ones remembered the plantations of Georgia with their wide fields, spacious mansions and toiling slaves. Three of them viewed the valley with utter distaste, and when they came of age, went back to their relatives in the bustling South. But the twins Reuben and Robert heard still another drummer when they wandered the faint paths that wound over the bristling ridges and along the wild tumbling creeks. The valleys were too narrow and the slave-worked South too effete for their taste. When they were twenty, they received new rifles and some money from their father and a motherly hug and kiss from the imperturbable "Ole Miss," then disappeared forever through the rocky gap where the sun set. Years later a few letters reported them in Oregon, alive and prosperous, the progenitors of a new tribe of Bonhams on the cold shores of the Pacific.

The others were content to remain behind and grow up with Slaughter County.

Most of the original settlers who built cabins along Indian River and its tributary creeks had come as members of close-knit clans. This was the traditional manner in which the frontier was shoved westward, and the threat of Indian raids made it essential in the Appalachians. Only a few were willing to go alone, as John Bonham's household had done, into a tangled wilderness where ambush and torture were ever-present threats.

When a new decade arrived in 1860, people of the Bonham blood were to be found in every part of the fledgling county, from tiny, dusty Blacksville to the head of Indian River and along all the deep, tree-choked valleys which fed the river for the first sixty miles of its length. And all who bore the blood and carried the Bonham genes were part of a larger clan or confederation of clans—that bound them by compelling bonds to a leadership that centered where the first of their name had built his cabin. In Slaughter County there were many clans and interclan affiliations, but the Bonham consortium was dominant and overriding. Those within it gained a strength and assurance from it and, not infrequently, people who were not "connected" with the Bonhams felt an envious hostility to those who were.

In the spring of 1861, the war so long deferred came to Slaughter County. It came at first, as it came to the rest of the nation, quietly and amid disbelief as communities and individuals pondered the reality of secession. Then came reports of the first battles, and attitudes hardened as men chose sides. The interminable years of endless argument in forums and around cabin hearths were to end at last, and even as they feared the future, men sighed with relief that at last and somehow the issue would be resolved.

Benjamin Bonham lived at the mouth of Muddy Fork in a gaunt, two-story house, the boards of which had been sawed and nailed together by the slaves who huddled in tiny cabins a hundred yards away. He was a drover who had prospered buying and raising sheep and cattle which he herded to markets in South Carolina and southern Tennessee. He believed with never a doubt in the divine right of white men to own black men, and embraced the cause of the South with a fanaticism that would have done credit to the slave trader. He had heard the strains of "Dixie" in rebel towns and had seen the new officers, in their gray uniforms, marching columns of raw but eager troops, and he resolved to lead a company of Bonhams and their kin to the battles looming over the Virginia horizon.

Ben Bonham bore the genetic imprint of Old John in every line of his face and form. His keen piercing eyes bored like gimlets, and his erect bearing and stern voice inspired confidence among the wild hill men who "heard tell" that soldiers were being recruited for the Confederacy. And they came, more than four hundred spare, rangy hard-fisted volunteers, in response to the muster call. Unsoldierly but supremely warlike, the unruly crowd clustered around the ramshackle courthouse, swore allegiance to the Confederacy, vowed to fight Yankee tyranny, and drank freely from kegs of whiskey. They called themselves the "Slaughter County Wildcats" and by shouted acclamation elected Ben Bonham their colonel. Before they started marching—or, more aptly, straggling—toward the training camps in Virginia a couple of days later, nearly two hundred others had drifted in from surrounding counties, and the new colonel was at the head of what would become one of the South's fiercest and most indefatigable cavalry regiments. Drilled, disciplined, uniformed, armed with carbines and decently mounted, their raucous battle cry would be heard on a score of battle fields. A few would desert, a third would die and nearly as many would hobble back on crutches or with empty sleeves. But the 15th Confederate Cavalry, as it came finally to be called, would fight to the last skirmish and its survivors would know unbreakable bonds of brotherhood until the last of them was dead.

These enthusiastic new rebels brought remarkably few family names to the muster rolls of the regiment. There were, of course, Bonhams in all grades and ranks, and they served beside men named Hampton, Potter, Early, Jordan, Fraley, Free, Baker, Markham, and Gibbs from the oldest clans. Then there were Johnsons, Callihans, Hensleys, Hayses, Wellborns, Turners and Maghardts out of later migrations into Indian Valley. From other counties came Rileys, Bashams, Dinkmans, Mays, Gilleys, Tanners, Nobles, MacIntoshes, Whites, Brewers and Fletchers. Two-thirds of them were related to one another and could claim some link, however tenuous, through the Bonham line to the man whom they had elected their commander.

But even in Slaughter County the Confederate cause was able to command only a slender edge in the contest for loyalties. To a man the Runyons were staunch Unionists, and they counted many friends. The Bonhams and their supporters were descendants of men who had come early and had taken up the best land—the broad, black-loamed bottoms and deep gentle coves. They and their lands needed and could support slaves and a sympathy for slaveowners. But the people who pushed into the labyrinth after 1820 were forced up the creeks and into the constricted hollows where bottom lands were ribbons a few yards wide and crops of corn had to be wrested from steep, rock-ribbed hillsides.

The war lay close to the border of Virginia, on whose battlefields southern hopes would eventually expire. The trail Old John-of-All had followed had gradually turned into what passed for a road, a pitiable twisting, rock-strewn affair that forded innumerable streams and wound through dozens of steep, wind-swept gaps. It ran generally from east to west, but near Blacksville, it forked and a prong crept away to the south. This road became an avenue for hard-riding rebel cavalry headed on terror raids into Ohio, for Union cavalry seeking to intercept them, for files of sweating infantrymen bound for strategic gaps and fords and, always, for foragers.

Affairs deteriorated with appalling speed. The relentless forage parties became supremely skilled at suspecting—and finding—secret stocks of meat and grain. The people were driven to the forests in search of edible roots, nuts, and wild beasts. Livestock disappeared and hundreds of families wandered barefoot and penniless to federal installations on the fringes of the Appalachians and begged for food and shelter.

Alone of practically his entire blood and name, "Little Ish" Bonham remained at home and a noncombatant. He lived in the brick house his father had built, and the patriarch, now far into his eighties, lived with him. Little Ish was diminutive and frail, and from birth had dragged a shriveled leg. The war had cost him much already, but on a bleak autumn day in 1864, it reached out to destroy him as it had already ruined so many of his kin. That day fifty Union soldiers rode past his door and the captain stopped and looked with pity at the slaves who stared at him from their cabin doors. He ordered them out, informed them that they were contrabands and by virtue of the Presidential Proclamation of January 1, 1863, were free to go or to remain. Colored army units were being organized and the young men would be welcomed. After the war they would be American citizens, would vote, own land and might even hold office.

The others remained rooted to the spot because they had never been out of Indian Valley and feared the unknown, but Big Dave, the carpenter and ironworker who had been bought in Roanoke for fourteen hundred pre-war dollars, stepped forward. He put his clothes in a sack and strode out along the road to freedom. The company camped near the forks of Dead Man, and when the fire burned low and the picket dozed, Big Dave crept out of the camp and returned to the little settlement near Fort Bonham. He carried a heavy stick, and because the watchdogs knew him, they did not bark. He knocked on the door, and when the diminutive white man who had once called him slave and nigger came to the door, he struck him in the face with all his strength. Then, as silently as he had come, he returned to the sleeping camp.

Little Ish did not die, but lay paralyzed and unmoving for the rest of his days. At dawn the next morning his wife gave birth to a boy whom she named William. The child's father could never name his assailant, and died before his lastborn was a year old. But now the fortunes of the people who lived at the mouth of Finn's Fork ran down quickly. The slaves drifted away. The last of the livestock was slaughtered and eaten or driven away by hungry Yankees. Old Isham, broken in spirit and shattered by the dissolution of his world, breathed his last and was buried by a handful of women and children a dozen steps from the grave of his father. Then, in the dead of winter, a band of men came over the icy hill, routed out the entire family and burned down the brick home Isham had built for his Georgia wife. Only a few heaps of bricks and two gaunt slender chimneys remained of it—that and a ragged woman, some ragged children, and a half-famished baby in one of the slave cabins.

The house burners were led by Jack Runyon, a grandson of old Sam and Esther, and a veteran of more Virginia battlefields than he could count. And the seven men with him were Runyons or their kin, and Little Ish's wife, Martha, knew and recognized them. When the snows melted and spring returned for the last time before the war ended, a little flood of the Bonham people came home to plow and plant for their families. Among them was Big Sol Early, a veritable giant of a man and a captain in the veteran 15th Cavalry. His wrath was immeasurable when he heard the story, and he and his followers moved with the speed and precision of steel traps.

Big Sol's lieutenant was his cousin, John Bonham—known across the hills as "Bad John" because of the dozen men he had shot down in fair and foul fights. They and their troops were in tattered butternut, their boots were worn through, their eyes and cheeks were sunken, they were lean to stringy gauntness and their horses were sagging skeletons. But before they turned eastward once more toward the finale of Richmond and Appomattox, they hunted down Jack Runyon and his men. One by one they captured them as they camped under lonely cliffs or skulked in thickets. Then when all were counted, they bound them together and marched them across the ridges to the mouth of Camp Fork where John Bonham had discovered the cold ashes of long departed hunters. And there, while their women and children looked on in horror, the captives were hanged. When their executioners rode away, the bodies of their victims swung and twisted in the late March breeze and dead reproachful eyes stared down the trail after them.

Within weeks, peace came to Appomattox and a nation began the fumbling task of binding up wounds. Benjamin Bonham did not come home, but the war in which he served so tirelessly never really left the stricken county until another half century had slipped away.

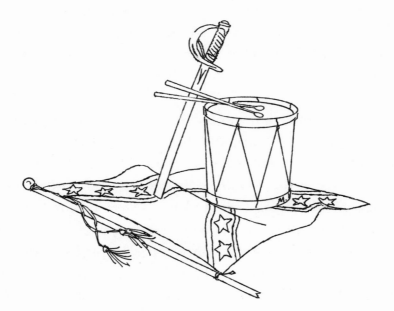

CHAPTER

4

The twenty-one years that brought William Bonham to his full age brought violent death to nearly five hundred men in Slaughter County. Newspaper men from far-off Cincinnati came into the hills from time to time to write accounts of the terrible, relentless, bloody feuds and gave the county its somber sobriquet of "Bloody Slaughter." As an editor at the state capital observed, "The county is aptly named because even more than the bloodthirsty inhabitants of the counties around it, the people of Slaughter seem to make the destruction of their fellow citizens their prime avocation."

The 15th Cavalry was a hundred miles southwest of Appomattox when Grant and Lee ended the conflict. The regiment—or, rather, the 118 officers and men left within its ranks—drifted westward for a week after they learned of the surrender. As a unit it never capitulated, but simply dissolved. One morning Ben Bonham thanked the men for their long and faithful service to the Confederacy and for their kindness to himself as their commander. Then he burned the tattered regimental colors, turned his back on all that had been and was lost, and rode away. Five others, all of whom had been among the first recruits at Blacksville so long ago, went with him. They headed for Kansas, and since they were a resolute lot, it may be assumed that eventually they reached the raw, wild towns and vast spaces of that new state.

Big Sol Early was slain from ambush on the bleak and bitter eve of Christmas 1865. His body was not discovered until the next morning, and it was frozen solid with a single bullet hole through the heart. The Bonham faction was remarkably restrained, encouraged to moderation, no doubt, by the losses of blood and spirit it had already suffered. The old men and women counseled peace and recourse to law, warning that a continuation of the wartime turbulence after the veterans of both sides had come home was unthinkable.

The world in which William Bonham grew up was one of unhurrying and unending nightmare. It was, in many respects, not unlike the Germany of the Thirty Years War— a world of ever-present peril in which stratagems and the foiling of stratagems were subjects seldom absent from mature minds. It was as if time had turned back for generations to a perpetual frontier war, but a war in which the foe was white and bore names one's grandfather had honored and esteemed. It was a world of nocturnal raid, of furtive but deadly ambush, and of dramatic confrontations and pitched battles. It was a time of marching militiamen seeking to restore order and blundering in pursuit of fleet-footed outlaws, of courts in disarray and flight and of public records put to the torch. It was an anguish-laden interval in which death most often claimed young and middle-aged men rather than the old and foredoomed, instilling a fatalism that would persist to plague many subsequent generations. It sent widows to the plow handles because no one else was left to plant and harvest for broods of voracious orphans. A mantle of oppressive foreboding gripped land and people and, except among the very old, and apathetic, wrath, vengeance and hatred consumed their passions and energies. Amid such frustrations the young passed from infancy to adulthood in a compressed span that left little or no time for the frivolous or childish. It was as if—to use a phrase coined by a sage contemporary observer of mountain life—"each new generation were born already old." But through it all the Bonhams counseled peace and order within the law, and sought to soften the passions that consumed the county.

In 1880, a new element intruded onto the brutal violence and hard, exhausting toil of mountain life. In the late spring, after the winds had dried out the almost bottomless mudholes along the abysmal roads, a red-faced Irishman named Wallace Horrigan appeared with a perfectly outlandish contraption. It was a lumbering steam-powered core drilling machine that six mules dragged along on its huge wagon. Horrigan and his two young assistants spent most of the next two years in the county, taking core samples at widely scattered sites. The mountaineers were fascinated by the machine, which was so utterly alien to their experience and background, and with few exceptions welcomed the engineers onto their lands. Usually the firebox was filled with white oak or hard maple, but occasionally a few bushels of coal were gouged out of a seam exposed by a landslide or a flooding creek. Most of the hill men and women were totally ignorant of coal, preferring to burn wood on their fireplaces rather than the foul-smelling lumps. They watched in open-mouthed wonder as sparks and clouds of black smoke poured from the iron stack, dragging out of the earth a three-inch cylinder of each layer of dirt, rock and sand to a depth of 194 feet. The indefatigable Horrigan filled many notebooks with precise records of his discoveries, and his eyes gleamed as they studied the cylinders of glittering black carbon that came out of the hills or up from the rich black soil of the creek-bottom cornfields. Pieces of each of these coal samples were preserved in carefully labeled canvas bags and from time to time a wagonload of them was dispatched a hundred miles over the mountains to the nearest rail head. There they were freighted to Cincinnati for analysis, and the chemists' reports were studied and discussed in the board rooms of a score of corporations which were zealously reshaping the nature of American life.

Horrigan and his clattering machine were all but forgotten when the warm winds of early summer in 1886 dried out the roads and trails that wound through the gaps and along gaunt ridges to the ungainly new frame courthouse at Blacksville. The building was constructed of hand-sawed poplar and housed a half-dozen offices on the first floor and a square, barren courtroom under the rickety bell tower. In those offices were kept such records as had escaped the wars and raids of two decades, including copies of land warrants, surveys, patents and deeds.

To these records rooms with their crude homemade tables and cane-bottomed chairs came two young men of a type never before seen in Slaughter County. They were lawyers, but of a different stripe from the self-taught advocates who followed the circuit judge from county seat to county seat. They were graduates of an excellent New England law college and carried themselves with a calm, efficient self-assurance and impeccable courtesy. They took lodgings in

Blacksville's tiny Wigwam Hotel and for three weeks studied the land records. During their sojourn, their affability gained them dozens of friends, and when they rode away their saddlebags bulged with notes and memoranda on the county's land titles. They knew the primitive indexing system and had learned to read the sometimes spidery script in which semi-literate clerks had inscribed the documents in the heavy, buckram-bound books. And they knew all the major lines of descent by which titles had come down through the generations from the early settlers. Their abstracts revealed glaring omissions caused by the burning of the old courthouse and by a cavalier failure to record essential papers. And they were able to recognize that in immense districts title patents had never been issued to anyone. Mountaineers had simply squatted on the wild acres, building cabins and clearing ragged fields for corn. But they were interlopers, nonetheless, with the enforceable, legal title still reposing in the state. This meant such lands—and all mineral substances within them— could be acquired by anyone who might survey them, file a patent application in the land office at the state capitol, and pay the state treasury a fee of five cents per acre. When they arrived in Philadelphia a few days later, they carried information that would drastically alter the lives of thousands of people. On the basis of that information, some people already wealthy would add greatly to their fortunes, and their descendants would inherit ease and station. Others, and they were legion, would be reduced to abject poverty and dependency because of it, but the two courtly young lawyers could foresee none of this.

William Bonham began to "read law" in his twenty-first

year. When he was a lad of fourteen, an unseasonal spring snowstorm caused Judge Dan Stamper and a couple of circuit-riding lawyers to find refuge for the night at the home of the widow Bonham, and he listened with rapt attention to their talk of lawsuits, the complexities of case pleadings and of famous courtroom arguments in which they had participated or which they had heard. William had attended a half-dozen three-month terms of the little one-room "common" school on Indian River, and he was an avid student. Because there were so few books to study he soaked himself in the handful of works available to him. The teacher was a self-taught surveyor who ground reading, writing, spelling, arithmetic, geography, and history into the score of students who turned up at the floorless log hut that passed for a schoolhouse. Because he was by nature a scholar with a keen thirst for knowledge of many things, William learned all the thin textbooks could teach, and pored endlessly over the Bible, a collection of Shakespeare's plays, an anthology or two and the six or eight other volumes he was able to lay his hands on.

But these efforts left him profoundly unsettled and unsatisfied. They aroused his appetite for intellectual achievement but offered small means of fulfillment. However, when he heard attorneys or a judge speak of the law and of the manner in which issues were resolved by study, logical argument and keen wit, he was thrilled and stirred and he drew near to listen and learn. He was drawn as a spectator to the infrequent court sessions and the affable judge soon found occasion to encourage his interest. He spent most of two years in the dingy, cluttered office of "Long Jim" May, one of Blacksville's two counselors, reading with single-mindedness intentness state and federal codes of practice, Blackstone's Commentaries, a six-volume encyclopedia of American law, and a long shelfful of reported decisions from the state's highest appellate court. At a term of circuit court in November 1888, Judge Stamper appointed two lean, stooped, mustached circuit riders to sit with him as a committee to "inquire into the fitness of one William Bonham to engage in the practice of law before this and other courts of the state." That evening they gathered around a fire in the judge's room, and while the committee sipped water and fiery moonshine whiskey, the applicant answered a couple of dozen questions they propounded to him. At nine the next morning, the judge entered an order admitting Old John-of-All's great-grandson to the bar and handed him a written certificate as a license to practice.

William Bonham's advent as a lawyer came at a propitious time. The prolonged and bloody "time of troubles" had been interrupted by few influences from the great world a-building outside the rim of the mountains. Incessant warfare and an unremitting emigration had prevented any appreciable population increase and the dreadful trails discouraged all but the most stout-hearted from visits to neighbors and friends. Introspection gripped the hill people, introspection and deepening poverty, and few new or modern things were to be found in the crude, dark cabins except the shiny Winchester rifles and Colt pistols borne by the lank, stoop-shouldered men and youths.

But the young lawyer hung out his shingle above the door of a tiny clapboarded building in the same year when

Mark Pellham came for the first time to Slaughter County. He was a suave, neatly dressed Philadelphian, lean of body and limb and dressed in the finest and most stylishly tailored cloth anyone had ever worn on the dusty streets of Blacksville. His voice and bearing gave testimony to a lifetime of easy familiarity with money, influential people, and the best of schools. There was a note of command and finality in his clipped accents and in the firm grip of his slender hand. Pellham rented lodgings in the Wigwam, and for years the courtly Pennsylvanian and his splendid sorrel stallion were familiar sights along the tangle of creeks that led outward to the limits of the county.

Within a month after his arrival, Pellham brought in a couple of young lawyers who set to work on title abstracts. They spent interminable hours among the frayed and dusty deed books, and there was much journeying by horseback over the hills to the nearest railhead, whence they reached the land office in the state capitol.

Pellham was a land agent for a group of speculators in Philadelphia who had put together the Northeast Coal and Iron Corporation. On his tireless forays across Slaughter County, he began buying the legal title to the vast mineral wealth which Horrigan's steam core drill had probed and measured. Nor was it long before his activities began to send a flow of questioning mountaineers to the office of William Bonham.

Pellham sometimes sought to buy tracts of land outright at places where his practiced eye told him time would see the building of coal tipples and whole new towns. But in the main, he wanted to "sever" the title to the minerals in the land from that of the "surface estate." By that means the real wealth of a selected territory could be made available for "development," while the eroded and old thicket-choked fields farmers had cultivated and abandoned would remain in the native populace to bear their separate share of future tax burdens.

Pellham's instrument for accomplishing his objective was a saddlebag full of printed deed forms. These documents came from the presses of a Philadelphia printer and contained blank spaces for dates, names of sellers, and description of land boundaries. When all spaces had been appropriately filled, and the deed marked with the cross of an illiterate mountaineer and his illiterate wife, and the whole duly certified by a notary public, the effect was awesome. The usual consideration for such a deed was fifty cents per acre and title passed to "all coal, oil and gas, and all other mineral and metallic substances of every kind and character, in, on and underlying the land." Then long, wordy, convoluted covenants granted to the Northeast Coal and Iron Corporation and its successors in title "forever," the right to enter onto the land and drill wells, sink shafts, drive tunnels, make excavations, make and leave heaps of mine wastes, divert and pollute water courses, withdraw "sub-jacent" supports and permit the surface to subside, cut and use for mining purposes the timber growing on the surface, and as a final clincher, "the right to do any and all things necessary or convenient" for mining. Then, in a last cataclysmic contract, the coal owner was relieved of all damages "and claims for damages" growing out of any action undertaken to withdraw minerals from the soil.

Yearning for the gleaming gold pieces proffered by the urbane Pellham was overwhelming. His arguments and inducements were tempting: the minerals had done no one in the mountains any good in the hundred years since the first settlements. They were deep in the earth unseen, and, perhaps, they were not even there at all. They would be mined by methods that would not disturb the farmers' use of the fields and forests. Railroads had been discussed for thirty years but had never been built, and without the rails mining would never occur. Hence the sale might put money in the mountaineer's pocket without ever bringing mines to burrow into his hillsides. Besides, if the rails were laid up the long and tortuous valley of Indian River, they would bring perpetual prosperity. A man and his sons could find regular work at high wages, the cabins would give way to larger and more comfortable houses, and the women could replace their drab "homespuns" with bright clothes from factories. Then schools would be built, and the young would learn trades. Even colleges might come to the hills in those days. Thus, to sign was to sanction progress and a new, good life. To reject the pen was to endorse the bleak and bloodstained present at a time when most men yearned for change.

Still, many did not put their marks to the deeds. The tall, spare Bonhams and their kin, in particular, were suspicious of the folded documents Pellham carried in his saddlebags of fine-grained leather. And it was they whose cabins stood above the thickest seams of black carbon the Irishman's core drill had ever penetrated. They brought the deeds to young Bonham for his opinion as to their meaning, and his advice was shattering to Pellham's undertaking. The documents would, he counseled, pass title virtually in "fee simple." All really important legal rights would vest in a corporation in another state, and the people in their houses and on their farms would be reduced to "tenancy by sufferance." Over and over he said, "My 500 acres are not for sale, and I advise you to keep your own. Pellham is not offering enough money to do you any real good, and once the deed is signed you will be helpless on your own land. You will own land you can't control, and he will control land he will not own!"

On the left fork of Dead Man Creek, Marston Early lived on 700 acres his great-grandfather had patented. He was nearly fifty and kept a tiny store which he stocked with goods his wagons dragged across forty miles of boulder-strewn mountains. And behind his store on days when rains swelled the waters of the creek, his millstones turned to reduce corn to meal and hard-grained wheat to a brown, coarse flour. He had been visited often by Pellham and his agents and had pondered the legal counsel of his youthful cousin. Now, on a bright day when the Pennsylvanian followed the creek road toward the Early place, he carried eighteen shiny new twenty dollar gold pieces wrapped in the brown paper from which they had left the mint, and beside the coins lay a deed ready for signing. Early's wife and sons had argued for sale of the mineral rights, and for a time he had yielded to their persuasions, but in the long hours of darkness in the preceding night, the miller had pondered afresh every aspect of the situation. His liking for the persistent Pellham had turned to suspicion, and with daylight he knew that the deed would never receive his mark.

The sorrel nickered at the hitching post near the millhouse

as his rider swung from the saddle. Pellham busied himself with the saddle girth for a moment before be turned toward the store. He understood the reticence and shyness of mountain women and wanted to give Lou Anna Early an opportunity to learn of his arrival before he approached to talk to her husband. When he found Early at the mill and walked with him to the narrow L-shaped porch, they found the place empty. Early's wife and her younger children had disappeared into the log kitchenhouse that stood a dozen yards to the rear of the dwelling, leaving her husband and the "furriner" to discuss alone the business of the deed. If he decided to sell, she would be summoned to make her mark beneath his own, but if the deal were rejected, she would remain out of sight and hearing.

The two men sat down on straight-backed, hickory-bottomed chairs, and Pellham tactfully cleared his throat. He spoke of the wild loveliness of the Early farm in the sheltering valley of Dead Man Creek and wondered how the place came by its name. He expressed pleasure at the prosperity of his host and hoped railroads and coal mines would bring an opportunity for him to become a rich man. Then he reached into his coat pocket for the deed, and with his other hand produced the shiny yellow disks imprinted with eagles which were calculated to buy seven hundred acres of the stony fuel on which the world depended for its steam and heat. "I think this is an excellent deal for you, Mr. Early," he murmured as the sun glittered on the coins slipping through his fingers.

But Early shook his huge head with its shaggy locks and frowned with a finality that abruptly ended the discussion: "Bill Bonham is a-kin to me by blood, and though he is a young lawyer, I believe he's a good 'un. He's read a copy of that infernal long deed to me, and from what he sez I'll be a fool if I sign hit. My mind is made up, and my hand'll not tech the pen, and as fer ye gold pieces, ye kin drap 'em back in yer pocket."

Pellham was a man of immense calm and self-possession, but as he rode back to Blacksville, his wrath and frustration mounted steadily. On the following morning at an early hour, he presented himself at Bonham's tiny office for a conference with the man who threatened to thwart his own plans and those of the financiers whose gold he dispensed.

He sat erect and dignified on a homemade comfortless chair and looked at William Bonham across a broad table, the boards of which had been planed and nailed together by some local carpenter. Behind Bonham on a few shelves nailed against the wall, were ranged the sixty books that composed his law library. The land he had inherited had been mortgaged to pay for these books which he studied with such tireless interest, but the man who smiled at him across the littered table held a degree from the law college at Harvard and his name was lettered across the door of one of Philadelphia's most prestigious law firms. When he spoke, the Pennsylvanian was the very essence of self-control except for the ends of the long slender fingers which drummed a light tattoo against the top of the table.

"Mr. Bonham," he began, "I need you, and my company needs you. The Northeast Coal and Iron Corporation has a great dream and great plans for this mountainous country. They are good plans, humane and generous plans, and if they can be realized, they will do wonderful things for the people of Slaughter County. Please believe me," and his voice took on a note of pleading and deep sincerity, "when I say that I have come to have a very real affection for the people whom I have met here. I know, Mr. Bonham, that you surely share my belief—and our company's belief—that the horrible feuds that afflict this county must end, and that the best way to end them is by making regular jobs at fair wages available to all alike, to Runyons and Bonhams, and to all their kith and kin."

He paused, and Bonham studied him for a moment and reflected on his well-chosen words. Then he continued, "We need you Mr. Bonham, in our work. You can be of much valuable service to my company, and the company can be of much help to you in your profession. Times are not prosperous, and we are compelled to operate on a tight budget, but Northeast Coal and Iron Corporation is prepared to offer you a salary of $150 per month if you will become one of our attorneys and help us in our title work and land acquisitions."

He paused again. "We can form here an association that can be of profit and advantage to our company and to yourself for many years, indeed for as long as you practice law."

Bonham was astonished. The proffered salary was munificent in Slaughter County in 1892. He was married to a beautiful and vivacious young woman, Delilah, youngest daughter of Ephraim Free, and heir to hundreds of acres of wild cliffy land on Marrowbone Fork of Big Greasy Creek. She was already pregnant, and his practice produced few fees. Neither his lands nor hers afforded any revenue nor, in their isolation, were they likely ever to do so. But William Bonham had seen some publications dealing with the mineral riches of the central Appalachians and he suspected that all such tracts would be of immense value if and when rails tied these hidden valleys to the rest of the world. And he remembered that old injunction that had come down from his grandmother and had sounded so many times on Bonham tongues: "Take good care of the land and the land will take good care of you!" He knew that, with his reply, he was crossing a personal Rubicon.

"I am pleased that your company is interested in Slaughter County," he ventured, "and I fully agree with you that the mining industry could do much to heal its old divisions. Every thinking man must be sick to his soul of these feuds and troubles, and the Lord knows I need the money." Here he paused as he remembered the many stories he had heard of Old John-of-All and the wars with the Indians the first settlers had fought for these rough, forbidding lands. He reflected for a moment on the men of his father's generation who had ridden so long and so hard with Ben Bonham, and he said as he looked into the land speculator's gray eyes, "I can't betray the people who trust my advice. I have to tell them the truth as I see it. If enough people sign your deeds, this county will become a vassalage to Northeast Coal and Iron Corporation. I must tell every person who asks me that he ought not to sign your deed."

As Pellham left the lawyer's office, the sun glinted on the steep hillsides beyond the courthouse. Bonham watched him meet "Black Alf" Runyon, generally regarded as the leader of his clan and its most murderous gunman, and walk with him through the battered doorway of the Wigwam.

CHAPTER

5

It was a spring day in 1900, and William Bonham had just turned forty. He was a relentless worker and had laid his hand to many enterprises besides the law. Men in his hire floated rafts of unblemished logs down Indian River for sale at the huge mills near the cities. His own sawmill screeched and whirred six miles from Blacksville at the mouth of Rum Creek, and his stack-dried lumber was carried on scows to the end of the little, narrow-gauge railroad that had been pushed nearly forty miles into the hills. His cousin, "Kittle Head" Sam Bonham, was an astute trader and used William's money to buy mountain cattle and sheep which the drover and his sons herded along the trails to stockyards in Virginia, Kentucky, and Tennessee. And though most of the people who sought his advice about Mark Pellham's deeds eventually disregarded it and accepted the Philadelphian's gold, Northeast Coal and Iron Corporation did not acquire all the titles that changed hands in Slaughter County. William Bonham was now sole owner of century-old Fort Bonham and three hundred and fifty of the acres Old John-of-All had claimed for his soldier's pay. He had bought a thousand acres elsewhere on Indian River and, using Pellham's form of deed and paying only slightly more than Northeast's standard fifty cents to the acre, he owned the minerals in eleven hundred more acres and the right to mine them by "any and all convenient" methods. When he found a client or kinsman who wanted to trade the uncertain future for the glittering gold pieces of today, the lawyer strove to provide the cash himself. "If you must sell," he would say, "then sell to me. My money is as good as Pellham's, and I am your friend and kinsman, while he is a stranger." Now a stack of the recorded documents lay in a small iron safe by his bed in the modest frame house he had built fifty yards from his ancestor's gaunt, weather-worn cabin.

This spring, William Bonham knew a few more years would bring a railroad and the rattle of locomotives to the valley. He was satisfied with his accomplishments and with the strong-willed wife who had borne him three sons and two daughters. Besides, he was tired, and found himself going with less zeal and less frequently to the cluttered and generally crowded law office. He had not spoken to Mark Pellham since their first and only conference nearly a decade earlier, but through all the years since they had been adversaries. Pellham had spent nearly half his time in Slaughter and other mountain counties and had built up a strong following. Perhaps a majority of the people had come to think of him as a dedicated friend who sought to bring jobs and a chance for real prosperity to the long-depressed backlands in which their history had stranded them. Pellham's friends considered William Bonham an obstructionist whose legal counsel represented a desire to hinder progress rather than an honest assessment of the law. Pellham had pointed to Bonham's land acquisitions as evidence that he himself was doing what

he sought to prevent Northeast Coal from doing. The prolonged struggle had cost Bonham friendships in circles his
forebears had esteemed, and he felt a growing despondency
about the future. The Pennsylvania speculators and a couple
of other companies now owned eighty percent of the county's
mineral riches. On business trips to mining areas in other
parts of the Appalachians, he had seen with horror the cluttered misery of mining towns with their smoldering culm
heaps, the endless accidents that killed men and widowed
women and, most startling of all, the abject dependency of
the people. This he foresaw as the future of his own remote
hinterland. Through a lumber dealer to whom he sold his
choicest walnut boards, he had acquired a prime building lot
in Louisville, and, he sometimes vowed, when the railroad
arrived at his lands, he would sell his holdings and move
away. They would then be worth a hundred and fifty thousand dollars—enough to build a good town house on the lot,
assure the education of his children and provide an ample
living for his wife and himself. He cringed from the kind of
"development" Northeast Coal Corporation and the railroad
barons were planning for Indian Valley and wanted no part
in it.

On this particular morning, he slept late after a restless
night. In midmorning, as he sat in the warming sun on the
long deep porch, he felt a strange indifference. If Pellham
and his Runyon friends had succeeded in shifting incalcu-
lable wealth from unknowing mountain farmers to the purses
of cunning speculators, well then, so let it be. He had done
his duty and had warned all who would listen that they were
selling fortunes for pennies, and had come out of the effort

with enough to secure his own future. He stood up and stretched, and called his four-year-old son Tom to his side. He would saddle a horse for the ride to Blacksville, and the child could walk with him to the stable.

Thomas Jefferson Bonham was William's youngest son. Even at the tender age of fifty-one months his face and form were uncannily like those of the long-dead veteran of King's Mountain whose sure swift hands had carved the thick logs of the old cabin where the children often played. The blood of a forgotten Cherokee squaw added the merest trace of a coppery tinge to his skin, raised and arched his cheekbones and thatched his head with thick black hair. He was tall for his age, and his hands and fingers were slender and quick. The nose was thin and loftily arched like the proboscis of a young but very imperious Roman senator. And the child displayed a boldness and self-confidence that had given him preeminence in the affections of his parent. More than once William Bonham had declared that this boy would go to a first-rate law school someday or, if he inclined that way, to a school of medicine. There were practically no doctors in the hills, and Bonham liked to suppose that he had begotten a physician. "That boy," he told Delilah, "will be able to do anything he sets his head to!"

He followed the path to the horse barn and saddled the spirited red mare that had cost him a long scowload of deeply stacked walnut and maple lumber. He stooped to kiss his son on the cheek, then swung onto the saddle. "I'll see you tomorrow, Tommy boy," he promised, as the prancing animal carried him through the open gate into the clear sunlight.

The sequence that followed was burned indelibly in the

child's memory and would recur as a heart-stopping nightmare as long as life and consciousness would persist. The hollow roar of a large-caliber Winchester boomed down from the new foliage cloaking the steep face of Big Laurel Ridge. William Bonham stiffened in the saddle, and his legs drove spurs deep into the flanks of the startled horse. The distressed animal snorted and reared almost straight up, and the man flopped flat on his back on the stony soil. The child ran to his father and stared down at him as the dying man's fingers tore convulsively at the earth and his heels kicked spasmodically against shards of rock. Then the lower jaw sagged, and the open eyes glazed to reflect the blue sky as a wide red stain spread outward to cover the center of the white linen shirt. With its mane and tail outstretched, the whinnying horse continued to run around the feed lot, and as the boy watched, realization came to him. He was still there, frozen in his tracks, when his mother raised her husband's head and murmured, "They've killed you at last, sweetheart, and may God help them! May God have mercy on the man who pulled the trigger for I will not have any!"

The chain of recollections, the storehouse of remembered things, began for Thomas Jefferson Bonham with that moment. In later years, all before it would be lost to him in infantile darkness, but subsequent things and happenings would accumulate on that stark and graphic beginning. He would recall the hundreds of spare lank Bonhams and their plain grim women who came to show their grief for the murder of their kinsman, the lowering of the cedar coffin into the deep narrow pit and the impassioned graveside invocation of the preacher, and then the loneliness after the crowds

scattered away and left the family with its grief.

He would remember also the tight firm set of her jaw as Delilah Free Bonham set to work on her husband's affairs. There was the lot to be sold in faraway Louisville and hundreds of acres of land in Slaughter County to be traded to Josiah King, a speculator who sought minerals for an outfit called King Koal and Karbon Kompany. There were visits by night and day from hard-faced men who sagged beneath the weight of holstered pistols. And there was talk, sometimes and in snatches, of people named Runyon—associates of an evil man named Mark Pellham—slain from ambush or in open affray. There was, on occasion, the handing out of long greenback notes or handfuls of glittering yellow disks to rumpled visitors who came under cover of darkness to conferences with Delilah in the lamplit kitchen. There was, too, what Delilah called the "halleluyah day" when Frobisher Roberts, William Bonham's first cousin, brought the news that Mark Pellham was dead. Pellham had been attending the trial of a lawsuit in the next county down the river when his time ran out. He had spent the night at the Four-Square Hotel, the county seat's only hostelry, and there were no witnesses to the episode. Charlie Bonham had been a guest there, too, and Pellham was shot through the spleen when the two met soon after daybreak on the dusty porch of the tawdry little inn. Charlie Bonham fired, he claimed, in self-defense, but, in any event, Mark Pellham was very, very dead.

The boy would remember, too, his mother riding grim-faced and properly side-saddled on a red mare to courthouses and trials with money to pay lawyers and court costs, and when he was nearly ten, the end of it all, William Bonham was properly avenged—the money gone and much of the land in other hands. But the place on Indian River remained, with stark old Fort Bonham beneath the beetling cliffs, and a few hundred acres of wild, tumbled land his father had said contained some of the finest coal veins in the world.

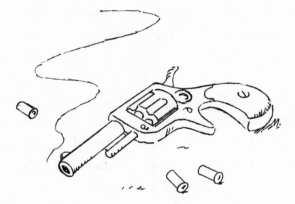

CHAPTER
6

The boy grew up amid hard times. A business slump slowed the work in the cities and the market for logs and lumber dried up. A century of tillage had worn out hillside fields. The feuds had discouraged and driven out even more than they had slain. Delilah Bonham fought hard against the weariness and dejection that settled over the hill country, for she was determined that her children would somehow rise above the ignorance and destitution that threatened to engulf all alike.

The sawmill and lumber scows were gone now, as were the spirited horses that once snorted in the pasture beyond the orchard. Gone, too, were the drovers and their herds of sheep and cattle, making up for the drive across the hills to market towns she had heard of but never visited. What remained were the old fields around Fort Bonham, a couple of plow mules, a cow or two, some hogs and chickens, and the hungry mouths of five children. The rough, hilly land with its coal veins added nothing, for Delilah was inflexibly resolved that it must remain the property of her children. So she and they plowed the bottom lands and assaulted the hill slopes with grubbing hoes. By their sweat, they wrung from Old John's fields enough corn and flesh for their sustenance, but there was nothing to spare. And the primitive, sagging little one-room school, with its semi-literate teacher that brought what passed for learning to Indian River precinct, inflicted an even more ruinous hunger on the minds and spirits of the forty or fifty students who attended it at uncertain intervals through a four-month term.

When Tom was seven his mother heard of a "strange woman" from Boston who had come down to the wild mountaintop at the head of Knob Fork of Rockhouse Creek. She had come with three other women younger than herself, and they had gotten a school started where none had ever existed before. Her "mission school" was supported by her own modest fortune and gifts from a dozen or so wealthy New Englanders, and was praised by all whose children had the good fortune to attend it. Helen Boyd and her staff were college graduates—the first women with that distinction ever to set foot in Slaughter County—and with the same determination that had sent Mark Pellham to his grave, Delilah decided to bring their work to Indian River. If these "neat and proper" women with their city ways could provide the knowledge poor old Jesse Banks so dismally lacked in his little musty schoolhouse, then she would have them for her own children. Not for a moment had she forgotten her husband's ambition for a lawyer or doctor to emerge from their brood, and she single-mindedly determined to see it done.

She rode the plow mule the dozen crooked, laurel-shaded miles to the huge, flat-topped mountain where a score of families had lived in almost total isolation for a century. When the Battle of Fallen Timbers crushed forever the hold of the original Americans on the central Appalachians, all but a few of them withdrew from the hills. But two Choctaw warriors built crude, unfloored huts on the high open country where for centuries red men had met in council and had buried their dead. They were there when Jason Gibbs and the other Melungeon families came sweating up the trail with their pack mules. Ten decades increased the numbers of this strange tribe to two-score families who lived in primitive cabins laid out in a long, fortress-like square. These sly, secret people never requested a school for their children, and the county trustees saw no reason for volunteering to build one. Then one day a newspaper reporter climbed to their misty fastness and wrote a fanciful description of their strange archaic world. The story was read by a heartbroken Yankee woman, and her life and theirs were drastically changed.

Helen Boyd was a beautiful and vivacious woman on whom Fortune seemed to smile in unstinted measure. Her marriage to Malcolm Boyd, a youthful heir to a banking fortune, produced no children, but resulted in a remarkably happy union amid charming, widely traveled and superbly educated people. Her world was abruptly shattered when he demanded a divorce and left her to marry a dancer whom she had admired and entertained. The knowledge that she was virtually the last to learn about the affair embittered her against the whole society in which she had lived. When she read about the forgotten people on the Appalachian hilltop, she saw an opportunity to escape and to put a Radcliffe education to work in a worthwhile cause. Six weeks later she startled the people of Knob Fork by dismounting in their midst. It was the first of many surprises she brought to them, for none had ever before seen a woman so bold as to sit astride a horse.

She carried a crusader's zeal, and tolerated few conventions when they hindered the task to which she had put her hand. She set about building a school for the children of "the dark people," and a combination of stern command, suave charm of a kind totally alien to the mountaineers, and a sudden burst of zeal for "book learnin" on the part of the community produced a two-room schoolhouse within six short weeks. It was a poor shabby thing of hewed logs—for the Knob Fork people knew no other way of building—but it was ceiled with planed lumber from a sawmill and admitted light through twin rows of tall windows. The homemade furnishings were as comfortless as they were clumsy, but Helen Boyd was unbelievably proud of them when she opened boxes of textbooks one-eyed Cham Gibbs had dragged all the way from Blacksville on a fodder sled. She had a tact and charm that enabled her to speak to both Cabots and Lodges of Boston, and with equal ease to Melungeon women who had never dreamed of journeying so far as the county seat. In her old age, she would see her creation grow to become a high school with three hundred students. Already when Delilah Bonham, in the third year of her widowhood, came to visit "the teachin' woman," the buildings were three in number, a modest "dormitory" was under construction, children from other valleys were making their way to the little campus, and three more young women from the East had volunteered at least a portion of their lives in service to the southern hills.

Whatever revulsion she may have felt against her new and uncouth surroundings, she, and her enlistees, kept to themselves. Shuck beds, uneven puncheon floors and foods invariably fried and swimming in grease were shattering contrasts to the glittering crystal, deep carpets and spacious homes they had always accepted as routine, but they bore the change with aplomb until one day they realized with a start that they had become inseparable parts of the Appalachians and that there could be no turning back.

The schoolteacher who had been born in a mansion on Beacon Hill poured coffee for her visitor—a woman whose advent had occurred in a log cabin on a rocky slope known locally as Scuttle Hole Ridge. And they understood one another perfectly from the beginning.

The mountain woman knew nothing of schools for she had never attended one a day in her life. Her husband had taught her to sign her name, but the complicated fines she traced on paper were from memory only and the letters were incomprehensible. But she knew the depths of her ignorance and that knowledge of the printed page brought power as well as understanding. She had seen too much of the unlettered mountain schoolmen and their untaught charges to expect anything from that quarter for her own children. She came to bargain for learning with the only people she knew to possess it.

"I am Delilah Bonham," she said with a calm, steady-eyed assurance, "and I've got a houseful of children who will live and die as ignorant as I am, unless I can get some help from you wimmin." The long ride in the warm sun had stained her ample garments with sweat so that she fanned her face with a magazine she picked up from a table. "People hereabouts give all of you ladies a mighty good name as teachers.

Things will change a lot in the mountains when the railroad comes, and there won't be any place for an unknowin' man. My own people have no learnin' and it's a mighty hard case for them now, plowin' and plantin' and clearin' for barely enough to eat. My husband read law and was a good lawyer, and he wanted his children to have schoolin'. I've come to ask you, will one of you run a school on Indian River if I will provide the house?"

The two strong-willed women parleyed across the table, and with the concurrence of the other teachers a bargain was struck. The huge square rooms of old Fort Bonham would be cleaned, painted and repaired by Delilah Bonham and her "hands," and a roof of new white-oak boards would be provided to keep the structure warm and dry. At least thirty children would be gotten together for a school term to start in October, and Helen Boyd, for her part, would undertake to provide a teacher. Nor would her task be too difficult, she believed, because she had been in correspondence with a young Vermont woman who was anxious to find a "purposeful mission" in the Appalachian backwoods. She would seek to divert her to an outpost on Indian River. There was, as she reflected, an ocean of need, and it was truly remarkable that, after her own Rubicon had been crossed, so many others should appear to take up tasks in her cause.

On the day she had designated, Delilah Bonham saw more than thirty of her kinsmen answer her invitation for a free "workin'" to rehabilitate the ancient cabin. It was cleaned thoroughly, sagging puncheons were replaced and interior walls were whitewashed. The tight new roof proofed it against rain and snow. But more importantly, work was begun on a neat round-pole cabin for the teacher's home, and the foundations were laid for a new schoolhouse. Nor was the work ever wholly suspended until the tasks were done and the little buildings stood intact in the shadows of the old huge hemlocks on their knoll—the same knoll where savage warriors had once hidden before their attack on John Bonham's sleeping fort. And Delilah Bonham rode the wearisome miles to the head of Knob Fork to hand a deed for the land to Helen Boyd. "We want learnin' for our little 'uns," she said, "and the Bonhams keep their word. We'll be much obliged to you and to your friends who come to teach our school, and we aim to do all we can to make your work among us satisfyin' to yourselves. We don't want any of the good wimmin who come here to leave dissatisfied on account of us." The Bostonian-turned-mountaineer looked long and steadily into the strong, handsome face, and tears of appreciation came into her own gray eyes. She had felt the fool many times since casting her lot among these strangely fierce and different people, but now it suddenly seemed wise and right, and she was happy.

The letters that flowed from the tiny Knob Fork post office were not without their effect, and in October when the frostbitten hills were aflame with every imaginable hue and shade of color, a surefooted mule brought a most unlikely character to inhabit the new cabin. Three other mules struggled behind, under mountainous burdens of trunks, bales and hampers stuffed with clothes and books. Miss Rose Quinlan, Woodstock, Vermont's gift to Appalachia, had arrived to do battle with the forces of ignorance, sloth and immorality. And having put her hand to the plow of progress, she would not look back.

She towered upward from the earth all of five feet two inches and wore the impeccable features of a cameo. She stood as erect as a field marshal, and her every gesture evinced perfect composure and an assurance that she was born to have her way on all major issues. Why she left the pleasant streets and spacious houses of her native village for the raw solitudes of the southern hills, she never once hinted. Whatever the cause, she never regretted it, and she bore her exile with few absences from Knob Creek and Indian River. But though she buried herself and her energies in her new work for nearly two decades, she did not sever contacts with the world beyond. She promptly loosed a flood of letters and notes of her own to points north and east and was struck in turn by a Mississippi of parcels that shattered the patience of "Hoss-head" Felix Bonham, the stooped, skeletal mail carrier who for twenty years had prodded lean, reluctant mules with thin pouches of letters from valley to valley. He delivered his burdens to postmasters at Skull, Eagle, War Hat, Ghost Rock, Gun Lock, Flint and Sycamore, and his pace had been leisurely and with a trace of dignity until its routines were turned upside down by "that air letter-writin' women." In utter exasperation, he exclaimed to the postmaster at Blacksville, "Haint nobody kin read all them books and letters she's allus a-gittin'. Hits all I kin do to lift 'em and my mule is sore all over from a-kerrin' 'em. I druther have the young'uns grow up without no teacher than to have to wear m'self out with all a this deliverin'."

Within a few weeks, shelves lined the walls of the "schoolteacher's cabin," and they sagged beneath two hundred volumes of history, poetry, mathematical treatises, encyclopedias, and novels. Overcome by curiosity, people crept to the door and windows to peep at her "liberry." Nor was that the end of their astonishment. From Sears, Roebuck in Chicago there came a long galvanized tub that clanged grievously against the aching sides of "Hoss-head's" mule, and there arrived, also, cakes of scented soap, and the word spread for miles around that she "took a bath all over" every day— and "sometimes twicet."

She was a stickler for perfection in herself and others, and the forty students who turned out for her attentions on the third Monday in October, 1903, soon found themselves under a regimen such as no rough-cut mountain schoolmaster could have imagined. The scholars ranged from six to sixteen and sat at homemade desks in four parallel rows over and about which she hovered like Nemesis. Her sharp eyes seemed to penetrate to the innermost cells of their brains and to divine every secret thought so that even fleeting mental infractions of her numerous rules brought dartlike glances and shattering scowls. Her little classroom had to be kept in complete order at all times, with each desk tidy, and the day divided into neat intervals precisely dedicated in turn to the subject of her curriculum. Maxims fell from her lips in an unending flow so that "Stiller Bill" Dingus, who donated a couple of days' work cutting wood for her fireplace, allowed that she had "swallered a book o' sayin's."

"A place for everything, and everything in its place," she admonished a boy who hung his cap on the wrong peg. "Haste makes waste" was flung like a lightning bolt on a redhaired girl whose quick calculations added up to the wrong sum. "Cleanliness is next to Godliness" and a tap with her long oak ferrule were the inevitable portion of any who arrived with dirty hands or faces. And to the frustrated arithmetician, who could not multiply by fractions, she murmured, "If at first you don't succeed, try, try again."

And her efforts produced something for every occasion. When Willie Potter stayed at his desk at recess to read a story, she routed him into the sunshine with "All work and no play makes Willie a dull boy." When he played ball so zealously he was last to reenter the door, he was struck with, "Slow steps lead to rags." In the afternoon when he dropped a tiny piece of chalk as too small for further use, she shook her head sadly and chided him with, "Waste not, want not." And when he prepared to walk the three stony miles to his father's cabin, he fairly quivered under a general directive not to tarry. "Dash home and help your parents with their work," she urged, reminding that "Many hands make light work."

But she was a teacher of awesome competence and total dedication who half drove, half led her charges to learn. Not all benefited equally from her efforts, of course, but some struggled successfully against the suffocating folds of their bleak backwoods environment and caught a surprising insight into the world of ideas, theories, and abstractions. And Delilah Bonham was richly rewarded for her own efforts by the progress of her children, and, most especially, that of Thomas Jefferson.

The child was called Tom, naturally, and from his first day within the renovated and whitewashed walls of the old fort, his tutelage was a glorious escape into new worlds that widened immeasurably as he advanced from class to class and from one book to another. Rose Quinlan loved to teach and Tom Bonham loved to learn, and their effect on one another was little short of magical. Except for his self-taught father, it was probable that not one of his forebears had ever learned more than the letters of his own name and the slender ability to draw the meaning from a few verses of Scripture. But Will Bonham's eight-year-old soaked up facts and perceptions as blotting paper takes up ink. The history of the United States and of America's antecedents in Europe, reading, spelling, writing and penmanship, arithmetic, grammar, and English literature—these were Miss Quinlan's subjects and her gratification was boundless as she watched the boy's progress. She would later observe many times that her mountain students had amply rewarded her decision to give up her other life, and that of all whom she remembered, Tommy Bonham, the lad with the imperious nose and keen dark eyes, was the best of all the lot.

As the students grew up, so did the little school, adding cabins for new teachers, a half-dozen clapboarded classrooms and a hulking weather-stripped "auditorium." In twelve seasons, the affair launched by Helen Boyd and Delilah Bonham acquired a staff of six, a dormitory for boarding students, a library, a primitive chemistry laboratory and a title. It became the Indian River Settlement School, and the wealthy Bostonians whose gifts sustained it found much pleasure in the light so brought to the inbred and feud-ridden people of the southern hills. Sometimes a few of them came to see for themselves, riding dust-covered and stiff-jointed over the ridges to spend a few days as honored guests, stared at in open-mouthed wonder by speechless students and their parents. Nor did the outpost abandon its graduates after Indian River Settlement School could do no more for them, but its letters and sometimes its teachers accompanied the ambitious to college campuses, arranging scholarships and loans, and in countless ways smoothing for shy, uncertain youths the transition from backwoods to the broad world beyond the hills.

Tom Bonham was the first graduate of Indian River to become a teacher in his own classroom. He passed the state's examination at nineteen with such high marks that the Board of Examiners issued him a first-class certificate. He taught his kinsmen for three years, being much patronized by visiting dignitaries and acquiring, in the process, the local nickname of "Teacher Tom." His salary was $50 a month, and he saved nearly all of it toward the three years of medical school to which he, his mother, and Rose Quinlan were so single-mindedly dedicated.

He was twenty-two when he passed the admissions test for the little College of Medicine in Louisville, a college quaintly housed in a smoke-blackened converted church. Before he left the hills, he had a final conversation with Rose Quinlan in her book-lined sitting room with its battered typewriter and unfinished letter. The years had changed her from a youngish twenty-seven to a plumpish forty-four and a little of the field marshal had ebbed away. She leaned back in her chair and smiled at him, the points of her collar neatly starched and as stiff and pointed as spears, her braided hair pinned in a coil on the top of her head. "I'm leaving, too, Tom, because the school is doing well and can go on just fine without me," she said in the firm, unarguable tones he had known so well as her student, "and it is proper, I think, that our work here should end in the same year. After all, we began together, when you arrived with your primer and I with my 'book o' sayin's'," and they both laughed at the recollection. "My years at Indian River have been wonderful, and I will carry with me many marvelous memories. Your mother came to Mrs. Boyd with a desire to see you become a doctor. God has answered all our prayers, and you have come so far that within a week you will be an enrolled student at a medical school. The dream of your mother, and long ago, of your father, is practically certain to be realized."

She paused for reflection, "Tom, don't just be a doctor!" she pleaded. "Be a physician here in Slaughter County. These mountain people are yours, and they need you very much. They will need you as a healer of sick bodies, and you can help them in that way. But they will need you in many other ways also. The railroad will reach Blacksville and Indian River within a few years more. Then the Bonhams and their friends and foes will become coal miners. Many, many changes will come to bewilder and confuse the people. Some—including yourself—will probably grow rich and others, as in every industrial society, are likely to be very poor. The hills will need wise compassionate leadership if much sorrow is to be avoided."

She paused again, tapping at her desk with a pencil. "Please consider devoting a part of your life to politics," she said, looking into him with the level gaze she used to skewer a lagging schoolboy. "If necessary, sacrifice other things to do it. Help the people find ways of building strong public schools, good hospitals, roads, just courts, just taxes—all the things they must have. These mountains will be a wonderful place for a young man to practice medicine, but it will be an equally good place for a young politician to play the statesman. You are related to half the people in the county; they admire you now as a teacher, and soon they will admire you as a physician. You'll have a duty, Tom. Please don't shrink from it."

"I won't," he murmured as they stood up. And he meant it deep in his soul.

CHAPTER

7

Tom Bonham graduated from the Louisville College of Medicine in 1920, and finished a one-year internship in a Cincinnati hospital and a three-month course in surgery in the autumn of the following year. He seized with sureness on courses in chemistry, pharmacy, and anatomy and was especially outstanding in studies dealing with the infant sciences of psychology and psychiatry. He brought a knife-edged cunning to diagnosis, his retentive memory enabling him to focus virtually all textbook knowledge on his every interview and examination. His professors were in agreement that Bonham was destined to become one hell of a fine doctor "Unless," as the Dean phrased it at a faculty meeting, "that imperious way of his gets him killed by a mere plebe." As things turned out, he graduated second in a class of thirty-three. Rose Quinlan's best student was inferior—though only slightly so—to but one of his classmates, a college graduate who had done all his premedical studies at Princeton. He promptly passed this information to Helen Boyd in a congratulatory letter. "In its infancy," he wrote, "Indian River may expect to run behind the Ivy League, but you and your teachers will soon make Indian River first."

His four-year absence had not been without its perils, however. There had never been enough money, though he worked three hours every evening cleaning up a flour and meal mill, and worked many Sundays at such jobs as could be found. His straits would have been much worse, however, had it not been for the assistance he received from the Bonhams. His mother required every penny she could find for the mouths still at home and to pay the yearly taxes on the land, but others answered her pleas with startling generosity despite the immense difficulty of finding even the smallest sums in the central Appalachians in those years. Soiled and wrinkled greenbacks from the sale of a few cattle or sheep and walnut and oak trees were delivered to Delilah as loans to "help Tom git through school." Old "Granny Jane" Bonham, a midwife who had pulled a thousand yelling mountaineers into the world, sent him a hundred dollars— her life's savings. "He kin pay me back easy enuff when he gits to be a doctor," she declared. And Delilah's unmarried sister, Mahala, who lived alone in a tiny cabin in Wild Cat Branch and acquired trifling sums selling ginseng, honey from her bee gums, and cakes of sugar boiled out of the sap of sugar trees, sent the student fourteen one dollar notes. Such small loans were witnessed by promissory notes the grateful recipient mailed to his beneficiaries and amounted to the astronomical total of $1,041 when the last day of his internship was completed.

Two days before he packed his few possessions for the trip to Blacksville and Indian River, he received a parcel from a Vermont village. It contained a beautiful, finely grained, black leather medical valise with "THOMAS J. BONHAM,

M.D." stenciled in gold across its front. Inside was a neatly penned and typically cryptic note:

Justice excels knowledge as knowledge excels ignorance.

Congratulations,

Rose Quinlan.

The three-hundred-mile trip home was vastly different from the journey down the river four years earlier. Then he had ridden a mule seventy miles to a railhead and a narrow-gauge logging train that carried him fifty miles to a connection with the Appalachian and Northern. Now the A & N had pushed its tracks all the way to Blacksville, and a prong thrust eastward up Indian River. The graduate was able to ride the stifling, closely packed cars to a whistle stop a hundred yards from Fort Bonham, while a full cargo of sweating and odoriferous humanity went on to the coal camp nearing completion around the bend.

He could scarcely believe his eyes and ears as the chugging locomotive dragged the eight cars up the winding valleys and around the rocky knuckles of ridges. Nearly half, perhaps, were mountaineers, men and women slouching in traditional homemade and ill-fitting garb—chewing, smoking and taking not infrequent drinks from bottles of colorless whiskey. Children sat on and around them in droves and babies sucked at bared breasts. Those were not surprising, of course, being the very essence of the society that had spawned and nurtured him, but the other people in the cars overwhelmed him with their differences of tongue and custom. Letters from kinsmen and from the ladies at the settlement school had warned him of almost unimaginable changes, but he found the reality both astounding and tremendously exciting.

The world, it seemed, had converged on the sleepy backwater that had long been Slaughter County. Two Albanians with black shawls and derby hats ate salami and onions and drank wine on the seats directly opposite his own. A little cluster of sad-faced and mustached Italians listened mournfully as one of their friends wrung a doleful note from an accordion. Immaculate and superbly tailored gentlemen kept their peace in the forward corner, occasionally exchanging a few well-modulated words or checking the time against glittering gold pocket watches. And poor whites in denim overalls or cheap cotton suits—men whose accents and manner betrayed their origins in the Appalachian outlands and the deep South—sat amid more confident appearing workmen from Pennsylvania and Illinois. An incredible babel roared and rattled through the cars, sometimes drowning the cries of the conductor as he shouted the names of brand-new coal towns, Rosskellan, Norbert, Ann Ellen and Shabtown. When the cars ground to a halt amid hissing steam and groaning brake couplings at the cry of "Indian River," Tom Bonham pulled himself erect, shouldered his bags through the crowded aisle and smiled as he climbed down the iron steps. Home had become one hell of an interesting place!

Delilah Bonham was fifty-eight when her dream of seeing her husband's son become a doctor was fulfilled. She met him at the little whistle stop and a grandson—Charlie's ten-year-old Jakie—helped them carry the suitcases to her house. She lived alone except for Jakie, who was assigned to stay with her "for company" against loneliness, but the next day all of William Bonham's children and grandchildren gathered to greet and congratulate the doctor and hear his accounts of what life was like in the city and in the medical school, and to marvel that one of their own blood had learned and seen so much.

All were married now, the sisters to mountaineers who had eagerly dropped the drudgery of farming for the perils and profit of coal digging. Julie's man, Jim Martin, was already a mine foreman at the Skull Fork mine of the Blue Jacket Coal and Carbon Corporation. Maude's husband, Jack Markham, was short and lean as a sawbriar and was one of the best coal loaders in the same mine. Randall Lacey was "about the busiest man in the county" as a tipple hand at the operation of King Koal and Karbon Korporation at the Forks of Indian River, but managed to find time to keep his wife, Dicey, continually pregnant. Tom's brothers Charlie and Tilford, too, had taken spouses and their tribes were increasing. Charlie's wife came from Middle Fork of Troublesome Creek, out of the old and crowded cabin of Nathan Cook, but Tilford, the oldest of Delilah's brood, had captured the vivacious daughter of Swede Dinkler, a subcontractor who had brought his family up from Alabama while he and his Italian workmen built stone railroad abutments and piers. Tom alone was unmarried, but the twenty-six-year-old bachelor counted ten nieces and nephews with a couple of pregnancies pointing to other imminent increases in the Bonham line.

A world war and its insatiable appetite for fuel had convulsed the valleys. The sinuous new railroad bed cut a slender raw terrace along the undulating folds of Laurel Ridge, leaped chasms on spidery wooden trestles, spanned creeks and rivers on scores of monotonously similar steel bridges, and bored through hills in tunnels already blackened by oily coal smoke, soot and ashes. New towns of four- and five-room wooden houses dotted bottom land Tom remembered as cornfields, and teams of carpenters stretched the frail, boxlike structures around hillside coves and spread them like dropped dice across rolling knolls and up narrow hollows. Commissary stores and payroll offices of sturdier brick, gaunt hotels, boarding houses, and recreation halls were in every stage of framing, sheathing and roofing. The pounding of hammers and the droning of saws echoed from ancient cliffs, and new tipples sluiced coal into railroad cars. In Slaughter County alone, seven coal towns sent floods of glittering carbon each year from the Moose, Gray Elk, and Splint seams to the markets on the Great Lakes, and men spoke with boundless confidence of an endless boom stretching into a coal starved future, of prices set in a seller's market and of an eventual production of fifteen million tons annually. And, wherever he went, Tom was welcomed by company officials whose communities would need his skills and wanted him to practice his profession in their towns where the corporations were building schools and hospitals much faster than teachers and physicians could be found to staff them.

But the place and the prospect that pleased him most was the camp being built in a bend of Indian River a mile above Old John-of-All's first settlement. The Northeast Coal Corporation held contracts to supply fuel to factories in northeastern cities and those steel and electrical firms held most of its stock. Its three hundred and eleven houses were nearing completion, half of them two-storied duplex affairs with porches front and back and a dividing wall down the middle.

Neatly painted privies and coal houses stood a few yards to the rear and drilled wells supplied water which hand pumps drew into the kitchens. Occasional trees had been left on a gently sloping hill and amid them rose the spacious houses of company executives. One of them, an eight-room, steam-heated structure would be the home of the town's physician, and directly below at the end of fifty yards of concrete side-walk stood a mighty enticement. Set twenty feet in from the street and surrounded by what would someday be a plot of grass and shrubs, the little hospital occupied the center of the brand-new village of Noreco. The building was complete and unopened crates of equipment lay in the newly painted rooms and corridors.

Ben Fleming was a Pennsylvanian who had lived the coal business and breathed coal-camp dust and fumes all of his forty-two years. His father and uncles had been in the mining business in a dozen counties in Pennsylvania and West Virginia and the disorder of camp living came to him as wholly natural and right. His clothing—whether a perfectly tailored suit or the denim shirt and trousers of his inspection forays—rode his spare frame with an easy nonchalance. Except for a neatly trimmed moustache, his face knew the discipline of a daily shave. He was quick to recognize the advantages that could flow from the recruitment of a doctor from the local populace—and out of the county's largest and most influential family at that—and showed off the waiting hospital and its possibilities with a true salesman's urbanity and polish.

The building was of the same white, yellow-trimmed weather-boarded construction as the rest of the sprawling camp, but was all on a single floor raised two feet above the ground on concrete posts. A ten-foot porch surrounded ten rooms, a huge square ward, a kitchen, a dining room, a storage room for medicines, a consultation room, and an operating room. The surgery was skylighted with frosted glass and tall eastern windows admitted long shafts of light onto a gleaming nickel-plated surgical table standing amid the splintered wreckage of its shipping crate. Glass-doored steel cabinets lined two walls and wooden boxes contained tools and implements. The floor was terrazoed and easy to scrub and disinfect.

Tom was astonished. The Slaughter County of his boyhood had contained 4,500 people. In four years, that number has soared to 20,000. Then there had been two doctors. One of them, old Dr. Elihu Free, had never gone to medical school a day in his life, but as a young man had ordered a couple of textbooks on anatomy, diseases, diagnosis and "curatives," and had gone about for fifty years distributing "papers of medicine" to his trusting patients, a surgical saw across the pommel of his saddle, and a collection of pills and potions in his saddlebags. His heavy-handedness was legendary, but he enjoyed a great reputation, especially as a "fever doctor." Dr. John Jenkins, on the other hand, was known as a "schooled doctor," because he had once taught for a few terms and had then spent a year at some sort of medical school in Indianapolis. He kept a yellowed certificate in a frame in his little office in Blacksville and traveled the winding trails to "fetch babies," set broken bones, probe for bullets and dispense futile medicines for that agonizing killer he called "cramp colic," which other generations would know as appendicitis. Unfortunately, Dr. Jenkins had fallen under the sway of his own medicines and came to the end of his years as a notorious addict.

Now this was all changed. Both the old healers were dead. Blacksville had attracted three university-trained physicians and the larger mining concerns were building treatment facilities that Free and Jenkins would have deemed palatial. In them a man could find time to study each problem and bring the best of his art and science to cure and restoration. If the new coalfield was an industrial frontier, it was also a social and political frontier, a land of new beginnings for the professions!

Ben Fleming laid his hand on the shiny operating table and looked at Tom. His quiet, assured tone and level gaze were those of a man who had long had his way and was confident that he would continue to do so. "This company needs you, Dr. Bonham," he began. "But, more important by far, the men who are going to work in our mines will need you. I know from long experience that the price of coal is pain. Some will be killed and many will be injured, and some of the injured will be your kinfolks because we have already signed onto our payroll a number of men named Bonham. The women and children will need you, too. And we hope that for the benefit of this community—and of your own career as well, you will join us here at Noreco." He lit a cigarette and drew a long draft. "Our stockholders have invested a generous sum in this building and its equipment, but they are nothing without a genuinely good physician. They can heal no one, but you can make them heal. Frankly, we have worked hard to recruit doctors, but the kind we want are hard to find. They have positions they don't want to leave or else they want to go to the cities with their glamor and bright lights. You are the kind of man we want and need. There is a house waiting for you, and this hospital will be yours to use and to run.

"And that's not all by any means. Your payroll assignments from the men will start you off at a thousand a month." He chuckled. "As a young bachelor, you'll find the women will have something for you, too. After all, we're going to have some hot-blooded fillies around here. They always turn up in coal camps."

The doctor moved into the big house behind the hospital a week later, filling three of the rooms with oak and walnut furniture from the company's huge commissary. And though Granny Jane always insisted a Bonham was "born with a hard on and never lived long enough for it to go down," he lived alone as a bachelor for three years, taking his meals at the little hospital and striving through eighty-hour weeks to bring an effective medical facility to a raw, brawling town so new no map showed its name.

The railroads were steel arteries which pumped people, lumber, groceries and other things necessary for mining into Slaughter County, and pumped out coal in an ever-rising flood. Towns sprang up like mushrooms—company-owned camps and shabby little crossroads trading centers—but there were no paved roads and even the county seat lacked so much as a single sidewalk. Everything came in or went out by the outrageously overloaded single-track line, and few were the physicians willing to ride the soot-coated passenger cars into this swirling industrial vortex. There were never enough of them, and like Tom Bonham, the few who came were promptly overwhelmed. There were no specialists and out of unavoidable necessity general practitioners turned their hands to every medical problem from fevers to obstetrics to surgery. The men borne from the mines with mangled limbs and broken backs and the pregnant women moaning in travail required immediate attention, and within a month after he hung a sign lettered with his name near the front door of the Noreco hospital, Tom Bonham was seeing and treating a variety and profusion of patients that on reflection left him numb with disbelief.

When Jake Bonham brought in his lovely long-legged daughter, Bessie, with a dreadful bellyache that could be nothing but acute appendicitis, the doctor and his nurses, Dora Compton and Mag Rierson, put her out with ether and removed the bloated, pus-filled pouch. When George Early killed a miner named Davis and was shot twice himself through the folds of his guts, the young doctor and his loyal henchwomen did not hesitate to slice open his abdomen, dip out the stinking offal, sew up the perforations and remove the hopelessly mangled parts altogether. This work was so successful the patient lived to "pull' seven years in the state penitentiary. The doctor was his own X-ray technician, and his only consultants were the score of textbooks on the shelves in his waiting room and the medical and surgical journals that came through the mail. The other doctors possessed no more knowledge and far less confidence, and there was no one to raise an eyebrow or perform an autopsy on his errors of judgment. His laboratory facilities were rudimentary in the extreme and could add little confirmation to his deductions. Diagnoses could be little more than shrewd guesses, but a large percentage of his guesses hit on the ailment or close to it, and the treatments afforded at the least a sufficient measure of relief. His successes and his absolute confidence in himself laid the foundation for his solid reputation as a "knowing doctor," and the sick and the broken came or were brought to him from dusty little camps with no physicians of their own and from shacks and cabins far back in the remote hinterlands. The operators and their wives continued to call him "Doctor," but the miners and their wives and the farmers with their cornfields and moonshine stills strung out along the rocky creeks referred to him with a mixture of familiarity and respect as "Doc" Bonham, and as "Doc" he would be known to a growing collection of friends and foes to the end.

His purse grew with his reputation and following. Six hundred men worked along the tunnels and in the dusty pits of Northeast Coal Corporation, and each of them was required, as a condition of his employment, to pay two dollars a month to the doctor and a dollar and a half to support the hospital. The capitalists who ran the corporation decreed a thorough-going system of socialized medicine for their men, and the payroll deductions sent a reliable flow of dollars to the man and the facility that provided medical care for the community. Fortunately for both, most of the men and women in the camps were vigorous and young, and their children were sturdy. Besides, they were unaccustomed to physicians and relied much on time and their own nostrums to heal their aches and pains. In their turbulent half-backwoods, half-industrial environment, it was considered a mark of weakness to seek the aid of a doctor except in emergencies where the necessity was apparent, so Doc, his two nurses, his cook, janitor and housekeeper were able to manage what otherwise would have been a wholly unmanageable situation. Besides the miners, their rotundly pregnant wives and the hordes of underwashed children that swarmed like brawling ants about the streets and across the eroding hills, he saw people from growing Blacksville and other parts of the county, and they paid in cash for his services and medicines. In his third year of practice, he collected twenty-five thousand dollars of a variety inflation had not yet sapped of their substance, a heartwarming sum in a time when income taxes were trifling, good steak sold for forty-five cents a pound and a thousand dollars would buy an expensive new car. The coal industry prospered and so did Doc. The little notes that had sent him through medical school were paid off with interest, and money accumulated in his account in the new and thriving Miners' Bank of Blacksville.

In one respect, he was a worry to his mother and the dozens of aging men and women who were his uncles, aunts and cousins. They were dismayed by his failure to marry and sire offspring. The Bonhams, they pointed out, always had big families and always stuck together. Big families and close ties to one another were the source of Bonham strength and ascendancy, and Delilah fretted over his failure to take a wife and add to the mounting score of her grandchildren. "It ain't natural and it ain't right, Tom," she warned him whenever he stopped for a visit. "You ought not to be livin' by yerself in that big house. You need a woman to live there and sleep with you and have you some babies. Mind me, now," she would plead, "get busy and find a wife!"

The warnings and entreaties were unnecessary as matters turned out. Until he finished medical school, Tom had been too poor to marry, and for a time thereafter he had been too busy and too engrossed in his work to really consider the matter. But all that changed in a mere moment one afternoon in 1923 when he encountered a young teacher named Irene Jackson.

The day was dry and hot and coal dust from the tipple drifted like a gray ghost through the town. Tom had gotten in his Model T Ford to make a house call when he saw her, a diminutive figure in one of those shortened dresses then coming into style. She carried a huge parcel and looked altogether very enticing. Could he help her with a ride, he inquired, trying vainly to recollect a line of poetry from Shakespeare or some other discerning observer about "the liquefaction of her clothes." He could and did give her a ride to her quarters in the huge boxlike roominghouse on the hill. Before she left the car, they were remarkably well acquainted, and the day ended on a note totally different from its beginning. Suddenly medicine and patients were of mere secondary interest. Not for a moment could he put out of his mind the firm arms and legs, the dexterous hands and fingers, the small perfect mouth beneath the straight little nose. And the tiny beads of sweat that had gathered just above her eyebrows made it all seem so ravishingly natural and wholly irresistible. It was not within his nature to cage himself with such an emotional torment for long, and a few hours later he was knocking on her door.

The dust and sweat of the afternoon were gone in the evening, and she greeted him with an aplomb and frankness that showed she had expected and wanted his visit. She wore a white starched dress, and he perceived at a single downward glance that her breasts were of the same firm and perfectly proportioned quality that had distracted him throughout the afternoon. As he would later phrase it, it was "lust at first sight," and as she stood aside to let him enter, he resolved to have this woman without delay.

Doc had never imagined anyone with such poise, such sureness, so much utter charm. She radiated self-confidence from every pore, but there was a self-effacing air about her that appealed mightily to his male ego. She sat him down on the settee by the window of her small but tastefully furnished apartment and put him completely at ease. While he learned about her, she made decisive mental notes about his own background. She was twenty-three and was a recent graduate of a teachers' college in Virginia. She had come up from a foothill county to teach the second grade in Noreco, a town with a new school system she had read about in a school journal. Her father was a politician back in James County and had been elected sheriff the year before. Her family had been in politics for generations, and she had heard talk of candidates and voters morning, noon and night as long as she could remember. She had two brothers and a sister, and was fascinated with life in the obstreperous, brawling world of coal. The company's schools and pay scale were much better than she could have found elsewhere. She concluded with a disarming and devastating candor, "There was only one thing needed to make me completely happy right here—" and then with a smile that dissolved him completely, "and I think I found that this afternoon."

To this Doc could only groan, short of breath and taut

with excitement, "How could I live to be twenty-seven years old without meeting you?"

What may have been the astonishment in the sheriff's household when the letter was read telling of her marriage to the camp doctor can only be imagined. She met him at three in the afternoon on Wednesday and was his lawfully wedded wife with all her possessions stored neatly in his house before dusk on Saturday. Ben Fleming and his wife got up a reception for them at the general manager's house, with a huge keg of mellow old bourbon that had survived the clutches of the Prohibitionists, and the short, decisive romance was toasted by nearly a hundred revelers. But Doc was too hungry for the woman he had already nicknamed "Twinkles" to dull his appetite with alcohol, and before the merriment reached its peak, he fetched her away. They escaped by a side entrance and fled along the graveled path to their own door. Safely inside he kissed her with a passion. She stood on tiptoe to return it, and he carried her off to his bed with a triphammer pounding inside his skull. After they had loved and loved again, he fell asleep, her naked body gently clasped in his arms, his last happy thought an unreserved approval of Delilah's admonition, "It ain't natural to live alone. You need a woman to sleep with!"

Nine months from that night, Twinkles presented him with the first of their children—a small but sturdy boy whom she named after the sheriff, Jesse Jackson. When Jesse Jackson was two, she brought forth their daughter, Tess, and the brood was complete. She served Doc with a single-minded but unsubservient devotion that left him happier than he had previously imagined anyone could be. As a lover, she almost never said "no" or "not now." She continued to teach through school terms the company's funds stretched out to eight months, adding her modest salary to the substantial income of her husband. And, besides the babies begotten on her body, Doc acquired other things. For one thing, he arranged to buy out the other heirs of William Bonham, and in 1927 became the sole owner of the six hundred acres still remaining in the estate. His brothers and sisters were willing enough to sell. Their fecundity was burdensome at the commissary counters, and there was little prospect that the land could benefit any of them within half a century. As Doc explained to them, the coal companies in Slaughter County already owned more than 80 percent of the minerals. The mining companies held thousands of acres in their own right and could lease practically unlimited territories from the land corporations. He pointed out that Northeast Coal Corporation could mine fifty or sixty years on its fee tracts without needing access to neighboring lands. He wanted to buy the old Bonham place for sentimental reasons and to avoid having it split up into smaller holdings, not because he expected to profit from it. It was all very reasonable and the deeds were signed, with $4,800 paid to Delilah for her dower rights and $12,200 divided equally among his three sisters and two brothers. Of course, his mother would occupy the house undisturbed for her lifetime. On the whole it was the best of all possible arrangements. The other heirs received their money when they needed it badly for many purposes, and their mother had money for her old age and continued security in her home. At the same time Doc assured that the ancestral lands to which all felt an affectionate attachment would continue in the Bonham line, intact and consoling.

Three years after he bought the Bonham lands, Doc and Twinkles commenced building a house for themselves and their two children. The site was a broad, moss-grown natural flat on one of the spurs that ran down like immense treecovered fingers out of the soaring side of Big Laurel Mountain. "King Arthur" Carerro and a half dozen other Italian masons were set to work quarrying gray sandstone out of the flank of the hill and cementing the pieces together again into a huge, castlelike box. There were ten rooms, including four big square bedrooms upstairs. A vast, gaunt, coal-fired furnace in the basement warmed it against winter storms, and broad, tall windows and high ceilings cooled it in summer. It luxuriated in two bathrooms fitted with dark blue fixtures and was roofed with red terra-cotta tiles and floored with unblemished white oak from Doc's own land. The stone walls were ten inches thick and smoothly plastered and papered. Two immense tulip trees and some hemlocks and hornbeams had survived the axes of loggers and now cast the lawn and deep porch in cooling shade. From the new wicker chairs on the porch, Doc and Twinkles could see the railroad with its endless coal trains, and to the east could look down on the ordered rows of yellow, white-trimmed houses, the commissaries, offices and clattering tipples of Noreco. They could see, also, the hospital where Doc toiled to restore his patients to health, and to keep them healthy so they could bring out the hard glittering lumps by day and then, by night, breed replacements for their worn-out and broken selves when they fell in the Stygian pits. And to the west Fort Bonham stood, restored and ageless, the center of the little campus where Helen Boyd and her friends brought Shakespeare, Latin and physics to a new generation of Appalachian children.

The house and its new furnishings cost Doc $29,000, and Twinkles, more radiant than ever, insisted on a reception to introduce the place to the community. Coal men and their bejeweled wives came from twenty coal towns, until their high, ungainly Cadillacs and Buicks blocked all the driveway and sank deep into the soft soil of the new lawn. They wandered gaily through the rooms and halls, their conversation enlivened by the keg of excellent whiskey one of Doc's patients had aged in charcoal for the occasion. Coal was king and the guests radiated confidence and assurance. Prices for the fuel were high, labor was abundant and wages modest Their world was aglow as Ben Fleming sat at the piano and played the "Buffalo Rag" and the "Sidewalks of New York." Everybody cheered so enthusiastically that he stayed at the keyboard for an hour. When he rose, he placed his hand on his host's arm with that easy mixture of familiarity and distance that had dissolved so many arguments and convinced so many opponents. "Doctor Bonham," he said, "it was a great day when you and our company got together. The years have been good to you, and you have been very good for us! Needless to say, we look forward to a long continuance of this happy relationship."

But Doc was not so sure of the future. As a child of Delilah Bonham, he trusted little and doubted much. He had neither time nor inclination to read economic journals in which learned and verbose experts proclaimed the shape of the future, but he watched developments with the same keen appetite for details with which he questioned and treated his patients. In 1929, he quietly sold the stocks a Louisville broker held for him and withdrew nearly all his money from the Miners' Bank of Blacksburg. Feverish speculation on Wall Street had driven share prices to fantastic levels and Doc felt safer elsewhere. He put the cash in a huge bank in Cincinnati, and he waited.

CHAPTER
8

Smoke from hundreds of chimneys eddied through the valley and settled like a grim deadly pall on disconsolate Noreco. A slow steady rain drummed against tarpaper roofs and sent rivulets along the sidewalks and streets. A dozen Model T and Model A Fords lined the driveway behind the gray, stone house on the hill. Twinkles poured coffee and served A & P cookies to more than a score of men drawn up in a huge ragged circle in the living room. Many of them wore opencollared shirts, cheap suits that fit indifferently and sat in stiff uneasy embarrassment on chairs Doc had brought from the dining room. Both host and hostess had met each of them at the door and made every effort to put them at ease. Then after a while, Twinkles sensed they would be more relaxed and communicative in her absence and withdrew to another room.

Slaughter County had lain in the grip of a tightening Republican machine for twelve years, ever since the railroad and huge sums of coal money had reached the thirty-four precincts. The operators felt more comfortable with the GOP in power at the county courthouse and had pumped cash into Jake Runyon's organization and put the clout of economic pressure behind his candidates. Runyon had been elected justice of the peace in 1917, a minor office indeed, but one that brought him to the monthly meetings of the fiscal court. The eight justices and their chairman, the county judge, had charge of the county's financial affairs, dispensing the meager road funds and doling out money to the school board. None of them was required by law to be a lawyer, or even to be literate; and as a matter of fact, four of the justices could neither read nor write their names. But Jake Runyon was different. He held a third-class teaching certificate and was a tolerable land surveyor. Short, ruddy, cautious and ambitious, he moved to assume leadership of the slouchy, tobacco chewing JPs. When county elections rolled around again, he ran for county judge, and the office's influence and patronage. Ben Fleming and his newly fledged coal operators' association backed him cautiously but skillfully, and despite the automatic and vigorous opposition of the Bonhams and their Democratic friends, Runyon won. His margin was a scant 2.3 votes, causing his Democratic adversaries to deride him as "little landslide Jake," but that was enough to put him in, and in 1930 his third four-year term was drawing to its end. He had proved to be a tough, resilient and cunning politician to whom victory was everything. Each race widened his margin and brought him more allies—and a growing number of detractors. But coal had been happy with him, for he had been willing to accept its support and to give in return low taxes and minimal services. Many people thought "Little Jake" Runyon was invincible.

The men Doc had gotten together in his living room were about all that were left of his party's leadership after twelve years of defeat and failure. They and perhaps as many more who had not made it to the meeting were the precinct chairmen and other local party officers who had struggled for years without funds or encouragement from the county seat and state capitol to elect a series of nondescript candidates. They were beaten, of course, by Republican chairmen who had cash for whiskey, cash to hire poll workers, cash for posters and handbills, and cash to buy the votes of numerous "floaters." Some were miners, a few ran country stores, one or two had held small offices at one time or another, but all lacked money or friends who could supply it. As they drank Doc's coffee and smoked his cigarettes, an air heavy with defeat and weariness pressed upon the shoulders of their rumpled coats.

Doc poked up the fire of hickory and hard cannel coal that blazed in an iron basket in the deep recesses of the fireplace, then turned to the men. The rain increased suddenly, beating against the windowpanes and sending a few drops down the chimney to sputter against the yellow coals.

"I'm sure all of you can guess why I've asked you to come here," he said. Then with finality, "I want us to start out and rebuild the Democratic party in Slaughter County."

Some of the men gazed with shifting and doubt-filled eyes into the flickering flames, but most of them straightened up in their chairs and looked about at one another and at Doc with mild approval. "Amen," sighed George Downer from Henry Ford's huge camp on Buffalo Creek.

Doc continued, "The Democrats ran this county for a hundred years. My people held offices in this county, and some of you had close relatives who used to win elections. But for the last twelve years the coal operators have been the government. They have a county full of captive men and women locked up in their coal camps and squeeze them into voting for Jake Runyon and his little clique of rubber stamps. Practically everybody in the courthouse takes orders from Little Jake—and Little Jake takes orders from Ben Fleming!"

"That's the damn truth fur shore," affirmed Tom Morton. Tom had lost a leg when a bank car crushed him against a coal rib and walked on a homemade hickory peg leg. He had run for JP and, on a wave of sympathy from other miners, had been elected. He took in a hundred dollars or so a month in small fees, and was the only Democrat on the fiscal court. He lived at the mouth of Poor Fork where he held a considerable following of miners and hard scrabble, hillside farmers. "I can't git nuthin fur my district," he allowed. "Ever time I ask fur sump'n, the judge sez they ain't no money, then goes and spends it to benefit some o' his sellouts." Then reflectively, "Jake musta bought three thousand votes last time around. It was reely a scandal!"

Doc nodded agreement. "You know what's happening, Tom. You're in the courthouse every day. You see and know about the things the rest of us just suspect! And you know what it is to run against coal company money, and how it feels to have a man come around with a satchel full of cash and hit you with it on the night before election."

"I know the feelin', myself," chirped a tiny birdlike man almost buried in one of Twinkle's overstuffed armchairs. "Spider" Smith made his living running a poolroom in Blacksville. He had served a term as coroner, holding inquests on dead bodies which turned up from time to time. "They shore beat hell outa me atter I thought I had it sewed up a second time. Jake sent old Lou Gibson around to sweeten things up, and peeple I thought was my lifelong friends turned agin me in a minute."

"Money is not the only tool in their chest," Doc said, settling into a chair. "They've got the jobs, in fact they've got practically all the jobs in the county. The operators control all work in the mines, and a man has to vote right as well as work right or he's soon off the payroll and blacklisted. Jake and his Republicans sit on top of the county's jobs, and if a man gets a job or anything else from any official in the court-house he's got to be cleared by Ben Fleming. A man can't wear a badge as a deputy or even draw a little pauper's voucher without Ben's approval."

"You caint hardly fart in this county, let alone git a job, unless hit's o.k. with the operators. Old Clay Morgan kin smell just about anything that happens in his camp and if hit's off the least bit he'll send a agent around to pay ye off and put ya outa yer house," gloomed "Bug eyes" Johnson, an aptly nicknamed merchant who also kept the post office at Dover on Jake's Fork. He had been appointed by Woodrow Wilson and sold groceries and dry goods in a store he had inherited from his father. The Bonhams and Johnsons had been friends and allies for a century, and a squad of Johnsons had fought under Ben Bonham in the Civil War. The Johnsons were, as a rule, huge of frame with broad chins, banana noses and long prominent ears. More importantly, from a political viewpoint, they were clannish and slow to forget an injury. Several young Johnsons worked in Clay Morgan's mines on Rummy's Fork of Jake's Creek and one of "Bug eyes" sons had been fired for trying to start a union. Something of the light of battle flickered in the postmaster's eyes as he contributed to the discussion.

"By God, somebody's got to stand up to th' operators and fight 'em," exploded Sam Chaney as he surged out of his chair. He was of middle height with the huge hands of a coal miner, but his one suit was neatly fitted to his frame, his brown ankletop shoes were brightly polished and his hair had been freshly trimmed. In better days his propensity for broad bright ties and fancy suits had tagged him with the nickname "Dapper Sam." He was always ready to make a speech, and his troublemaking had brought his expulsion from a halfdozen camps in West Virginia. His black eyes flashed under heavy eyebrows and a lengthening forehead as he continued. "We are Democrats, and this means we've got nothin' except strong backs and weak minds and, generally, wet asses. We've got votes, too, but because we've been weak-minded and never smart, we've let the Republicans take over this county and this state and the whole damned country. And they've throwed us into the worst damned depression anybody ever heard of, and now we're all about to starve to death!"

He stared reflectively about at the circle of faces and his voice sank to a low dramatic murmur. "I am a union man, too, mornin', noon and night. In Pennsylvania and West Virginia and here in this pore benighted state, I've fought to get out of bondage and to help other people get out of bondage, and God knows I've suffered for it. I've been gunwhipped by comp'ny thugs; I've been jailed by comp'ny judges; I've been fired by comp'ny bosses, and had my family set outa comp'ny houses onto the roadside in the dead of winter to freeze and starve. I've put eighteen years of hard labor into the mines diggin' coal for companies and today I've got a wife and four kids, some worthless furniture—" he ran his hands into his pocket and pulled out a crumpled dollar bill and some tarnished brass disks, "and a dollar in cash and eighty-five cents in scrip! I've got nuthin' to lose but that," as he dropped the money back into his pocket, "and, by God, if Dr. Tom Bonham will help us get goin', I'll follower him to the heart of hell if we can break the grip of these damnable comp'nies and get to be free men agin!"

"Tell 'em Sam," "Ain't nobody can talk like Sam," and "That's the truth if I ever heerd it told" came from his approving listeners. Doc's older brother, Tilford, puffed on a pipeful of Prince Albert and stared from one face to the next. He had dropped out of school after eight grades and wandered away to Oklahoma and Kansas, then served a hitch in the army. Now he worked for the railroad company as a train dispatcher. Unlike Doc, his waist was expanding and he saw the world through thick, steel-rimmed glasses. He lacked Doc's quick decisiveness and was slower of speech and action, but he was an omnivorous and insatiable reader and a shrewd judge of men and circumstances. He traded and trafficked so skillfully that he had acquired a row of small houses which he rented to miners, and some other property besides. When the Depression struck, he was prospering as part owner of a tieyard, supplying hewed white oak timbers to the A & N's section crews. But the tieyard was gone now, and he lived on a salary of twenty-five dollars a week. "Everything you men have said is the truth, but hell, that ain't enough! You can't win just 'cause you're right and tell the truth. Oh brother mine, did you come through the crash with any money? And if you did, are you willing to spend it in an election?"

Doc did not answer directly. "I want to be county judge," he began. "Under the state constitution a man doesn't have to be a lawyer to hold the office, but he ought to be honest and he ought to be loyal to his friends. If I am elected, I can do some highly beneficial things for this county—and I can help every one of you. You Democrats can hold the jobs and draw the salaries now tied down by Jake's gang. Our friends can wear the badges and carry the guns. We can decide where the roads will be built, and we can throw Dick Jones out and elect a Democrat circuit judge, a man who can try a case without calling the coal operators to ask their advice about how he ought to decide it. The Democrats in this county are outnumbered and poor and the Republicans have all the advantages, but a lot of Republicans work in the mines for their bread and are fed up with things. They will join us if we can get a decent campaign going. They can't join nothing; we've got to give them a cause to vote for."

The little group listened with complete attention. It was apparent that each man was pondering how his own affairs might change for the better if Little Jake Runyon went back to his farm on the Camp Fork and Dr. Tom Bonham became the county's executive officer in the front office of the crumbling county courthouse.

Doc waited a moment for his words to sink in, then continued. "This county has been good to me. The people have trusted me, and I have prospered. When I left medical school and came here to practice, I was less than a pauper, for I had nothing and was in debt. Now my debts are paid, and I have some possessions. In this respect I may be better off than some of our Republican coal operators who have, as you know, been going broke at better than a fair rate during the last year or two."

The men looked at one another and giggled. The thought of a bankrupt mine operator was not a heartbreaking one for most of them.

Doc continued. "I am willing to lay a substantial sum on the line in a race for county judge if you and my other friends will give me your wholehearted support. It goes without saying, of course, that I can't win without you, and it is just as clear that none of you has any political future in this county unless I do win. We can all win together or..." and he opened his hands in a gesture of hopeless futility.

Steve Dominic chewed his fat black cigar and scowled at Doc through a veritable thicket of downward swooping eyebrows. As a young man in San Andrea, Italy, he had been a fiery socialist and had fled to America to escape conscription for a capitalistic war. He was still a Socialist, but because there was no Socialist party, he was perforce a working Democrat. A dozen relatives had followed him to the Appalachian coalfield and had clustered with still other Italians on the hill above the little Catholic church in Dicco, a town owned by Diamond Iron and Coal Company. Their community was known to white miners as "woptown" and the stocky, volatile people were regarded by most of their neighbors with good-humored disdain. But they had a sense of unity, they voted, and Steve was their acknowledged leader and spokesman. His huge nose, sturdy teeth and thick calloused

hands betrayed generations of peasant blood, and he sometimes shook with indignation when he spoke of workers robbed
of their rightful place and legacy by landlords and industrial
magnates. He was honest, and he could be brutally frank.

"Doctair Bonham, you bin doctair in company hospital,
you bin on company payroll, you bin big friends with company officials. You made lotta monney out of alla this. How
come a-now you wanta help these-a people and this-a county?
Why you say these-a things now and did not say it when
times was good and da coal companies was alla reech?"

Doc did not blink or blush, but leaned back in his chair and
studied the stonemason's face. "You are right, Steve, I have
made money, I have prospered under the system the coal companies have set up. I have worked in a company hospital just
as you have worked on company buildings and some of our
friends here have worked in company mines. After all, the
companies owned all the hospitals as well as all the mines." The
men murmured their approval as he went on. "The officials of
this company—and of other companies—have been good to
me. But they needed me, just as I have needed their hospital
and their support. I was in debt, as you were in debt when
you got here from Italy. I have always resented their iron
domination of this county, but what could I have done? I had
no money until I worked it out! They had all the jobs and we
all know, Steve, that until the Depression struck, they had
the miners solidly on their side. In most camps they told the
men the candidates who would be friendly to the coal industry and the men voted for those candidates. Hard times have
caused the miners to change and, by God, Steve, I've changed,
too!"

"Thats good enuff fer me, Doc," came from a curious figure sunk deep into one end of Twinkles' red plush sofa. Joe Carr was five feet, six inches tall and his circumference at the navel was about the same. His father had been a staunch Republican and had brought Joe up accordingly, but when Joe was twenty-three with a wife and three children, he was forced to abandon the Grand Old Party. Then as slight as a sourwood sapling, Joe worked as a slatepicker on a tipple. One morning his gloved fingers strayed too close to the whirring gears that sent the endless conveyors roaring upward with their torrents of coal and slate. The meshed cogs seized his fingers and slowly and implacably devoured them, then crunching the bones, flesh, veins and tendons, a half inch at a time they ground his hand, wrist and arm to an indescribable sausagelike appendage. The tipple foreman heard his shrieks and turned off the power, but the momentum of the machinery sent the steel teeth upward past his elbow. He would have died on the spot if Big Jim Miles had stayed home that day. The burly, round-headed black leaped from a catwalk ten feet above Joe's head, rupturing himself in the process. The agony in his own vitals was gut-closing, but he rammed a steel crowbar into the gears, bringing the monster at last to an abrupt, clattering halt.

Joe Carr did not lose consciousness as a sputtering Model T ambulance carried him along rutted, cinder-strewn streets and three miles of abominable potholed roads to Doc's little hospital. He knew precisely what was going on about him when four men dashed with him and his blood-soaked canvas stretcher through the swinging double doors into the receiving room. He would never forget their heavy, labored breathing and the beads of sweat on their foreheads, nor would he ever forget Doc as he thrust a needle into his intact right arm and the relief that came with the morphine.

Joe left the hospital in four weeks with a five-inch stub and memories of an agony that clamped into his flesh like steel claws. When he remembered the unspeakable horror of his flesh and bone jarring into a ghastly ruin—and the memory came often and unbidden, like a psychological lightning bolt—it hurled him into a search for escape, for refuge. He eschewed alcohol and his wife was a patient bore, so he turned to food. In the taste of food on his tongue, he found a measure of relief from his torment, and he ate endlessly. He ballooned outward, discarding heaps of out-grown clothing in the process. In a curious reaction against the pain that jabbed so remorselessly at the end of his stub and seared excruciatingly at his psyche, he took on an aspect of serene jocularity. Miners liked him and their wives giggled at him, and the "Fat Man," as he came to be called, felt a call to public service. The Republicans could find no niche for him in the courthouse, so he ran for recorder of county records—as a Democrat. In a year when all his running mates were swamped by a Republican landslide, Joe swam through to a handsome victory. After four years watching his depu-ties copy deeds into the huge vellum-bound books, he ran for the legislature, promising to promote more generous com-pensation benefits for crippled miners and their widows. Again he won, and made a number of helpful contacts with state and big-city politicians. His fund of quaint tales and outlandish yarns made him a favorite of the governor and his aides, but at the end of his two-year term in the House of Representatives, a determined drive by Jake Runyon's disciplined organization turned him out. His friends at the capitol found a series of state jobs for Joe so that he was able to devote most of his time to keeping together at least some semblance of a countywide political organization. He had talked to Doc many times in recent months and pressed with every artifice known to his nature to induce the man who had saved his life into the race for county judge.

"Yes, friends," he continued with a broad smile and dulcet tones, "the doctor is right. There is a time for all things, just like the Bible sez. There was a time for Doctor Bonham to lay low and practice medicine, and now a time has come for him to run for judge. And Doc's time in his hospital was necessary, 'cause he was makin' friends an' plowin' the ground. As a doctor, he has made hundreds o' friends who owe him everything and will stick by him now. I know, fer I happen to be one uvem. He saved my life, no question about it, and I'm goin' to campaign straight out fer him till the last ballot is cast."

He pulled himself nearly upright and waved his pudgy hand in a conciliatory gesture. "Why, if Doc had fought the companies afore now, they would a put him out o' the hospital and I, for one, would not be here." The hand patted the huge paunch. "Let's git down to brass tacks and figure out a organization precinct by precinct that can fill the courthouse with Democrats, with Doc leadin' the way, and then build and finance that organization. We can win if we do our groundwork first. Elections ain't won at the polls, they're won days and weeks afore the polls ever open! We can start winnin' here tonight!"

"How do you think we ought to start?" Doc asked matter-of-factly.

"There is only one way to start, we've got to come up with some good issues, things most run-of-the-mill people want, then take the issues to the people. We stir 'em up to push fer the things we offer and see that they git to the polls and mark their papers."

"Alla right, then, whatta you plan to do? What are zee issues?" rumbled from Steve Dominic's thick throat.

"There are two main issues in these mountains, and I intend to run on both of them. First, there is the question of who really runs this country, and second, who pays the cost of running it. Jake Runyon and the other men he has put in the courthouse are shadow officials running a shadow government. They attend to the little things, the details, but policies are reached and all the important decisions are made by the county coal association. For all practical purposes, Ben Fleming is the chief executive officer, and he runs the county. If I am elected, I will change that. Ben Fleming wants captive courts and a captive sheriff so he can arrest and run out of the county anybody who challenges the coal association. And he wants low taxes, so somebody else can be made to pay the bills for the county. The county judge appoints the Board of Tax Supervisors. Ben picks 'em and Jake appoints 'em! The board are company flunkies." Doc breathed the last sentence with scorn curling his thin lips and heaving his arched nose even higher. "These flunkies have practically exempted mining property from taxation. Damn it all, here in Noreco a four-room company house with two porches is valued for tax purposes at $200. Fifteen thousand acres of coal land carries a value of $30,000. Mining machines that cost Henry Ford $5,000 are on the books at three hundred. At the same time, a private citizen who happens to own a little something pays three or four times the industry rate. These low taxes keep schools sorry as hell, keep the county from building any roads, make us the laughingstock of the whole damned world. People in other parts of the country think we are nuts. They read that we've got the best coal and the worst schools in the United States!"

"And our children pay for it all because they grow up ignorant. Our teachers pay because they have to scrimp along on disgraceful little salaries. Everybody pays anytime he's in the courthouse when it rains; the place leaks like a sieve."

"I am going to change all this. I'm going to appoint decent men to the tax board. We're going to tax coal and raise three or four times the amount of money the county is collecting now. We will give a teacher a fair salary—and pay it on time every month, too. We will build new schoolhouses. We will make jobs and put the right men and women in 'em. We'll have something good for everybody who believes in good government and nice little tax increases for everybody who doesn't!"

Sam Chaney smote his palm with a clenched fist. "Now that's one helluva platform to run on, Doc. You may not win with it, but you'll sure stir up a ass-tearing storm with it!"

Doc went on. "I was a little luckier than some of the companies," he chuckled. "I've got a little money left, and they lost theirs when their own little banks went broke. I want to make an outlay for each precinct. I believe when people understand the issues, they'll vote for us, in their own self-interest, but we have to take our story to the camps and up the hollows, and if a few have to be sweetened a little, we'll try to have some sugar."

Joe Carr said blandly, "I have a list of ever' vote seller in the county. The trash'll go fer the man that pays 'em, and if we don't buy 'em, Jake Runyon will. He shore knows how!"

Joe turned to a tall slender black man, stooped, narrowshouldered, big-handed, bald, with deep-set reflective black eyes. "Deacon Timmons," he inquired with consummate unctuousness. "You preach to our colored friends all over the county and know their needs. What will it take to make good Democrats out of them this fall?"

Jesse Timmons had been nearly fifty when he left the cotton fields of the floor-flat Mississippi delta and boarded a train for the narrow valleys and steep hills of Slaughter County. The train was chartered by United States Steel Corporation and its eleven cars carried three hundred "transportation men" and their cotton-garbed women and children to a totally alien world. They brought their few possessions in bundles and in pasteboard boxes, and the men gave up the plow handles and the hoe and the bright sun and blue skies for the pick and shovel and the cramped and deadly darkness of the mines. But coal proved to be as oppressive as cotton, and the prayers and sermons of the preacher sometimes consoled the loss of another promise.

He put his immense gnarled hands together, then interwove and flexed his fingers. The gesture emphasized the almost grotesque slenderness of his wrists and arms. He wore a black serge suit, and his high-top, black patent leather shoes were the most brightly polished in the room.

"We have 953 colored voters in the county," he said, and his voice was low and solemn like a high priest's at his altar, "and times is mighty hard!" and he shook his head and sighed. "You know how it is, even in good times the colored' is the last hired and the first fired. Times been hard every where now for more than a year. People ain't got no money, ain't got nuthin. If they vote wrong, companies will set 'em outta their houses onto the road. How we goin' to be able to talk to 'em under circumstances like that?"

"Well, for one thing, preacher," broke in Sam Chaney, "with Doctor Bonham county judge they're not goin' to be throwin' people out of their houses like that. The new judge won't issue the orders t' do it. That oughta buck your people up a little."

"But still times be mighty hard," he reverted, "and colored people has been fooled a heap o' times already. Still, money goes further than it use to. We'll have to have a dollar bill for each voter, and hand it to him just when he goes to the polls. And then they's at least twenty leaders among the colored who's goin' to have to get at least ten dollars a-piece in their hands. An' we needs to have a few barbecues in the right places, and some whiskey for the ones who likes a dram. Course I don't touch it myself, but just a sight o' folks won't vote unless they gets a good dram, a halfa pint, say." He paused and ruminated for a long moment. "I 'spect you'll need about two thousand dollars for the colored!"

"The colored are in a mighty tight place," Joe Carr concurred, with a nod of agreement toward the preacher. "The comp'ny police are a lot rougher on them than they are on the whites. But Jake Runyon's crowd has done nothin' at all to help the colored. The colored has great respect for the preacher here, and he's our trump card. If Deacon Timmons will go to the mat for us, we'll hold the colored for Tom Bonham, I'm dead certain o' that."

Doc looked at the preacher for a long moment. "Reverend, you'll get your $2,000 as you need it. And let me say something else here before these men who are your friends and mine. If the colored people of this county stand true and vote for me, it will be remembered because I know I cannot win without them. If they back me, you will have a place in my administration and things will improve for them. We'll see they get justice in the courts, and there'll be no more lynchings. Deputies who pick on colored people will be fired. And they'll get the schools they've been promised for fifteen years but never did get! They'll get their fair share of everything the county provides, and you'll be there to see I keep my promise." Doc held out his hand and shook the old preacher's hand to seal the covenant.

"Praise de Lord!" exclaimed the deacon, clasping and unclasping his bony fingers. "I never 'spected to hear dat from a white man, and said in front o' other white folks, too! I'll work night and day, dats fer sho', an' I believe we'll win. I'll pray dat we'll win; we'll have Tom Bonham prayer meetin's and pray and pray! Praise de Lord."

An hour later the meeting broke up. Twinkles reappeared and thanked the departing men for coming. She shook hands again with each of them and said she was grateful for the support they were giving her husband. And each man deemed her enticing and lusted after her in his own heart and in his own way.

Then she and Doc and Joe Carr sat by the fire for two hours longer, discussing the coming campaign precinct by precinct, and the strategies that would be required to capture their votes. They talked of the old precincts with the primitive backwoods names—Bear Wallow, Dead Man, Gun Lock and Gouge, where men still held resolutely to the old politics of their fathers and voted straight Republican, and of Elk Creek, Salt Lick, Dead Sticks, Camp Fork and Indian River, where descendants of old John Bonham were still numerous and most people resolutely marked their ballots once only and that in the Democratic circle under the crowing rooster—and they talked of the new precincts born of coal and the industrial age, Noreco, Fordco, Low Sulphur, Black Diamond, Henrietta, Mary Ann and a score of others where men spoke a dozen tongues and sullenly waited for jobs and leadership. And when he left, Joe Carr had in his mind a blueprint that would elect Doc Bonham to the county judge's office if an organization could be built to its plans and its loyalties held together while it worked.

CHAPTER

9

Blacksville's weekly, *The Mountain Courier*, was published every Thursday by Tim Elkins, a cadaverous slab of a man and a devout Democrat. He was a pauper whose press and home were mortgaged and escaped foreclosure only because his creditors knew no one who would buy either. His paper carried a notice of Doc's candidacy in its first issue in April, "subject to the action of the Democratic primary" scheduled for August 3. The publisher ran the ad with twofold joy: he hoped Doc would win, and he needed the advertising revenues a heated campaign was sure to generate. His strongwilled and opinionated wife Katy was a daughter of old "Maje" Bonham—so-called because he had been a major in the rebel army—and his editorial enthusiasm for his wife's kinsman knew no bounds. In May he opined in a front-page commentary that "Dr. Bonham is an honest man charging a citadel of corruption run by Jake Runyon. The doctor will need a sharp scalpel to cut out this deep-rooted carbuncle." In June he tried another tack. "Poor Jake Runyon," he observed, "has got many things since he left surveying and went into politics. He has got rich and got the support of the coal operators. He has got Slaughter County in an awful mess. He has got high taxes for ordinary people and has got low taxes for coal companies. Now he has got one of the best men in the hills to run against and has got to have a lot of luck if he is to fool enough people to win again!"

Jake Runyon had also gotten wise to the moods and perversities called public opinion. One morning he handed the astonished publisher a statement to be carried as a paid politicial ad. In it he thanked the good people of Slaughter County for their kind support during his years as a public official and informed them that he would not seek reelection as county judge. He had done his best in that capacity, he told the public, and now the affairs of the county were in a sound and sensible condition. The time had come for him to stand aside and allow a new man with fresh ideas and abundant energy to take over the task of managing the affairs of the county. He was sure that the Republican party—the party of Lincoln and freedom, the party of fiscal responsibility and the party dedicated to an early return to prosperity and full employment—would offer a fine candidate. Jake Runyon would support that candidate and would oppose any Democratic political quack whose pills and salves might crush the county's coal companies and take the bread from the tables of honest, hard-working, God-fearing miners and the Christian businessmen whose investments had made those jobs possible.

Despite Elkins's personal and political antipathy, Runyon remained a few moments in conversation with the lanky editor. To Elkins's delight he paid for the ad in cash, assuring a kettle of stew and some biscuits for his family's supper. With a smoothness that would have disarmed practically anyone except the ink-stained journalist, he commented on the frustrations and satisfactions of public office and dwelt with pleasure on the coming return to his farm.

He left with an expression of good wishes for Mrs. Elkins and the children, and before the nonplussed editor could rush to the telephone and inform Doc of the unexpected development, a new caller appeared at his desk. Arthur Hall was thirty-five, short, neatly suited, with a red bow tie and a white shirt starched stiff as cardboard. His wavy black hair was neatly trimmed by barber Syd Wright on a regular schedule every Saturday morning, and was plastered securely into place with generous applications of rose oil. He polished his black shoes each evening and shaved with a fresh Gillette blade and a cupful of hot lather regularly each morning at 6:30. He was a graduate of something called the Jefferson School of Business. A bachelor, he belonged to Elks, Moose and Masons and attended church somewhere every Sunday. He was a bookkeeper for Ben Fleming's mines and ran an office with a couple of clerks in Northeast Coal's main office building across the street from Doc's hospital. He was utterly square, a son of old George Hall whom Jake Runyon had elected a school trustee, an unflagging and ultraconservative Republican and a man whom Doc instinctively and deeply disliked. He drew a chair up close to Tim Elkins's incredibly cluttered desk and pulled a sheet of neatly typed paper from his coat pocket.

His clipped little moustache curled and his black eyes glowed with scorn as he handed the paper across the desk. It was a political announcement to be published in ensuing issues of the *Courier*. Arthur Hall was a candidate for county judge. As a Republican he promised that there would be no waste of taxpayers' money, sane and conservative taxing policies would be followed so industry could prosper and create jobs. He would continue the general policies of judge Jake Runyon and would canvass the county thoroughly to see and talk to all voters. Finally, he would support the coal industry because "Whatever is good for coal is good for Slaughter County."

The call from Tim Elkins astonished Doc. Jake Runyon had built a formidable political fortress, but like all citadels it had weak places and Doc and Joe Carr had studied them all. They had developed a plan that would exploit every old grievance, each unkept promise, all thwarted job seekers, the frictions and jealousies among Runyon's toadies in the court-house. The judge was vulnerable because he had held and dispensed power a long time, an exercise that alienates all whom it injures or offends. Suddenly by a single stroke, Doc's devious and cunning adversary had created a totally new ball game and Doc was at bat. The foe, formerly so tangible and in many ways so vulnerable, was now elusive and indis-tinct. Arthur Hall was regular as sin and the Republican organization would find no reason to oppose him. He had found time to join and fraternize, to attend the high school ball games that so intrigued the coal miners and to support and boost the teams. He had worked hard in a half-dozen "community betterment" projects involving boy scouts and the "service clubs." He was too young to have fought in the World War, but he was an "honorary" member of the Ameri-can Legion Post on the hill outside Blacksville, which gave him drinking privileges with its members and the opportu-nity to drop an occasional coin into its slot machines. And he could count on every vote the coal operators' association could persuade, coerce or buy.

Doc knew himself to be vulnerable in the very respects that made Hall formidable. For ten years his work had kept him in his hospital early and late, and even in the last six months after young Doctor Omar Moss came up from Indianapolis to work beside him, he found little time for work outside his profession. The Depression which cloaked the coal counties had pushed a pall of sickness into the flimsy camps and up the smoky creeks and cramped hollows. Children suffered from itch and malnutrition, pellagra, and scurvy. Too much reliance on a diet of dried beans left people listless and sent them to his office. Hard times caused bosses to take chances that produced a rash of accidents. And scarcely a week passed without the inevitable case or two of appendicitis. Doc had felt a surge of confidence when his opponent was Jake Runyon, but was apprehensive when he assessed the new situation.

His high-strung Bonham temper was outraged by the sure knowledge that his new opponent was a reactionary, who, by comparison, made Jake Runyon appear progressive. Hall was tightfisted, strongly anti-labor, and saw no need for improved coal-town schools. Still he had no record to pin him to these positions, as Runyon did, and to the end of the campaign might wear a veneer of moderation capable of fooling a far more discerning electorate than the simpleminded voters of Slaughter County.

Never in his life, except when he first met and thirsted for Twinkles, had Doc wanted anything so much as he now wanted to win this election. For twelve years, whining coal trains had dragged coal—one hundred and fifty million tons of it—out of the tortured hills of his native county. Homes and offices had been warmed by it and factories and mills had hummed to its heat. The glittering lumps had powered the nation's industrial surge through the twenties, and colliers had unloaded them in huge dusty heaps in the ports of half the world. But through it all—the building of thirty towns, the rattling of a hundred tipples—Slaughter County had remained strait-jacketed in the same primitive habiliments it had worn when the first locomotive whistle resounded from its crags. Most of the larger companies had organized "independent" school districts to which they paid the school taxes assessed against their houses, commissaries and mines so that they not only determined the amount of taxes they paid, but controlled the spending of the meager funds so collected. Their hand-picked trustees hired teachers, set salaries and influenced the quality of teaching. Sometimes extra sums were donated to the schools, but such gifts were rarely generous, and outside the "independent" districts, the tiny log and flimsy frame schoolhouses persisted, decaying huts whose teachers drew salaries ranging from fifty to seventy-five dollars a month—and sometimes not even these pittances were paid.

It grated against Doc's very soul that the county's immense outpouring of indispensable wealth had bought so little for the county itself. The tottering old frame courthouse with its crumbling vaults and dilapidated furniture, which had been built as the center of a vast backwoods, now rotted and stank at the heart of an industrial powerhouse. The coal cars with the stenciling of New York banks on their sides rushed to market over unimpeded ribbons of glittering steel, but the wagons and Fords of miners and farmers sank to their axles in mud. Blacksville boasted no single foot of concrete street. The county had never established a health department, and there was nothing resembling a sewage or water treatment plant anywhere in the county.

Doc's remedy for this disastrous and outrageous situation was simple: tax reform. All property would go on the books in a systematic new assessment—and the rate of levy would be doubled. Even this would leave revenues at a trifling level. Next, a Democratic fiscal court would impose a severance tax of a dime a ton on all coal mined in the county. Every ton hauled away would leave a new brick or two for schools, libraries, public hospitals, a new courthouse. Each sixty-five-car trainload would deposit in the county treasury a month's pay for a teacher, and at a living rate. The young would go to school, roads would be built for their parents, the whole county would move into the twentieth century with its enlarged aspirations and expectations.

He had visions of modern tree-shaded schools and hospitals such as he had seen in Louisville and Cincinnati. The shy children in ragged denim and calico would change to assertive, self-confident youngsters sturdily clothed and shod and with the red cheeks of ample nutrition. He wanted a county hospital set on broad grounds, generously equipped and endowed, and with proven specialists on its staff. He wanted libraries, at least a dozen of them, to carry the best of art, science and literature to a people who had never glimpsed them. He wanted the befouled streams with their stench of filth to sparkle again. Above all, he wanted mountain men and women to stand up and assert themselves, free of the twin yokes of poverty and ignorance. He was convinced all these things and more could be achieved with the reforms he visualized.

There was no doubt of it; Jake Runyon had become vulnerable. He had appointed weaklings and ignoramuses to the board of tax supervisors, and they had taxed as he suggested. He had let the county rot while coal companies made millions in the 1920s. Then came those jarring days when the world trembled and darkness came over the sun. Newspapers told of bankers and brokers who jumped out of skyscrapers or sent bullets crashing through their brains. The farmers in the West had suffered for a long time, producing meat, grain and cotton for a glutted market and going broke in the process. Suddenly the steel mills went to a two-day work week and coal collapsed overnight. Long lines of empty railroad cars were sidetracked under silent tipples and miners idled away interminable hours in the bright rays of unaccustomed daylight—hours that lengthened into days, then months. Miners and managers looked at one another dazed and dispirited. Then in their new idleness, men looked about them and saw that ten years of toil had brought them little. The mansions raised by coal fortunes stood in New York and Philadelphia, the shanties proliferated for sixty dreary miles along Indian River. Suddenly men and women saw that schoolhouses were dilapidated, that teachers were shabby and uninspired, that their children had learned little. They saw that coal had brought many tragedies and no triumphs, and they were angry. Jake Runyon had served the forces that had made the mess; he had, they now realized, betrayed the people whose votes had made him. They would have defeated Runyon, Doc knew, but now Runyon was out of the battle. But, actually, he was not out, for he would mastermind the campaign, fighting a rear-guard battle to put a new set of men in office for four more years, and they would resist and stifle every cry for equal treatment of mining man and mining company. Under them the established order would remain intact and company-paid police would drive out of the county those dissidents who opposed them.

The coal companies were in a hell of a fix, no doubt of that. A dozen had bankrupted and others were about to do so. But, damn, somebody has to pay taxes, Doc thought. The miners are broke, too, and always have been. The prosperity of the Roaring Twenties was phony for them. They ate beans, slept on thin, worn mattresses and found their recreation on the haggard bodies of their harried wives. Things had to get started again and somebody had to pay the bill. The companies would have to dig it out of the same emergency funds, contingency funds, and loan funds that were paying their presidents and board chairmen. Somewhere they would have to find funds to support the county their operations had created, or the county would die. Doc knew merchants, doctors and lawyers who lay awake at night and sweated blood over their own taxes, and he intended that the masters of Noreco and thirty other coal towns would do the same. He told Sanders Redwine, an Associated Press reporter who interviewed him about his race, "By God, the little man has been doing his duty, and his children have paid for it. The big man is going to do his duty, too, and his stockholders are going to pay for it!"

When plans for Doc's race had first reached Ben Fleming,

he had not believed the report. Jake Runyon told him about it, stopping at his office early on a misty morning when dense clouds and a dearth of coal orders swathed Noreco in a deep layer of gloom. "He aims to run," Runyon reiterated in a slow mountain drawl. "He aims to run agin me and agin you, and agin the coal association. He aims to lay everything that's wrong with this county on what he calls 'discriminatory taxes' and he could become a mighty hard man to beat!" He shook his head. "It depends on how the idea ketches on. Right now, people are mighty dissatisfied."

Fleming shook his head in turn. "Tom Bonham has done well for himself since the coal industry opened up this county. He lives in a big house and is well heeled, and he wouldn't be making $30,000 a year without coal. He can't be serious. Your information must be wrong," and a pained disbelieving quality was in his voice.

"He's serious, and my information is correct. Not much happens in this county without me hearin' about it pretty soon." Runyon chuckled, "He has friends who are my friends, too."

A couple of days later Fleming turned up at Doc's office. It was late in the afternoon, and there were no other patients. He was promptly admitted into the huge square room with its high frosted-glass windows where for nearly a decade Doc had talked to an endless stream of the sick and lame. Fleming seemed shrunken and gray. A half-dozen pounds had melted away, and his sparse frame was sparser still. His neatness of dress was as punctilious as ever, but the weariness of discouragement lay over him. He complained of a sore throat and of feeling "very, very tired." Doc listened to his chest, measured his blood pressure, and gave him a tiny envelope full of pink pills. He swabbed Fleming's throat with a fiery germicide and told him to spend a couple of days in bed. "Rest is the best curative," he ventured, "for both colds and business frustrations."

"You're right, doctor," he sighed, stuffing the pills into a vest pocket. "We're going through frustrating times. I've been in the coal business all my life and thought I knew it inside and out. But never did I suppose the present situation was remotely possible. Here I sit with a camp full of good workers and serviceable machines on top of seams of first-rate coal. The world needs goods, and half the people in it are freezing and half its cities are dark half the time, and if I find orders for three days a week I'm lucky!" He clucked ruefully. "My stockholders are raising hell and so are my bankers." He spread his hands in exasperation, "As the old saying goes,'When it rains, it pours,' and right now I'm just one coal man who is wading in a deep flood of cold and bitter troubles."

He cleared his throat and continued with a subject that was obviously distasteful to him. "When our company and other mining firms moved into this field, we had to make an enormous outlay in everything—houses, commissaries, machine shops, tipples, machines. Everything was new, we had to start from scratch, so we cut corners to recover as much of our investment as possible, as quickly as possible. I am sorry to say that we did this on local taxes. Our industry has not contributed enough to the county and its needs. With the benefit of hindsight we recognize the mistake. I have heard about your concern in this respect and as a citizen—a permanent citizen—of the county I share it. I want Slaughter County to have a better future and am willing to join you in working for it, but, damn it all to hell, doctor, the taxes you have been talking about will totally bankrupt and destroy every mine in the county! It's too late for that. We could have stood them in the twenties, and I wish now we had paid them, but the industry is nearly flat today. What you are proposing is to lock the barn door after the horse has been stolen. We've already mined the best of our seams; our heyday is behind us. New taxes now will ruin us and sink the county at the same time. I hope you can see this and change your position on this issue."

He paused and looked around at the rows of medicines on the shelves, the medical textbooks in the oaken cases, the medical diploma on the wall, the yellowing, grinning skeleton in the corner. Lines of fatigue were etched into his forehead and at the corners of his mouth, and his fingers drummed nervously on the corner of Doc's desk.

Doc pondered his answer carefully, realizing that he was prescribing drastic medicine for a sick industry. Fleming had organized the Slaughter County Coal Operators Association and had served as its president for at least half of its twelve-year history. Doc knew that his weariness stemmed in part from the difficulties facing his own company but even more from the disaster churning its way through the association. Doc knew Fleming's political enmity was inevitable, but he hoped to retain his respect and, in a measure, his personal friendship.

"When I have replied to the things you have just said, you will probably decide that I am an ingrate." He looked into Fleming's tired eyes and tried to manage a smile of sympathy. "I hope you won't feel that way, but if you do, I hope time will prove you wrong. Sometimes a man finds himself caught between two conflicting obligations—a gratitude to old and proven friends such as yourself, and to old benefactors like Northeast Coal Corporation, and then, on the other hand, an obligation to public duty, to schoolchildren, schoolteachers, the miners with their picks, the people, the future. And if we do the right thing, when we choose we will come down on the side of public duty instead of personal inclination."

"We know in our hearts, you and I, that since the beginning coal has been a slow and reluctant taxpayer. A tipple that cost $200,000 goes on the rolls at $20,000. A four-room camphouse pays a hundred and fifty dollars a year in rent—and is assessed at $200. A seam of coal is six feet thick and the company that owns it collects $6,000 an acre in royalties—and is assessed at $20. And besides their coal, the companies' own ledges of iron ore and limestone, and oil and gas and brine reserves that have never even been tapped, let alone taxed! Low taxes on industry saddles private citizens with unjust burdens. A farmer at the head of a creek living in a four-room house without electricity, and with no road except a walking trail, finds his house assessed at a thousand dollars."

Doc's eyes narrowed with indignation and his voice took on a hard, harsh edge. His sympathy for Fleming evaporated and he continued. "I won't blame a man or a corporation for being frugal, but I resent the evasion of responsibility. The Slaughter County Coal Operators owe a great duty, a great responsibility to this county and its people. The mines brought people here from the ends of the earth. The mines caused schoolchildren to jam these streets. The mines made the hundreds of cripples like Joe Carr, and the widows and the orphaned children. A handful of scrip and some uncertain shelter are not enough. The people need leadership to put the natural resources and the human resources to work together to build a prosperous society, and the first part of that duty is a fair tax scale. Without that, everything else fails."

He remembered Rose Quinlan's admonition of many years ago, and the little school on its campus by the ancient cabin. He felt a deep compassion for the people whose endless efforts found the small—and dwindling—gifts that kept its doors open. "Here we sit," he flared, "in a shrunken, futile hulk of a county whose public services would be a disgrace anywhere in the world and a lot of our children going to charity schools, and beneath our feet and all around us are the world's richest deposits of natural resources." Fleming's eyes shifted away from his own. "It makes no sense," Doc went on. "We will be criminally culpable if we let things go on as they are."

"Damn it all to hell, Ben, I don't want to put new taxes on Northeast at this time. It's too much like kicking a man while he's down and out. But there is another side to this coin and I see it every day right here in this room. I see children with scurvy and pellagra and whole families who have the itch for six months at a stretch. All of it comes from malnutrition. Their teeth are falling out. The kids are too weak to go to school, and the men are too weak to do a decent day's work when the company gets a few orders. So what do we do? Give up and starve?"

Fleming stood up and thanked the doctor for the pills. A little of his old jauntiness and self-confidence came back and he laughed. "I hope the pills work," he said, "for if they don't, the things you've said are going to make me sicker than ever." He passed through the door, and Doc heard him speak to someone in the hall. His voice had resonance and his words the uncondescending concern that had kept peace on a raw industrial frontier through a turbulent decade.

The interval that followed—a half year that ended when the vote count was finished on November 8—was the most hectic, crowded, challenging, and provocative in Doc's lifetime. He was thirty-six, at the peak of his physical and mental alertness, and absolutely determined to win. His cause was a passion with him—tax reform and the building of a modern and progressive Slaughter County. He carried the amateur's naive conviction that because he was right he would prevail, that because what he advocated was logical men would believe it. He had the quick and endless energy that had always marked the Bonhams, and he poured his strength and his very soul into the campaign to capture the voters and to hold them against what were certain to be terrific counter pressures.

But in his task he toiled under almost unimaginable difficulties. His very popularity as a physician—the bedrock on which his campaign was based—swamped him with patients through many long hours of each day. They came out of the mines with their broken bones and unspeakable agonies, and the women and children came with their coughs and their diarrheas, their pallid faces and their sunken eyes. For them he could prescribe what they could not buy or beg or steal or borrow—fresh fruits and vegetables, milk and cod-liver oil. Even with Dr. Ross to aid him, a luxury he had never known before, he could rarely leave the hospital before one o'clock; often he was there until three.

Of course, he electioneered with the patients who were able to hear him and with their kin and friends who brought them to him and received countless pledges of support—but he was hindered in the organizational work he knew to be vital. When he could escape the pinched, drawn, sallow faces of the sick, he aimed his Chevrolet up the abominable creek roads that followed the winding railroad tracks to the dusty camps, and far beyond them along widened and slightly improved Indian trails to the remote outlying precincts where the tempo and tenor of life had been much less affected by the vast industrial upheaval spawned by coal.

He sought out the influential people whose opinions set the drift and tenor most would follow when they carried their ballots into the booths—the miners, merchants, schoolteachers, sawmill owners, cattle dealers, petty officeholders, and, by no means least, the ubiquitous moonshiners who, despite Prohibition and its swarms of agents, sent torrents of fiery liquor down the throats of all who could pay fifty cents a pint for their wares. He sought them out and appealed to their Democratic loyalties, their immeasurable hunger for roads, their lesser but appreciable desire for schools where none existed, and for better schools than the pathetic institutions that brought "learnin'" to most communities, to their often-expressed craving for progress and a better life. And always be appealed to the loyalties of blood, for everywhere he found the Bonham genes, the high cheeks, the thin arched noses, the slender tallness of Old John-of-All's issue and the families into which they had married. This skein of blood relationship was tough and strong and had about it a quality of primal insistence. There was an ancient, feudal reverence and affection for "the blood," and time after time in camp shanties and the spare crowded houses of crossroads store-keepers, he heard the observation from men and women alike, "Why, we're jist a little bit kin, me and you, and it's hard fer a body to vote agin his own people, his own flesh." Though he had always known the mountaineers' ingrained respect for consanguinity, he was sometimes astonished anew by the tenacity with which it had survived so far into the twentieth century.

Doc took the utmost advantage of his wide relation-ship, exploiting it at every opportunity, and he took pains to make sure there were many opportunities. He set the aging Delilah—now a nimble and wholly dedicated sev-enty—to recollecting every branch and ultimate terminus of the Bonham line, together with similar information on all who bore the genes of old Ephraim Free. So numerous, so widely scattered and so mingled with the settled, deep-rooted families of the county were his near and distant kin that he could—and did—claim relationship by blood or affin-ity with nearly a third of the inhabitants.

Doc's brothers and sisters and old Delilah turned out on every day they could spare from other tasks to canvass the precincts for him. In their Model As and by horseback they went to the voters—wives of miners by their grimy stoves, miners loafing in front of commissaries or black with coal grit at the end of a shift, farmers plowing in their steep and rock strewn fields, store clerks leaning on their counters, "com-pany men" dispensing scrip and recording payrolls in grimy flyspecked offices near dusty mine portals, an occasional teacher on his way home from an overcrowded and cheerless classroom. They, and a small swarm of Doc's uncles, aunts and nearer cousins, promoted their candidate as a tent preacher promotes salvation. Each had his own favorite pitch which was varied somewhat from one voter to another and in different parts of the county, but invariably the nucleus of the argument was progress: "Dr. Bonham is agoin' to do somethin' fur the county. He ain't anybody's captive and aims to put taxes where they ought to be—on the people who are able to pay 'em! He's got a plan fur building roads and schools and other things we need so bad, and how to pay fur 'em. We've had enough gover'ment by the coal association and the New York companies, and it's time now to give an independent mountain man a chance at our problems. He went away to school, but come back here among us to live and work, and a many a man is alive because he stayed in Slaughter County. He has showed good judgment as a doctor, so let's let the doctor be the judge!"

The phrase, "Let the doctor be the judge" became the slogan of his campaign, repeated countless times by the determined men and women who took up his cause. It leaped at voters from ads in the Mountain Courier and underlined his name and photograph on three thousand cardboard posters nailed to utility poles, roadside trees, storefronts and the sides of barns. Some of those who worked for him so tirelessly did so because he was their kin or their wife's kin. Some were for him because his scalpel had saved their lives or his medicines had brought wife or children past some brush with death. Others owed him a debt of gratitude be-

cause he had helped them with a loan, or had signed their note for a few dollars at the Miner's Bank of Blacksville—small but important funds that stayed off a mortgage foreclosure or kept a son or daughter in college on a faraway campus in the "flat country" beyond the hills. Miners had worked and lived for a tumultuous decade on terms dictated solely by their employers and many rejoiced to see those autocrats challenged at last and were for Doc simply because the enemy of their enemy was their friend. By no means least in numbers or importance were those souls weary of laboring in dripping haulways and amid creaking timbers in vast hollows of the earth, and who hoped for political jobs of some sort topside in the sunshine. In the aggregate, they were an impressive lot.

The men, who strove to put all this support together into a reliable force and to assure that its votes arrived properly marked in the thirty-six galvanized steel ballot boxes, were the group—and a few others—who had gathered in Doc's living room on the rainy afternoon in February. Joe Carr was Doc's campaign manager, and there developed between them a rapport, a firm and abiding friendship that made them almost one—so much so that Arthur Hall once sniffed, "If Doc farts Joe smells bad." Joe had put together somehow an intelligence apparatus that reached into every cranny of the county, including the headquarters of the coal association, and which would have done justice to the spy ring of a Russian czar. He fed Doc an unending flow of essential information, counseled him as to his strengths and weaknesses as well as those of his foe, and often moderated Doc's abruptly formed and sometimes imprudent decisions. He was a born organizer and the structure he began putting together was based to a large degree on young men, for Joe Carr planned for the future and the long haul. He rose early and retired late, and every waking moment was single-mindedly centered on the garnering of votes, and even as he swallowed his gargantuan meals he weighed the number of votes in this family or that and cogitated on how best to prevent their falling prey to Republican machinations.

Doc was fortunate in that the efforts of the coal association to provide him an opponent in the primary were unavailing. Democrats had won so few contests in so many years that it required a rare blend of ambition and foolhardiness to enter the lists. Joe Carr was able to anticipate the men whose background and family connections could make them serious contenders and strove to turn them into allies. Some he persuaded to join Doc's slate as candidates for other offices—sheriff, tax commissioner, clerks of county and circuit courts, county attorney, justices of the peace. Still others were pledged jobs in the lean years ahead, with assurances that in four years their time would come and they would be on the ticket themselves with strong support from a rejuvenated party. And one, youngish Coots Whitaker, was seduced into going back to Appalachian State Teacher's College in pursuit of a master's degree, his soul titillated by a brand-new dream of someday becoming county school superintendent—and with a few hundred dollars of Doc's money nestling in his tattered billfold. "Anything is better," Joe Carr assured his candidate, "than a primary. That would wreck ever'thing fur certain. Stir up a awful lot of trouble. The man you beat would bolt and take most of the losers in the other races with 'em. This Whitaker feller could be a real problem, and yore money is well spent." An expansive smile spread over his amply padded face and the jowls that hung under his chin. "Besides helpin' yoreself you're helpin' to edjicate a man. Make ye feel good to promote edjication," and he stuffed a handful of roasted peanuts into his mouth.

Nor were Doc's attempts to get a serious challenger on the GOP ticket against Arthur Hall any more successful. A couple of likely prospects were approached through Doc's third cousin, "Long Link" Bonham of Gallagher's Fork, but they shied away from the enticements that were dangled before them. Lincoln Bonham was a genuine rarity, a Bonham who generally voted the Republican ticket. His father had limped back from a Yankee prison camp to find his wife dead and his cabin burned. He married a woman nearly twenty years younger than himself and she bore him a spate of children. He died when the oldest was seven and their mother brought them up in the political faith of her father, Joshua Gallagher. She taught them to be frugal, hardworking and acquisitive and one of them, at least, prospered. Link, the youngest, was a trader who trafficked in everything from pocket knives to livestock and tracts of land. After the mines were opened, he made a modest fortune supplying locust, hickory and black oak props for the tunnels. His influence in his party grew, and for a time he was county chairman. But he nourished the hill man's attachment to family ties, however tenuous, and he shook Doc's hand and gave him the answer the candidate had expected from the beginning. "I have to put blood afore party, so you kin count on me, Doc."

Long Link approached Mart Gallagher, who had once

been sheriff and still hoped someday to return to the court-house, and urged him to make the race. But Gallagher was a cautious man and discussed the proposition with Ben Fleming and a number of other kingmakers whose support he considered vital. They convinced him that Link Bonham would never fight his cousin and that his appeal was a du-plicitous attempt to set Republicans to fighting one another. So both candidates entered the general election campaign with claims of solidarity and undivided party loyalties flow-ing in their wakes.

In August, Joe Carr brought a visitor who conferred with Doc for a couple of hours. With two exceptions the state's governors had all been Democrats since the Civil War, and Governor Cash Bishop wanted to encourage Doc's efforts to return the county to the fold. He sent a youngish and ambi-tious henchman, State Representative Carl Rutherford from Whitleyville, in the far-off western tip of the state, to express the governor's best wishes and offer the support and encour-agement of the state executive committee. He could bring no funds of course—the committee was quite broke and was struggling hard to raise money for the upcoming gubernatorial race—but Doc's victory might send Joe Carr or some other de-serving Democrat back to the House, and the committee wanted Doc to know his efforts were watched and appreciated.

Carl Rutherford was thirty-six and had been a first lieu-tenant when the firing stopped in France. He was tall with thinning strands of brown hair and pale blue eyes that peered through round, steel-rimmed glasses. Despite his six feet two inches, he carried a round little paunch that promised to swell to generous dimensions beneath the buttons and pockets of his vest. His suit was of a cautious gray with a thin blue stripe, and despite its starch, his white shirt had begun to wilt at the collar. Whitleyville lay five hundred miles away where the land stretched flat and steaming like a freshly turned pancake and men grew white cotton under a burning sun. His voice carried the soft and courteous inflections of the Southland. As he talked he occasionally distracted Doc by grasping his vest and shirt and pulling them outward as if they clung too tightly to his flesh—a mannerism, Joe later explained, that had caused his fellow savants in the House to dub him "old titty-pullin' Carl."

Doc and Carl studied one another carefully and each decided the other could be useful in the years ahead. When Carl was gone, Doc could not tell himself that he actually liked the man or that it was probable he ever would, but he recognized a strength, cunning, and persistence that he could admire. Tilford came to Doc's office while the visitor was there and was introduced to him and shook his hand. He was moved to remark, "You'd do alright up here in these mountains, my friend, because you're just a leetle bit like us Bonhams yourself."

Carl laughed good-naturedly at this sally and left with laughter and handshakes and pledges to return. "We'll see more of each other," he predicted in gentle, courtly tones that contrasted strangely with the harsh archaic drawls of the mountaineers.

For several weeks, Doc was confident of the outcome, and in their frequent talks, he and Joe Carr found much to fuel their optimism. Hard times and the oppression of the bosses fired rebellion in miners and their wives, and it appeared that they would vote for a new chance for themselves and their families. When Doc appeared at gatherings his reception was warm and friendly, and outclasped hands, pats on arm and shoulder and fervent promises of support were routine. The candidate calculated the precincts one by one and concluded that a smashing victory was building up. He told Joe Carr as much, but that worthy ate a candy bar and cautioned Doc against overconfidence, the greatest stumbling block on any political trail. "Don't count yore chickens yit, Doc. Wait till they hatch out and come home to roost."

Then a change came—a slow and scarcely perceptible cooling which Doc's best efforts were never to slow or reverse. He could never pinpoint its beginning or its immediate cause, but it began to manifest itself in averted eyes and in moments of silence or hesitation when he asked for votes. And when he sponsored barbecues and set cold watermelons and cool kegs of home-brewed beer before the paupers whose labor—now rarely more than two days a week—brought out the coal that had earned their valley a measure of renown, they began to express skepticism about his schemes to improve the county by taxing the coal they dug. The words and phrases that began to reach his ears were not theirs, he knew, but were couched in the slogans and arguments carried daily from the graceless brick headquarters of the coal association in Blacksville. Actually, very few ever challenged him directly or argued a point with him, but their expressions of sentiment came to him through Joe Carr, Steve Dominic, Tom Morton and other devoted pulsetakers who invariably knew every shift in sentiment that blew through their precincts. Dominic reported the situation in the bleak camp where he sometimes found a few days' work as a mason, and observed, "Coal miners are fools, doctaire, and after all, I guess zat iss why zey are coal miners! Zey zink if zis God-forsaken county puts a little tax on a-coal peoples will quit a-burning it!" He sighed in sheer and utter disbelief.

The company propaganda flowing from the offices of the bosses met no effective organized rebuttal from labor simply because there was no organized labor in Slaughter County. When the coal field was first opened, the mountaineers knew nothing about the hardships of an industrial society and had no appetite for united and concerted undertakings. The immigrants who had learned trenchant lessons in the mills and factories of Italy and Austria-Hungary had little influence with the individualistic mountaineers and the timid southern blacks. In the twenties, a few brave souls from the United Mine Workers and the Communist-leaning National Miners Union tried to organize locals, but had met virtually no success. They encountered only apathy in most miners and lead pipes in the hands of company-paid policemen. Furious and unrelenting in his efforts to enlist men into unaffiliated locals to bargain company by company, Sam Chaney claimed to have had the hell beaten out of him fifteen times—"Once for each of the twelve disciples and three times for Jesus Christ!" as he phrased it. In the main, the listless workers swallowed the propaganda that unionism would mean joblessness— "Labor unions will force the closing of every mine in Slaughter County" and "A little bread is better than no bread."

The same tactics that had turned men away from joint action, their sole hope in dealing with their united employers, were now directed against Doc. Nor did the operators couch their counterarguments in strident, vicious assaults on the camp physician who proposed to build a respectable county government at their expense. They were much too smart to set him up as a hard-pressed underdog certain to attract sympathy. Instead they discussed his proposals in the gentle terms and tones reserved for an old and dear friend who has, for incomprehensible reasons, gone astray and fallen from grace. Doctor Bonham's plan came too late; it would have been fine and logical when the mines were new and there was a boom, but now the Depression made the scheme totally impractical. All the mining companies were striving to stave off bankruptcy and any new tax burden—such as the doctor proposed—would shove them over the brink. Most operators were keeping the mines going "just to accommodate their miners" because low prices ruled out profits. With the mines closed, the commissaries would be shut up and total starvation would replace near starvation. Besides, Doctor Bonham was a fine man and a wonderful physician whose services should be continued—in his hospital. He could cure a sick man, no doubt about that, but what he proposed would kill the county.

In numberless sessions, Doc rebutted these propositions. Either poor miners or poor coal companies must bear the cost of government and from any viewpoint, the companies were less poor than the miners. Unless better schools were provided, the children of miners would never be able to go beyond the pick and shovel of their fathers and they, rather than the present taxpayers of the county, would eventually pay the price of failure. Over and over again, he repeated that schools were shacks, teachers poorly paid, the courthouse was leaking, bridges were rusting for lack of paint, and past it all every day rolled trainloads of coal that had never felt the tax collector's touch. He spoke of neat, new schools with comfortable desks, of better paid and better educated teachers, of a public health office with a doctor and nurses to immunize children and ward off the ravages of diphtheria, smallpox and measles, of a county farm agent to help farmers coax larger crops from their fields and improve their livestock with purebred sires, and of smooth, paved roads to connect the county seat with such isolated places as Dead Man, Coonskin, and Eagle. He urged unionism on miners as an indispensable device if they were ever to draw decent wages, and pledged that the power of the county would protect them in their right to join unions and bargain collectively. All of these things and more were possible, but only if his tax reforms could be secured. As he told a crowd at a rally at Black Bottom, "The choice is between the operators and me; the choice is between the operators and yourselves. What I'm asking you to do is vote for your own dinner bucket, for pork chops for your own belly, for your own wife and schoolchildren, your own right to good health, good roads and a good income. The only place where you can get these things is at the voting booth, and a vote for me is a vote for all of them!"

Good rhetoric, perhaps, and sound and much-needed proposals, but they were directed at confused and frightened people, and people who had had no experience with the things he dangled before them. Besides, small driplets of money from the coal association began to reach many of them, a few dollars and the endlessly repeated admonition,

"Things are bad enough as they are; don't vote to make them any worse. Bonham's platform will take the beans off your table and the fire off your grates."

The state had a "sobering up and cooling off law" that required a delay of twenty-four hours after the polls were closed before tabulation of the ballots could begin. This legislation resulted from the tendency of enraged election losers to kill the winners when the results were announced, so that the impounded ballot boxes reposed in the county clerk's office for a night and a day before they were opened. They were guarded by a couple of Republican sheriff's deputies, who were guarded in turn by Doc's cousin, "Big Bill" Bonham, and his two sons, Jupiter and Jesse. When the count began in the circuit courtroom on Thursday morning, it proceeded, as 11,000 paper ballots required, with numbing slowness. Six tables surrounded by six sets of tabulators received the boxes, gravely saw to their unlocking, stacked the "straight tickets" in two separate heaps, then droned through the tedious process of counting the crossovers. Each table was surrounded by packs of highly partisan and usually armed onlookers determined to see that their favored candidates were not "counted out" of ballots to which they were entitled. Bonhams and Frees, scores of them and from every part of the county, watched the count for Doc, and as the tabulation continued, their long faces began to sag beneath the realization that he had lost. From the beginning, their kinsman fell slowly but surely behind.

Doc did not go to the courthouse himself, but stayed at the hospital seeing patients and striving to appear engrossed in his work and entirely satisfied with the results of the election. He was weary past comprehension of shaking hands, exchanging inane pleasantries, asking for votes and explaining over and over to dubious, slack-jawed, vacant-eyed men and women the advantages he wanted to bring to them and their children. He was weary unto death of the indignity of appealing to brains and a public concern that did not exist, to a concern for children that found little response in the fathers who had begotten them or the slovenly camp women whose travail had propelled them into the world. Doc could never forget the monotonous, unswept cabins he had visited by the dozens and scores, nor the stench of urine, sweat, coal smoke and boiling beans that almost always pervaded them. "O what a damned mess is this thing called democracy!" he said over and over to himself and to Twinkles.

At noon on Friday, he slipped out the rear entrance, leaving the hospital and a horde of patients for Dr. Ross to look after. The gray house was rainwashed and a continuing drizzle sent water rattling through the downspouts. He paused on the broad, deep porch and looked up the valley to Noreco, huddled sodden and lifeless beneath a cloak of smoke and fog. That precinct, at least, had stood by him despite the threats and pressures Ben Fleming and his henchmen had brought to bear on each man and woman within the town. The battle had been ruthless, for Doc had determined that regardless of cost in cash and energy he would not lose his own precinct. Joe Carr had shown him the count the night before, 383 to 271, and he had enjoyed one small morsel of triumph.

But the house was cheerless. Joe slouched before the fire eating a ham sandwich Twinkles had brought him. Twinkles was still in her nightgown and housecoat, her hair baked into a frizzled "permanent wave," falling in a somewhat sinister flap over her right eye. She had partaken of more than a little of Doc's election whiskey, and she hiccuped when she poured coffee for him. She sat on the sofa by Doc and looked across his shoulder at the slip of paper Joe drew from his coat pocket, and passed to him. All the precincts were listed, with the outcome in each of them. Doc had carried 11 and Arthur Hall had won in 19, in some of them by wide margins. Doc had gotten 4,823 votes—in response to years of toil as physician and surgeon to a county, and to a careful plan to serve the county's people in many other ways. But the lackluster bookkeeper who promised them nothing had garnered 6,298. There it was, defeat by 1,475 votes.

Joe did not drink, not even a thimbleful, when his fondest hopes had been dashed to ashes. He could offer Doc nothing more than a few words of consolation. "We tried hard, Doc, and we learnt a lot. Next time we'll win." He struggled with his one arm to get into his threadbare overcoat and trudged down the steps to his battered coupe. His son, seventeen-year-old Denver, drove him away to what Doc knew was a houseful of dashed hopes. Joe had no money and his home was mortgaged; he had counted on the political job Doc had promised him and it too was gone, leaving him with debts to pay, groceries and fuel to buy, a family to hold together. And this with no skill, no job, no education, no right arm. No wonder that he sagged as the rain beat against him.

Doc grieved for his friend who had worked for him so long and so devotedly. He also felt sorry for himself, a leaden self-pity that seeped into his very soul and spread like a gray miasma into every crack and cranny of his mind. The children were at school and would not climb the stone steps to the front porch for three more hours. He poured himself a stiff drink from Twinkles's bottle, poured water into the glass and swallowed the fiery liquid in two or three huge drafts. He wanted sympathy and so did Twinkles, so he grasped her by the wrist and marched her off to their bedroom. Her warm, firm, shapely body pressed hard against his own, and he made love to her as the alcohol spread from his belly and sent its glow of reassurance into his depression and misery. When he finished and fell back onto the bed beside her, the nightmare of his humiliation swept over him again. He ground his face into the pillow and for a long moment held his breath in vexation.

The long months of campaigning came back to him in their every detail. The weariness and labor of it all, the meetings, the promises, the broken pledges of support, the double-crosses by people he had befriended and trusted, the idiotic willingness of people to vote for the very people who oppressed them, the sorrow of his kinsmen, the dismay of his especial friend, Joe Carr, the revolting knowledge that he had been outwitted by Ben Fleming, the certainty that Arthur Hall would smile condescendingly at him when they met again, the certainty that across the county people were gloating over his fall.

"No, damn it all, never again," he moaned, "not for the damned sons of bitches who are the people!"

"What is it, honey?" Twinkles hiccuped from the dresser where she was pouring herself another drink.

"Nothing," he said, "nothing at all." But the first faint glimmer of a new determination had already begun to sprout in the dripping cave of his despair.

147

CHAPTER
10

Doc took Twinkles and the children and went to Florida for an escape he found imperative. He lay on the hot, white beach and watched Twinkles as she helped the children build castles and walled villages out of the sand. One was a fort for King Arthur's men, and it grew so complex that it needed a well to provide water for the garrison. It was dug, a smooth round pit a foot deep, and the children shrieked with pleasure when water filled it nearly to the brim. Twinkles was lovely against the background of sea and sky, and her vibrant breasts and hips half tempted him out of his gloom, but when the sea came up and swept away the walls with their towers and domes and gray gulls swooped across the sunset, his depression came back dark and overpowering. He sank into folds of self-pity as deep and dank as a rainy sky. His life as a coal-camp doctor with a huge stone house on a grassy hill, myriads of complaining patients and a county full of stupid voters seemed utterly oppressive and unbearable. He yearned to turn over a new leaf, go somewhere else and make a fresh start in a totally different setting into which the smell of ether and disinfectant and the moan of misery would never penetrate. He pounded the sand in frustration as he weighed the world into which he was so securely stitched and from which he could see no avenue of escape. While thousands of penniless Slaughter County miners sat before smoky fires listening to chill rains beat against tarpaper roofs and saw the future as virtually hopeless, the only man they knew who had had the good sense and sound fortune to survive the crash with fifty thousand dollars in a solid bank lay on a warm beach beneath a bright sky and weighed a future that was without a single flicker of hope. Trapped, defeated, sapped and disconsolate, he was a weary warrior ringed by implacable spears.

But a Florida beach in the company of a sexy and sympathetic woman is a difficult spot for the nurturing of melancholy, and on the fourth day his spirits abruptly improved. From the vantage point of a new morning, he suddenly wondered what the cavelike gloom of the previous week had been about. He turned with a healthy appetite to the rest of his vacation—the first he had ever taken—and his spirits and vitality returned as he rested. For the first time he realized how tired he had become in thirty-six years of unremitting work. Healing crept into him with the relaxation and freedom from pressure. He soaked in the luxury of a couple of murder mysteries, helped his startled and delighted offspring raise new forts and castles, and slipped into a hypnotic daze as they buried him beneath a mound of warm, dry sand. He could not free himself from the encumbering weight and begged for help when the foaming tide swirled up to his chin. His family happily and hurriedly dug him out and he and they romped in the sea exhilarated to intoxication by a sudden burst of new freedom.

For the first time in their lives, really, Doc became ac-

quainted with his children. Always before he had been too busy to see them as more than living bundles of flesh and blood that ate and slept and sometimes cried. He glimpsed them for a moment or two each day when he was hurrying away to the hospital, or when he returned for a hasty lunch, or in the evening over the edge of a newspaper or medical journal. Twinkles, too, had become something of an abstraction because so much of his time with her was only partly devoted to her. There were unbidden mental departures to his patients, or to investments he expected to make, or to voters he planned to entice. She sensed these absences and was saddened by them, and now rejoiced to have him restored to her fully, even if only briefly.

To the children Doc had been a benevolent stranger who sent food to the house, saw that their mother had a woman to help her with the housework, gave them medicines on the infrequent occasions when they were sick, and was generally seen coming to or leaving their home. When he found a few uninterrupted hours to stay at home, he read something or listened to the raucous croaking of the huge, walnut-cased Majestic radio. Then, too, there was an unending procession of callers, some of whom claimed to be sick, while others wanted to talk politics. With all such persons he would disappear into the somber, paneled "second parlor" which had been fitted up as an examination room. Certainly he had found little time for the girl and boy he had fathered. They took him for granted, generally ignored him, and harbored only the mildest order of affection for him.

Within a few glorious days, this was all changed. He learned many things he had been too preoccupied to notice before, and they made equally interesting discoveries about him. Tessie, he perceived, was a Bonham, pure and simple, and a beautiful child whose distinctive high cheekbones, slightly dark skin and keen penetrating eyes were combined with the imperiousness that had long been associated with her family name. She was slender, quick, and sharp-tongued, and from the family's brief sojourn in Florida, she would idolize her father and receive his unstinted devotion in return. Thence forward she would be denied few things he was able to bestow.

Jesse was a different proposition. Physically and mentally he inclined toward his mother, with brown wavy hair and small, perfect features. Already he liked books and stories, and his sister's temper and capacity for hauteur were missing in him. He was introspective, sometimes brooding and more likely to observe than to comment. It was not within his nature to show affection as unreservedly as his sister, and so it would never be as warmly and generously rewarded.

When their ten days were up they came home on the Andrew Jackson, one of the country's crack express trains. It brought them to Cincinnati, and they rode the rest of the way on a dusty little six-car affair that pounded its way along an interminably crooked track past innumerable smoke-shrouded mining towns huddled in a labyrinth of bleak, rainwashed valleys. On the train, they ate in the dining cars and were served by waiters in starched uniforms. Doc saw that their plates were loaded with delicious foods and the children deemed themselves the essence of elegance as they drank cups of hot chocolate and watched trees, telephone poles, roads, cars and houses slip past like impressions on an unfolding canvas. Doc and Twinkles took turns reading to them stories of knights and princesses, and black men in rumpled blue uniforms with red braid on their caps made up beds for them on soft, shelflike bunks where they giggled and romped behind the dangling curtains that cloaked their tiny compartment. They fell asleep to a metallic lullaby as the wheels clickety-clacked through a windy night. When Doc awakened his son next morning, the child still clutched a couple of pink shells from the Gulf strand and Doc bent to kiss his cheek. Doc was a thoroughly skeptical freethinker with little sympathy for notions of deity and prayer, but at that moment he spontaneously whispered a small expression of thanksgiving and a vow to keep his new family relationships alive and glowing. "From this day this family comes first with me!" he vowed; and the vacation that had commenced in such gloom ended in happiness as Doc returned to the cluttered little hospital and its waiting patients with pinched faces and ancient tattered clothes.

Doc's vacation was a marvelous restorative and he went back to work with a royal will. His shoulders were erect again, his voice strong, even and commanding. Out of his defeat and despair had come strength and renaissance so that it was widely reported he was "a good loser and didn't seem to care a-tall." Doc encouraged this notion and at every convenient opportunity remarked that, in retrospect, he was actually glad he had lost the election. "I ran because I wanted to do something for the county and the people," he said. "It would have cost me a lot of money to live in Blacksville four years and fight the coal companies all the time." Then with a nod and a smile, "This way I stay here and work and get the money. Arthur Hall is the one to feel sorry for. He's got all the troubles I missed!" And as the county continued to wallow in a Depression that deepened day by day, Doc came to believe his own rhetoric and rejoiced that he did not occupy the moldy little executive office in the decaying courthouse where each morning brought an avalanche of new complaints and a torrent of new demands.

Dr. Ross had saved the daily newspapers for him and in one of them Doc read that Carl Rutherford had moved from the state's house of representatives to the senate. He had won by a substantial margin and now represented three counties. One of them contained a city of 20,000, and, on the whole, Rutherford's district was an effective power base. Reflecting this fact, the new senator would serve on the committee on ways and means, and would have a voice in organizing the new session. Doc sent him a letter of congratulation and good wishes. He pointed out that while his own race had ended in defeat, the margin was not crushing. "We have made progress for the party in Slaughter County," he said, and then, "Let's keep in touch. There are important things ahead for you, and I want to help whenever I can."

Doc not only brought back new vigor from Florida, he came back with a new philosophy. Two days after his vacation ended, he met Ben Fleming in the post office across the street from the hospital. Fleming was a bit uneasy, but Doc set him at ease. He shook the hand of the startled operator and declared that by-gones should be by-gones. "I was wrong, Ben, in what I tried to do. I was wrong and I lost—thanks to the good sense of the people of this county—and I can't blame you. Coal is the future for Slaughter County, and I realize

154

now what you knew all along. We must promote it instead of knocking it!"

The astonished Fleming gripped Doc's hand in a fervent grasp and murmured a number of startled comments, all of which reflected most favorably upon the man he had opposed so stringently at every polling place in the county. They parted with most of their old friendship restored and with Fleming promising to drop by Doc's office for a visit within a few days.

But Doc abhorred the memory of days and weeks spent as a candidate. In his soul, there was an iron resolve never to see his name printed on another ballot. Politics was no more than a struggle for power, and the thirst for power and dominance was in his Bonham blood—as it had been in the blood of so many of his forebears. Power could be asserted through others, and by more subtle ways. And henceforth he would seek it for himself and his wife and their children and for their profit and advantage. In politics, too, the tenets of Darwinism were sound, and the nameless and faceless would have to serve often and well before they would be served. These, he perceived, were the first and ever-abiding rules of the game.

As Doc climbed the steps to the waiting patients, he mused that it appeared a lot easier to win with Ben Fleming's support than with his opposition. After all, he concluded, if they can't be licked, they can sure as hell be joined.

CHAPTER
11

Doc was busy with his practice and avoided all political involvements, but circumstances which he could not control combined to enhance his prestige and influence. He was not oblivious to them—to the contrary, he noted them carefully and marked their course and progress—but believed his future would be best served by a period of withdrawal and inaction. "These ignorant people," he told himself, "have made their bed, and now, by God, they can lie on it!"

The bed was hard and the lying a misery. Arthur Hall was, at best, an affable non-entity whom coal company money and coercion, and a gross measure of stupidity in the electorate, had elevated to a position whose duties he was wholly unprepared to discharge. The disasters that fell upon him like an avalanche of Damoclean swords were part of the collapse of a nation, but the suffering people of his county blamed the near and the evident for their woes rather than the distant and speculative. And as a chorus of criticism and denunciation welled up in the precincts, the man whom the voters had denied the office profited immensely in their esteem. Since Hall was blamed quite automatically for their troubles, people came to believe with equal ease and supreme illogic that things would somehow have been better if

Doc had won. Doc did nothing to counter this fast-spreading notion, and Hall was powerless to do so.

Hall entered the office with a pledge from the coal operators' association that the companies would help him to mount a general improvement program. Doc had so alarmed the operators with his campaign to increase their taxes and curb their powers that they resolved to contribute enough funds to give teachers a pay raise, start a rural road maintenance program and set up some sort of public health service, but such good intentions dissolved in the flush of victory and as the operators' own burdens burgeoned.

If 1930 had been bad for an industrialist with a million dollars invested in a coal mine and a hundred and fifty families huddled in his houses hungrily waiting for the work whistle to blow, then 1931 and 1932 were terrible. Orders for coal practically vanished as the economy of a stricken world ground toward utter breakdown, families starved, companies bankrupted, and Slaughter County became a hell.

Along the streets of Blacksville, stores that had opened amid high hopes in the boom closed their doors in the bust. A contractor went broke in the middle of a paving project, and the drab county seat lay for years in a scatteration of rotting wooden forms and intermittent stretches of unfinished concrete. Farmers could find no markets in the town for their produce, and stayed at home to ponder the land-tax bills they could not pay and ease their frustrations with libations of whiskey made from their unsold corn.

Amid this riot of deterioration Arthur Hall was expected and compelled to hold up his little world alone like Atlas on his mountain. He economized first; God, how he did economize! The plan for a county health office and a physician remained just a plan. Schoolhouse roofs went unrepaired, and rain dripped onto the heads of teachers whose pay sank to a monthly average of $55. Then came March 1932, and there was no money at all. No bank would cash a county voucher, miners rioted and robbed commissaries, and Judge Hall, with no other alternatives open to him, ordered the sheriff and his deputies to collect all delinquent tax bills, wherever and by whomever owed. They levied attachments on automobiles, sewing machines, law libraries, dental drills, the tools of mechanics and the cows and wagons of farmers. Nor did they spare the coal baronies, for their mining cars, tipples and power generators went on the auction blocks too. The squeeze worked after a fashion; a few score thousand dollars were rounded up and the schools reopened in May. The judge's Draconian measures saved the county from total collapse, but there was no escape for himself. He became the most hated individual in the county's history, a joyless, haggard, shrunken figure who crept into his office by a side door and avoided every possible encounter with his constituency. Their antipathy was palpable, and its bitter edge took the spring out of his step and bent his shoulders into a sagging stoop.

Everybody blamed Arthur Hall for everything that was wrong. Schoolteachers denounced him for their shriveled paychecks and for that dreary month when there was no check at all. Farmers held him responsible for unrepaired roads and bridges that stranded them along creeks and mountainsides. Paupers by the hundreds cursed him for suspension of their "pauper vouchers" that would have put a few beans and some corn pone on their tables. Coal operators said he was ungrateful and a failure because county-paid policemen no longer patrolled the camps and protected commissaries and storerooms from pillage by thieves made desperate by hunger. To save money, Hall even stopped sheriffs deputies from seeking out union organizers and expelling them from the county. As much as he was scorned for these omissions, the sentiment was mild by comparison with the sheer hatred that washed around him when he imposed and collected the taxes used to restore some of the services. Every taxpayer, it seemed, wanted much and was enraged when it was not forthcoming, but damned as gross injustice the notion that he should pay any portion of the costs.

With the fall of the county judge, came the collapse of the Republican machine that had ruled the county so ruthlessly for nearly two decades. The GOP incumbents felt power slip through their fingers as a new era dawned in the spring of 1933.

If Franklin D. Roosevelt did not know how to overcome the national malaise, he pretended that he did and acted so confidently that most Americans trusted him. After an effort to cure a grossly deflated economy with spending cutbacks, the new President adopted a new policy and commenced spending on a huge scale. His "pump-priming" outlays coursed across the nation and reached Slaughter County in a good generous flow with the gentle days of autumn. The money would do good things for many distressed people, but among those it was destined never to benefit were Arthur Hall and the other unfortunates who had ridden to victory with him.

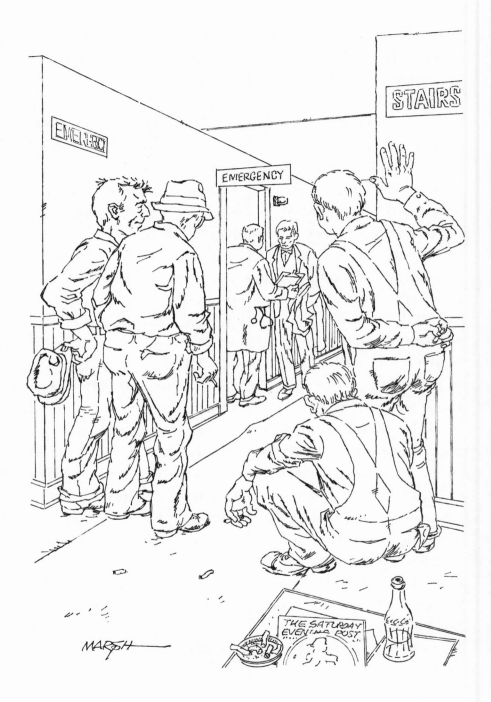

Doc had had a rough day beginning with an emergency call that took him to the hospital at a quarter to four in the morning. His eyes were heavy with fatigue when he climbed the dingy steps, their boards creaking after two decades of hard use and few repairs. A half-dozen Fords and Chevrolets were drawn up in front of the building, yellow beams from their headlamps pushing through the cold white mist that eddied along the cinder-coated streets. On the steps and in the waiting room upstairs huge uncouth men hovered anxiously. Doc knew them all—sons, grandsons and sons-in-law of Rex Ballard, a grizzled and grim old moonshiner who lived with his tribe on the head of Owl Fork of Viper Creek. His stills had turned out whiskey through all the years of Prohibition, a smooth, decently distilled product that was filtered through tanks of charcoal, then delivered to an underground railroad run by Irish and Italian gangsters which conveyed it to the speakeasies of Cincinnati, Chicago and Detroit.

Ballard lived in an ancient log cabin his grandfather had hewed from walnut and poplar trees, and so many of his kin lived close by and voted at his whim that Viper Creek was aptly known as "Rex Ballard's precinct." They were a truculent lot whose cabins and ramshackle houses were festooned with pistols, shotguns, and rifles, and understandably, state and federal officers had ignored their operations. The Ballards wanted no reformers in office and Doc had garnered only three votes out of the 97 cast at the ballot box set up in their rickety one-room schoolhouse. Besides, they were staunch Republicans, a circumstance that dated from 1861 when a Bonham killed a Ballard with an ax. Rex's great-uncle, Jake, had claimed that "niggers are human, not jist kinky-headed animals with wool instead of hair." Colonel Ben Bonham's brother, Aleck, considered such a proposition "a damned lie and an insult," and when Ballard reiterated it with much heat and added, "In fact, a nigger is as good as you are and some of 'em is a damned sight better," Aleck clove his skull and spurred his horse southward through the gap. His people buried Jake Ballard and Aleck Bonham was decapitated by a cannonball three weeks before Appomattox. Still, there had always been bad blood between the two tribes, and Doc had an eerie sensation when he saw the overalled men crowding his premises, their pockets bulging with pistols and sweatstained wool hats pulled down over their eyes.

Old Rex stood in the hall near the frosted glass door to the operating room. The huge form of his son, little Rex, lay moaning on a table. Draxie Davis, Doc's night nurse, had cut away and pulled off his shirt and pants and draped him with a white sheet. The sheet was soaked with blood, and in his agony, the man chewed on a corner of it with huge teeth that ground together like broken gears. He was about thirty-five, and Doc knew him for a cold unflinching killer who had shot "Round Rube" Elkins to death in a squabble over a batch of whiskey and had served a stretch or two in the state pen. In recent months, he had worked as an "industrial peace officer" hired by the county coal operators association to guard tipples and mine portals against sabotage and his reputation had worsened in the process.

A day's growth of grayish beard was on Rex Ballard's face and a solid paunch rounded out the faded bib of his overalls. His eyes narrowed as he looked at Doc and back at the writhing man on the stretcher. Both threat and entreaty bubbled in their depths. "Hit's my boy, Doc. Hit's Little Rex. He's shot twice, square through the guts."

Little Rex and the bloody cart disappeared through the swinging doors. Draxie Davis had called Dr. Ross and Doc heard the young physician's steps on the sagging stairs. As he took off his overcoat and hat and hung them on a peg, Doc asked what happened. "He was a-guardin' a mine at Big Seam," Old Rex replied, "and some men come by in a car and Little Rexie took 'em fer Union organizers an' agitators. He tried to arrest 'em, er at least scare 'em outta the county, and one of 'em let loose with a .45. He may have killed my boy, but he's already dead hisself. Rexie shot 'im atween the eyes after two balls had already gone through his own bowels."

There was pride in the moonshiner's voice and Doc sighed with the silent reflection, "We'll probably save his life so he can go on and commit other outrages until he is as old as this old bastard." But his reply was a soothing pat on old Rex's arm. He looked for a long moment into the agitated eyes and promised with a show of sincerity Rex Ballard would never forget. "I'll do all I can. He won't die if it is within my skill and knowledge to save him!"

While Dr. Ross and Draxie Davis injected morphine and checked blood pressure, Doc washed up and pulled on anti-septic gloves. Ross poured ether onto a cloth and put it over the patient's blood-flecked mouth. The electric bulbs glared down on the perforated belly, and instruments clinked as they were laid out. When Ross signaled that the man was unconscious, Doc went to work. Ross listened to his chest with a stethoscope and murmured, "Heart like a horse. Beat steady and strong." Then in the primitive little surgery where so many shattered coal miners had been patched up, Doc foiled with scalpel and needle on loops of intestines.

Antibiotics were yet to be developed and excrement from the severed bowels had oozed into the body cavity. Doc lifted it out with a hastily boiled spoon someone brought from the kitchen. "Not much use to sterilize it," he growled as beads of sweat gathered on his nose. "There can't be anything on the spoon as nasty as the stuff I'm dipping out with it!"

In two hours they removed a yard of bowels and a quart of nauseating excrement. Doc sluiced down everything with hydrogen peroxide after the ends of the shortened gut had been rejoined. Then the huge incision was closed with a dozen stitches and Little Rex was rolled away to a bed. Doc leaned against the wall and sucked on a Chesterfield before going out to give an account to the waiting Ballards.

Doc did not get home again until eight in the evening. He felt good about Little Rex, and about the cash the moonshiners had gotten together and laid on his desk. Patients were easier to come by than dollars to pay for the medicines and services they required, but there was no problem about payment for services rendered to Little Rex. His kinfolks paid for the operation and promised more and, into the bargain, Doc thought there was a chance the patient might live. Peritonitis would probably set in and carry him off in a vast fog of delirium—but again, it might not. Dink Brown had been machine-gunned in the guts in Belleau Wood and had lain out on the ground all night with no medical attention, and now he loaded coal alongside other men. His belly was as rough as a washboard from the scars. Doc calculated Little

Rex to have one chance in four, maybe even one in three. One thing was sure though, Doc had made some friends that day, and even in his weariness, he made some calculations as to how he could best use the altered situation on Slate Creek.

That evening Doc found that Old Rex had sent a half gallon of his best spirits to the house as a gift, and Twinkles giggled as she poured him a generous drink and added water and ice to the glass. The whiskey and a supper of pork chops and potatoes left him in a good mood. He eyed Twinkles speculatively, then called the hospital for a report on Little Rex. Temperature nearly normal, pulse steady and strong, still sleeping. "The sonofabitch is going to live sure as hell," he muttered as he reached for his wife, but his carnal plans were thwarted for the moment by the jingling of the doorbell.

It was Joe Carr and he entered humbly, apologetically. His shirt was frayed at the collar and his suit had laid no claim to newness for nearly five years. His empty sleeve descended in a pathetic limpness and was tucked into the pocket of his coat. The shoulder above it was shrunken and thin, sticking up under the blue cloth in a sharp peak. Doc worried a lot about Joe and had helped him in a number of ways. Joe fed his family and sustained his own endless appetite because Doc had made him a loan of a few hundred dollars to buy some pool tables and set them up in an empty store in Blacksville. Too many of his customers, though, paid him in coal company scrip so that ends often did not meet for Joe, but, in whatever befell, he was a friend of Doc; the doctor would someday lead the Democrats to victory in Slaughter County, and then Joe, and many another deserving sufferer, would find jobs and largesse. In all he thought and undertook, his candidate's advancement was Joe's one perpetual aim.

Doc motioned him to a chair and Joe said he was sorry to bother Doc at home after a hard day at the hospital. "Folks have been sayin' at Blacksville that Little Rex's guts was riddled like a sieve and that you cut out a basketful before you sewed him up."

Doc laughed. "Well, the guts and the rest of the stuff almost filled a slop bucket. You know, Joe, Rexie Ballard is a pure unadulterated rascal who ought to die in the public interest. But he's not going to. He's going to live."

Joe's face brightened and rows of white teeth gleamed as the huge mouth curled into a happy smile. "If he lives it's worth a hundred votes and them all Republicans ninety-nine percent of the time." He calculated a moment, "If he dies, you've picked up fifty, anyway forty, and that ain't bad either."

Doc shook his head. "Votes don't seem as important to me personally as they used to, Joe. I don't think I will ever run for anything again. You know what I went through for a whole year, and all because I wanted a few thousand nit-wits to get a fair shake in their own courthouse." He sipped the whiskey and allowed, "I think I'll let other people do the running from now on."

Joe eased his round carcass into Doc's leather armchair and sighed. "Sometimes a blessin' comes disguised, so disguised, in fact, that it's mighty near impossible to see that it's a blessin'. And that's exactly what happened to you and the Democratic party three years ago. You got beat but you got your name and principles into ever' house in the county. The people know you now, ever'where— not just as a doctor, but as a politician. And they wish to their God's good name they had voted for you."

Doc snorted. "That blessing cost me nearly thirty thousand dollars!"

Again Joe delivered himself of a deep and solemn sigh. "If you had won, though, you'd be in the same shape today that Arthur Hall's in. These hard times have killed him politically, and they would have killed you if you had his office. You'd have to keep the schools open and enforce the laws. People would demand it and then hate you fer raising the taxes to give them what they demand! The ways things are now, you're in a perfect position to run and win. People will vote fer you 'cause Arthur Hall beat you and they hate Arthur Hall!"

Doc eyed him closely but said nothing. Joe continued. "The federal government is a-goin' to spend a lot of money in this county. It's got to or people will die by thousands in another year. Relief works are comin' on a big scale, soon. And, since Roosevelt is a Democrat, a Democrat is goin' to decide who gets relief in Slaughter County. And that Democrat can come close to bein' a king. He can make the coal operators look feeble."

Doc continued to study Joe. Joe heaved himself upright and looked Doc in the eye. "Carl Rutherford is on his way up here from the state capital. He is makin' a kind of tour of all the coal minin' mountain counties. And Doc, my friend, he is bringin' tidin's of great joy!"

He got up to go. "I've already talked to him, and I know what he will say to you. He will be at your office about two tomorrow. After he leaves we will have what it takes to make this county Democratic forever. Ain't nobody can fight the federal treasury, and it's a-goin' to be on our side."

Joe's deliberate footsteps faded as he crossed the porch and went down the steps. Doc sat for a long time, his eyes closed as he considered the blessings a national relief program might bring to Slaughter County.

Carl Rutherford did not reach Noreco until after four o'clock. It was raining, as it had rained all day, and his rumpled suit and muddy shoes testified to the inadequacy of raincoat and umbrella. His belly had enlarged since their last meeting and he was tired, but enthusiasm for his mission buoyed his spirits.

Doc knew a future governor when he saw one, and invited him to his house for one of Twinkles' steaks and to spend the night. After a drink of Rex Ballard's whiskey and a sturdy meal, Rutherford slipped off his shoes and stretched out on a sofa. He stacked the cushions in a heap, clasped his hands behind his head and closed his eyes for a long interval of reflection. His host had anticipated most of what he said.

"A doctor who practices in the coal field doesn't require me to tell him that the Republicans have got this country in a hell of a mess. They took a boom and turned it into a bust, and Hoover did everything possible to make the situation hopeless. That poor sap couldn't find a ham in a smokehouse. Maybe he was God's gift to us Democrats."

Doc nodded, and Rutherford went on. "We've got a different President now, but the important thing is that we've got a different kind of President. The governor just came back from a conference with Roosevelt, and he is a Roosevelt man all the way. The President convinced him that he intends to lick this Depression and get the United States moving again under a full head of steam. There is a lot stirring in Washington, and things will soon start stirring here."

One arm lay across his eyes, shutting out the light from a glass-beaded floor lamp. "For a long time the Democratic problem has been money. The coal industry is tied to the steel and power companies that burn its product, and to the railroad and barge companies that carry it to market. They all have friends, stockholders and employees. They can influence their customers. Together they make a mighty big kettle of fish. They have been able to raise enough money to control the legislature and the delegation to Congress. The combine is Republican, and it is the real government in the state. It elects and defeats. A Democratic governor can't fight the combine because it always manages to control the legislature." Then after a little pause, "It turned Joe Carr out of the legislature, and it beat you."

Rutherford sat up and looked at Doc. "What do you need to turn Slaughter County Democratic and keep it that way? We may not be able to get you all you need, but we'll try. The governor and the President are on your side."

Doc laughed. "We need jobs, about two thousand of them, and control over the jobs. We need grub for thousands of people who are tired as hell of living on soup from these poor little greasy-spoon soup kitchens the Quakers and Salvation Army run. To put it sweet and simple, we need what the coal association has had for years, and to use it the same way: the stick and the carrot — temptation and chastisement."

Rutherford loosened his collar and pulled off his tie. "You are right in the middle of real good sense," he agreed. "But you have to have two other things to go with the things you've named. Since the money will be federal, it will be watched, and someday there may be investigations. You need to be discreet, and you need to turn this county around and put the game rooster back in the courthouse without putting any Democrats in a federal pen."

"No doctors, at least," Doc ventured, "but it might be a good thing to send up a few dozen sons-of-bitches who pretended to be for me and then sold me down the river like a black slave for a job or a dollar or two."

"Doctor, my friend, a cousin of mine named Reuben Humble is coming to Blacksville. He is a discreet and reasonable man, and a dyed-in-the-wool Democrat whose grandfather was a rebel captain at Cold Harbor. You can trust him because he knows the ropes and the rules. I picked him myself, and he is going to relieve the misery of the good people of Slaughter County. Josh Wynn, the state's relief administrator, served in the state senate with the governor twenty years ago, and they understand each other. He has appointed Humble as relief administrator for Slaughter County, and he will get the job done—if you and Joe Carr help him."

"I'll help him. I'll be his most devoted assistant," Doc chuckled.

"Your attitude is constructive and just what we need to bring relief to the indigent people of Slaughter County. I think we can do a wonderful lot of good while helping the poor. We can make the county Democratic, send Joe Carr back to the legislature where he is badly needed, put you in the county judge's office if you want it, and help to send a couple of Democrats to the U.S. Senate. These are noble goals for Samaritans like ourselves who share the President's wish to fill empty bellies and clothe naked backs."

They laughed and lit cigarettes. As the smoke drifted about them and eddied toward the ceiling, Doc told Rutherford about Little Rex Ballard and his gut shots. "I think we ought to use a little more of the old man's liquor to toast our enterprise."

"Who knows?" Rutherford mused as he savored the malty taste of the moonshine. "Your Little Rex may become a straw boss and a registered Democrat! Stranger things than that have happened."

"I've got bigger plans than that, by God. I'm going after all of them. I'll turn Viper Creek Democratic before Old Rex goes to hell."

Doc dreamed considerably that night, though he slept less than usual.

CHAPTER

12

Reuben Humble's ancestors on both sides had been Democrats since a dozen years before the election of Andrew Jackson. They had come out from the Virginia tidewater, with slaves, some beautiful cherry furniture, a collection of silver spoons and a bag of gold coins, passing through the mountain gaps and hundreds of miles beyond to the sun-washed flatlands. They—his great-great-grandparents—had built a brick house with white Doric columns on a bluff overlooking a huge bend in the Mississippi. Cotton growing in profusion out of the black soil, and cattle and hogs for the river trade, had made them rich. But in later generations numerous descendants divided the eight thousand acres of Far View plantation into many farms, wore out the land and frittered away their money on travel, books and college educations. Far View Hall was bombarded and burned by a Union gunboat in 1863, its copper roof dripping in yellow globs onto the ashes of oak timbers and ash floors. Of the great beginning, the years had preserved for Reuben Humble only the political faith of his fathers and the four scarred columns in a weedgrown grove.

His father was a dealer in lumber and sent his son to Yale to study engineering and architecture. For a while after his marriage, he found commissions and designed homes, schools, a few college dormitories, and a multitude of courthouse memorials to heroic doughboys. Then came the hard times in the late twenties and the incomprehensible dreariness of 1930, 1931 and 1932. The commissions disappeared, a mortgage wafted away the house he had built under twin elms on a quiet street, and his wife took their two children and went home to her father, a banker who managed somehow to keep his doors open. Humble sent her money when he could which was not often—and his well-tailored suits and shirts turned thin and threadbare. At forty-three he was delighted when Josh Wynn, an old political crony of his father and the state's newly appointed federal relief administrator, remembered him and offered him a job in Slaughter County. As he sat in the paneled office in the Federal Building above the stricken streets of the state's largest city and heard the offer of employment at a robust $250 a month, he would manage only a single comment. "Where," he inquired with a laugh, "is Slaughter County?"

He and Josh Wynn had sprung from the same soil and their thoughts instinctively ran in the same channels. Wynn was twenty-one years his senior, a lawyer who had been a state circuit judge, a state senator and, under Woodrow Wilson, U.S. collector of internal revenue in the state. He was tall and courtly, with longish talcum-colored hair, white linen suits and a black string tie. He and Reuben Humble spoke in the same soft, gentle, old-South tones that for generations had marked the people of the state's western reaches.

They talked for a while of other times and of a vanishing way and pace of life. The older man reflected aloud on

Jefferson, Jackson and Wilson, the party's ancient coalition of northern workingmen and southern farmers, and of the persistent oppression of "little people" by Republican bankers and monopolists. The country had drifted for a long time, leaderless, chaotic, and depressed, and now Franklin D. Roosevelt and a revitalized Democratic party offered a last chance to draw back from the brink and preserve liberty and liberal institutions. Every county, he noted, was important in the struggle to avoid a Mussolini-style fascism in America. He leaned back in his leather swivel chair, pondered the toe of his brightly polished shoe for a moment, then looked up to study the younger man's face. "Rube," he said with a steely grimness and persuasiveness Humble would never forget, "Do all you can to save the people of poor godforsaken Slaughter County from starvation. The government wants every man to have a job as speedily as possible, and every stomach to be filled. Save them for the party too, Rube. Make Democrats out of every God-damn one of those hillbillies! Don't just fatten them up so they can keep on voting Republican."

Humble brought to the two-room office above Callihan's Feed Store in Blacksville a quiet manner, a distinguished appearance and an old-fashioned charm of a kind that had sent a number of his kinsmen to legislative halls. He combined courtliness with a genuine concern for others. He was urbane and civilized, and almost childishly determined to succeed in the unusual task that had fallen into his hands. He was, also, a deeply partisan Democrat who adhered without a quibble to the opinions of Josh Wynn. He had seen starvation in the eyes of hundreds of young men and women on the icy streets of Hamilton, Cleveland and Gary, and in the cotton rows of his native county had seen farmers stumble from famine. The instincts for order and grace that had turned him into an architect were repelled by the evidence, visible on every hand, that America was deteriorating into a vast slum. Innovative and liberal, he found the inventiveness of the New Deal much to his liking. He came to his work with a fervent determination to turn Slaughter County into a citadel of Rooseveltian democracy. Withal, he was cautious and unobtrusive. The New Deal had chosen wisely in sending him to the camps and hollows of the coal industry.

He had seen distress in many places, but the conditions his inspection revealed in his new bailiwick defied description. King Coal had been dethroned, and his domain was in anarchy. In many camps there had been no work for more than a year. In others —the fortunate ones —the work whistles on top of the commissaries wailed once or twice a week. Ten hours "at the coal face" rarely paid a miner more than two dollars. A dozen companies were gone entirely, long since defunct in bankruptcy, their tipples still, their stores empty, their streets thronged with threadbare scarecrows. The Miners' Bank of Blacksville was still operating, but the county's other two banks, the First National and the Slaughter State Bank had collapsed. Their doors were padlocked, and Humble stared through grimy windows into their dust-covered, paper-strewn little lobbies. Gangs of flat-chested and hollow-eyed boys and young men loafed at every crossroad and slatternly, emaciated girls and women stared from countless sagging porches.

The physical environment was as ruinous as the social and economic debacle. Immense heaps of slate and waste coal had piled up in or near each of the county's twenty-seven mining camps. Slow fires consumed them night and day so that clouds of sulfurous smoke lay in the valleys and crept in foul mists up the coves and along the ridges, killing trees and leaving the land as naked as the cheeks of a skeleton. Hunger had sent men, women and children to scratch the hillsides for corn, potatoes and beans. And predictably, rain had washed away the loosened soil, gullying the slopes and choking the creeks with mud.

Chastened and depressed, Humble called at the office of the county judge to enlist the aid of local officials in what would have to be a complex and massive effort to provide food, clothes and jobs. In the dingy office with its crumbling plaster and ancient, rickety, scarred furniture, he found a beaten man who could suggest no solutions and lived only for the day when his expired term would enable him to seek a living elsewhere and otherwise. The eight justices of the peace who sat with him as the fiscal court on "court days" were attired in denim overalls and tattered, unclean suits, their collars bereft of ties, their cheeks stuffed with tobacco. All except one were Republicans and none was fruitful of ideas. All were eager, however, to get "grub and jobs started afore ever' body might' nigh starves t' death," as one of them phrased it. Judge and justices alike pledged prompt approval of such resolutions of local support as were necessary to get relief projects underway. As he left the filthy, stench-filled courthouse, Humble's gloom deepened to match that of the sere, gray hills.

He found a house and rented it and called his wife to tell her of the arrangement he had made. She promised to have her brother drive her and the children up to Blacksville within a few days, and Humble breathed a sigh of relief for the crotchety old banker who was his father-in-law. He ate a grease-tainted supper at the nearby deserted Indian River Hotel and, buoyed somewhat by the prospect of having his family together again under a roof of his own choosing, went to his room. He wanted to call some of the men his friend, State Senator Carl Rutherford, had mentioned to him. The senator had come to him after his conversation with Josh Wynn and congratulated him on his appointment. "The governor," he said, "is very pleased that you are going to direct things in Slaughter County. He knows you will get the job done if anybody can." He mentioned the names of Dr. Tom Bonham and former State Representative Joe Carr as men of integrity, foresight, and knowledge of the situation. "They are Democrats, and that little fact won't hurt anything. Then, too, they know what is going on in the county and can provide you with contacts you would require months to make yourself." Rutherford assured him, "They'll give you only good advice, you can count on them for that!"

As things turned out he did not have to call them. There was a rap on the door, and when he opened it those two worthies stood before him. He recognized Carr at once from Rutherford's precise description: "He's a big fat man who eats all the time." They introduced themselves and Humble invited them into the huge square room with its worn carpet and hideous brass bed.

After the manner of the old South, he called them—as he always would— "Dr. Bonham" and "Mr. Joe." And they, after the fashion of the hills where nicknames spring up like mushrooms in a cave, accepted his invitation and called him

"Rube." They got along well from the beginning, forming a friendship that remained unshaken during the seven years he would remain in Slaughter County. "Rube" had clothes, food and jobs to dispense, and they knew multitudes who needed them, and how the largess might bring the most relief to the destitute without any benefit to the party of Lincoln and Hoover. There occurred what diplomats term "a frank exchange of views," followed by a series of Joe Carr's most outrageous yarns about traveling salesmen and their adventures with the daughters of farmers and miners. Carr's huge belly shook with laughter at his own tales and Humble, who had had little to laugh at for a long time, chuckled also. The doctor happened to have about him a bottle of fifteen-year-old "medicinal spirits" which a Pennsylvania distillery issued in limited quantities for victims of sundry ills. Doc allowed that a medicine that would cure a disease would probably ward it off, and prescribed a few precautionary drinks. When they left and he heard Doc's Model A Ford coupe chugging down the deserted street, Reuben Humble turned the light out and went to bed. The visit had left him feeling better than he had for years, and the task of relieving the distressed seemed considerably less formidable.

The New Deal moved speedily to get relief to the cold and hungry. The warehouse of a bankrupt wholesale grocery was filled to the rafters with dried beans, cheeses, canned fruits, evaporated milk, sides of salt pork and bags of potatoes. New boxcar loads were trundled inside each week, but with equal dispatch the "commodity grub" was passed on to the long lines of men and women who came in old cars, on mules and afoot to claim "food vouchers" at the office across the street. They went away bent like so many ragged Santa Clauses beneath stuffed gunny sacks and long, striped meal bags. These "pokes" brought to cabins and windy camp shacks the smell of sizzling side meat and potatoes, quenching the nagging hunger that gnawed at young and old bellies. At many a scarred dinner table gaunt men and women wept with relief and gratitude when they realized that their children were experiencing something new —they were going to bed free of the pangs of hunger. Radios brought them the mellow, strangely accented voice of Franklin D. Roosevelt telling them that there was an administration in Washington that cared about them and was determined to bring them better days. They were thankful to FDR and all his busy legions of brain trusters who were "priming the pump" and doing so many other incomprehensible things away up there in the nation's capital.

They were thankful to Joe Carr, too, and to Doc Bonham. Joe sold his poolroom and assumed the title of Director of Commodity Relief Food Distribution, though a Republican wag expressed concern that "with Joe's appetite the poor folks won't get much." He moved his rotund frame into the oak swivel chair behind the steel desk, took on a roomful of typists, bookkeepers and other assistants and began receiving applications for food vouchers. He issued them too, in a stream that quickened into a flood. Joe minded Humble's admonition of "no politics, everything on the up and up!" and never mentioned the forbidden subject to anyone—never certainly during office hours at least. But this was a light burden for Joe to carry. He knew practically every man in the county, and most of the women as well, and those who had been loyal allies in the past saw their applications for the coveted vouchers whisking to the rubber stamp of approval. Others were delayed, then approved, then slightly delayed when they next appeared at the "voucher window." The recalcitrant, the iron-bound and rock-bottom Republicans were sometimes difficult cases to process and so their claims languished while hunger deepened. The word spread quickly that the hand that held the carrot grasped the stick also, and a man ate better if he was a friend of Joe Carr. The director was jollity itself—the salary and regular employment had restored his spirits completely—and every applicant was asked a friendly question or two, and most became the target of a compliment. But men remembered Joe's close ties to Doc Bonham, and applications seemed to move with never a hitch if a commendation could be gotten from the doctor himself or any one of his close and special friends—a score or two of men and woman scattered across the county. And those men and women in every precinct turned out to be old and faithful supporters of the doctor, and many were his blood relatives. Generally they held no official positions, drew no salaries, possessed no power to command. But they could suggest the course of discretion and wisdom to the frightened and desperate. And the frightened and desperate learned that things were eased for them when they acted affirmatively on those suggestions. It was so when the icy autumn winds began to stir along the crags and the newly fed lined up for sweaters, jackets, underdrawers, socks and shoes. It was so when the work relief projects were organized and men turned out to pile stone walls, build roads and schools, and plant tens of thousands of trees on eroded hills. If a man was a friend of Doc Bonham, the rough spots were smoothed down. The sacks of food, the shapeless clothes, the all-important jobs came easiest to those for whom someone "said a word to Doc." And the desperate came to Doc in his office and sought his aid in a room where portraits of Franklin D. Roosevelt and John Nance Garner smiled down from the wall. There were other photographs too, all duly signed—the governor, both senators and Carl Rutherford. They bore such endorsements as "to Dr. Tom Bonham with kindest regards," and "for Dr. Tom Bonham, a fighter for people." All were Democrats, and Doc often tapped Rutherford's solemn likeness and assured his callers that "here is a close and good friend of mine. It will be a great day for this county when he becomes governor." Yes, when Doc got behind a man things got better for him. Doc had friends, no doubt about that, and could deliver when he wanted to. Generally he wanted to, but sometimes he did not.

Doc had come out of his disastrous race against Arthur Hall with a goodly number of scores to settle. He had learned, also, that kindness does not always pay, and that the errant must be chastised. He had a memory like a bear trap, and it hung doggedly to every affront and wrong. But he was, in the final analysis, not actually vindictive or cruel; rather, he had come to think of voters as abstractions, as a chess player may think of pieces. He was perfectly willing to lay aside—while still remembering—a man's past derelictions if he "straightened up" and became reliable. Doc was a pragmatist, and Arthur Hall had taught him to forget sympathy, antipathy, gratitude and confidence. Men would behave out of self-interest only, and he intended for them to learn that their self-interest lay with him and in no other quarter.

Rube Humble needed a man to head an office to hire men for the dozen Civil Works Administration projects that had been authorized for the county, and Doc suggested that his brother Tilford possessed in full measure all the needed qualities and qualifications. Humble demurred a little on the ground that Tilford's job with the railroad was one of the best in the county. "We ought to give that job to a good man who is already out of work," he suggested, but Doc laughed and allowed that would be against the Scriptures. "To him who has will be given—" he maintained, and Tilford put together the "work relief" office. He staffed it with Bonhams and Frees and Earlys and Callihans galore. Tilford's eyes had weakened with the years and the lenses of his glasses had thickened so that as he sat behind his desk and studied the faces of job hunters he looked distinctly owlish. Still, rueful Republicans soon had occasion to point out, "He can see some things better and a damn sight quicker than others. In fact, he can see Bonhams and Democrats in no time a-tall!"

Tom Morton came to see Doc one morning, his peg leg thumping on the hollow stair. He waited among the sick and afflicted until Doc could get to him, then shook Doc's hand as the physician closed the door for privacy. "Tom, you old vagrant, what brings you over here from Poor Fork? You can't be sick, you never looked healthier in your life!" Tom laughed, showing twin rows of huge yellow-stained teeth. One hundred and ninety men were digging a road up Poor Fork, and one of his sons was a straw boss and the other the timekeeper. They were doing the work with picks, shovels, wheelbarrows, a few mules and "main strength and awkwardness." Tom was furnishing the mules for the project fifteen of them at $2 a day. This was the same pay issued to a man and Tom was not complaining.

He sat down and crossed his legs so that the peg stuck out like a blunt and muddy rapier. "Road work's comin' fine," he began. "They're right in front of Old Man Haint Jones's place." Doc was pleased. "I'm glad to hear it, Tom. People need roads, people need jobs; Roosevelt kills two birds with one stone. What about our friends out there? Is that brother of mine taking good care of them?"

Tom twisted in his chair and leaned back so that the peg pointed straight at John Nance Garner. Three weeks earlier his wife had presented him with a nine-pound son whom he had promptly named John Nance Morton. He pondered the vice president's likeness and licked his lips before he began.

"Doc, I think we ought to do somethin' for Old Man Haint Jones. Now, don't git me wrong, I know he and his whole bunch voted agin you, and fit you. He's always been straight Republican. His old man was a Union soldier and lost his leg at Cold Harbor and spent forty years on a peg, like me. Me and Old Haint are neighbors, though, even if we always did disagree on election days, and he's damned near starvin' right now."

"I don't have too much of a grudge against him, Tom. I think he needs to suffer a little while longer, though. The coal association put eighty dollars in his pocket two days before he helped screw me, and I want to make sure he has used up his election money before he draws any relief money."

Doc laughed and smote his knee in appreciation of his own sally. Tom looked pained but managed a weak chuckle.

"It's already gone. He ain't got a cent. He sold his mule and shotgun. He even sold his pocket watch. He give a right of way through his old wore-out land, and it seems kind of wrong fur ever'body else on the creek to be buildin' a public road through Haint's place and him and his bunch the only one's that caint git to do any work on it."

Doc laughed again. Tom's great, bland earnest face amused him. Besides, Morton had been his friend too long and too loyally for a favor to be denied.

"Tom, we won't let Haint's bunch starve to death. It's unhealthy, and as a doctor I have to prescribe food for the hungry. But you know," and here his tone became confidential and intimate, "there is a time for everything. A time for an old son-of-a-bitch like Haint to starve, and a time for him to eat. The time for him to eat is close at hand. I think Haint can be helped." He stood up and clapped Tom on the shoulder. "Wait till Monday of next week and then suggest to Haint that he come and see me. After we have had a little talk, maybe Tilford and Joe can see their way clear to help him and his whole bunch. Jobs and grub, that's the ticket!"

Tom left in an expansive mood, much pleased with himself. His wife was a Jones, Old Haint's first cousin as a matter of fact, and Tom had been under severe pressure to do something for her kinfolks. Only that morning she had caustically commented that it was a great mystery to her why he was able to get Tilford Bonham to hire "every last piece of trash" in the precinct, but could do nothing for her "own blood people," she said, who had always been "decent and hardworking." Now he could mollify her and bring peace to his roof. The Joneses would soon have work and three or four boxes of food. If Doc handled everything properly, Haint would be grateful to his dying day—and twenty-six votes could be counted in that cluster of weather-beaten little houses in the Big Bend of Poor Fork. Doc would work everything just right, Tom was confident of that. The votes could be relied on in the future, and Tom would get a good liberal share of credit for straightening things out. His plans broadened. Old George Smith was about ready to die or retire and give up the Poor Fork post office. With Doc's help Tom could be the new postmaster. He could set up a small store with the post office to draw customers. The peg leg sounded an ambitious note as it pounded down the stair and across the heavy timbers of the porch.

On Monday, Doc had long lines of patients, and it was three in the afternoon before the last of them was gone. Finally he sat down to relax with a Chesterfield and a Coke. There was a slight movement at the doorway and he looked up to find Haint Jones hovering half in and half out of the waiting room, his battered hat turning uncertainly in his hands, and a quizzical, almost frightened expression on his thin face. Doc, who had previously and carefully calculated with both Joe Carr and Tilford how long Haint should go without help in order to "work him best," rose to greet him with a smile and an outstretched hand.

"Come in Haint, come in, come in!" he repeated, the essence of pleased surprise. He betrayed no indication that he had expected Jones, but beckoned him to one of the yellow oak Bank of England chairs that lined the walls of the waiting room. He gave his caller a cigarette and inquired about his family and the people generally on Poor Fork. He asked about the roadwork and commented that the relief projects were bringing many improvements that the county could never have made. Jones remained restive and uneasy and a small silence fell. At last Doc inquired, "What can I do for you, Haint? You don't look sick, so what's on your mind?"

The small, spare man looked at Doc through round, blackrimmed glasses. He licked his colorless lips and pulled on the cigarette. His reply required a visible effort.

He stared around the room with its pictures of smiling politicians, a stricken look about him like a trapped bird. "Really, I never did know much about you, just what people said. Always heerd you was a good doctor. I just took the word of the leaders of my party, and so I voted for Arthur Hall." Then with great earnestness, "I shore hope you won't hold that agin' me."

Doc said nothing.

Haint went on, "You said I don't look sick, but I am. I am sick to death with worry. I've had the worst run of bad luck a man ever seed. No job of any kind for a year, now, Farmin' brings beans and bread and 'taters, but no money. I can't pay the tax on my old place, can't buy shoes for my girl who is still tryin' to go to school. Can't buy sugar er coffee. We're up agin it, and I ain't got no place to turn fur help. I can't git no relief work, and my application for this relief handout food has jist been held up week after week. Now things are so bad they can't git no worse."

Doc said, "Times are mighty hard, Haint. I'm afraid Hoover has wrecked the country."

"It looks like it. He er somebody else wrecked it fer me. But folks say you can help me out, and I hope with all my heart you will."

Doc asked, "What do you want me to do, Haint? I'm not in the relief business. I'm just a doctor who made the mistake of getting into politics and got beat for his trouble!"

"You're a mighty important man right now in Slaughter County. You're a heap more than a defeated candidate. You're a friend of this here man, Humble. Your brother hires men for CWA jobs. Joe Carr is like a brother to you and is settin' down there with a warehouse full of grub to give away. They've helped a sight of people and no doubt ever' one of 'em needed it, but my family needs it too, and not a one of 'em has been able to get a nickel's worth o' anything."

Doc lit another cigarette. He looked at Jones's imploring face for a long moment, then leaned forward and patted him on the shoulder. "Haint, I've got no grudge against you. You had a right to vote the way you did, and no man will ever lose my friendship for being a man of independence and courage. The people of this county have made me what I am. I owe them my gratitude, and that goes for you and all the others."

Jones looked relieved and his face brightened. He accepted another Chesterfield. "I have no control over any of the relief work or the food programs. They are federal and I am not connected with them in any way. My friends may or may not listen to a request from me; and since the days of Cain and Abel, one brother has rarely done much for another. I doubt that Tilford would think much of any recommendation I might make."

Jones smiled. "Two Bonhams never have fell out with each other in this county. They stick together like burrs on a horse blanket. He'll listen to anything you say fur me!"

Doc stood up to indicate that the conference was over. "I'll talk to all of them, Haint, in strict confidence, mind you. I'll tell them that you and I have talked and that we are friends, and that I want something done for you and your wife and children. I'll ask them to cut out the red tape and get you something to eat, and some jobs for the Joneses. Your sons and the men your daughters married need help, too, and we'll keep all of them in mind."

He gripped Jones by the arm. "Let's keep this just between ourselves. It may not work. On the other hand, things may be in good shape for you in a day or two."

Jones wrung his hand. "I'll be your friend to the last day o' my life. I won't ever fergit yer help. When I can do somethin' fer you, you won't even have to ask."

Doc listened to him as he passed softly down the hall, then closed the door. He called Joe Carr, then Tilford. To the latter he said, "That little dried-up horse turd, Haint Jones, just left here, and it looks like the time has come to issue some work vouchers to him and his gang. Starvation has softened his heart, but if he goes much longer he'll be too weak to work."

Over the wire came a grunt. "We had some delays processing job applications for Mr. Jones and some of his relatives, but everything has been cleared up. It looks like they can report for work Thursday morning. The Good Lord truly blesses a sinner after he repents." Doc grinned and the phone clicked against his ear.

Doc had Tom Morton keep an eye on Haint, and to feel out members of his "generation" from time to time. He and they were truly grateful for Doc's timely intervention, and the reports Morton brought in always reflected it. "He put meat and bread on our tables!" Haint said over and over; and in 1936 when Joe Carr left his desk in the relief office and ran for the legislature, he was elected by a whopping majority. The Joneses of Poor Fork remembered the free food his vouchers had brought them—as did thousands of other people—and Joe went back to the state capital. There he loyally supported the Democratic governor and helped Carl Rutherford organize the assembly along regular and disciplined lines.

Doc did not run again for judge. He no longer wanted the office for the reforms and reorganization it would enable him to achieve, and its power could be exerted quite as well through another man. Woodrow Bonham was his first cousin, and had made some money as a bottler of Nehi soft drinks. Doc persuaded him to run "for the good of the county," and added, "With all these jobs and a trainload of free grub every week or two, we could elect the devil." The new judge reveled in the office and carried out its duties as Doc and Joe suggested. Since the county was broke, his principal task was to approve the work projects Reuben Humble brought to his desk.

The projects multiplied and roads pushed slowly up the creeks past thirteen new schoolhouses. At one time in 1937, 2,283 men were on the federal payroll and Doc's lieutenants in the precincts were able to hold nearly all of them, and their wives, uncles, aunts, parents, cousins, nieces and nephews, in line for the reborn Democratic party.

In that same year, old Delilah Bonham died of a stroke.

It happened on a lovely spring morning and Charlie's son, Jake, brought Doc the news. He went at once to the gaunt, weathered frame house where she had lived so long as a widow. He found her firm jaw relaxed for the first time and drew down the lids over her glazed eyes. She had become a member of the ancient Southern Church of Regular Baptists, and no fewer than five preachers came to "say a few words" at her funeral. They talked about the resurrection and the life, and how the worn and wrinkled body in the walnut coffin would rise from the grave and lead her children and grand-children to glory.

They prayed at inordinate length, and Doc sat through it all pondering the things wrought by her will and resolution, and counting the grandchildren and great-grandchildren who had sprung from her loins. They ranged in age from bawling babies to twenty years or more, and Doc studied their faces for indications of personality and character. Nearly all bore the high thin Bonham nose, black hair and high cheekbones. As the lid was screwed into place above his mother's face, Doc concluded that she and his father had generated the equivalent of a fair-sized precinct. They buried her by mur-dered William and a dozen yards from the crumbling grave-stone of Old John-of-All. Doc had brought many of them into the world, and as they straggled away from the graveyard, two or three dozen of the younger ones came by to call him "cousin" or "Uncle Tom" and to shake his hand. Clearly they knew of his influence and growing power and were pleased to acknowledge their relationship to such a man.

In that year, also, the legislature abolished the public school trusteeships based on the ancient system of "English hundreds." Hence forward, it was decreed, a county's super-intendent of schools would hold a degree from an accredited college of education and would be employed for a four-year term by a five-member board of education whom the people would elect. Doc calculated the amount of political patronage that could be extracted from the schools—even in an impov-erished coal county—and decided to sponsor a slate of can-didates in the board races. He had in mind a most likely and promising candidate for the desk behind which old Hugh Thompson had humblingly mismanaged the county's mea-ger school funds for the last twenty years.

He and Twinkles went to work. Joe Carr was prospering mightily as a legislator and could not be spared to run him-self, but he helped with some excellent suggestions.

They first talked to the redoubtable Tom Morton, whom they found stumping around on his wooden leg behind the counter of his new store on Poor Fork of Indian River. Tom, too, was prospering. His house had been freshly painted and his storehouse was crammed with groceries, dry goods and hardware. Practically every man in the straggling commu-nity was working on a relief project—now supervised by the WPA—or had a son, father or brother who was doing so. They knew of his influence with Doc, and of Doc's influence with the men in the "main office" in Blacksville, and were anxious to buy from the man who had befriended them, and could do so again. It was a slack time in the store, and the jovial Morton handed each of them a cold Dr Pepper. After a swig of the soft drink, Doc got down to the matter that had brought him out of the hospital in the middle of the after-noon.

"Tom," he began, in the trusting and confidential tones always employed when he was about to share a secret or bestow an honor, "we've come out here to ask you to do something that will cost you some money and take up a lot of time you could spend more profitably right here in your store."

Tom cocked a wary eye and waited. He was tight-fisted where money was concerned and was much more inclined to take it in than to pay it out. "What is it, Doc? What do ye want me to do?" Then, to strengthen his position somewhat against any request that might prove too costly, "I'm still pretty hard up, jist sorty gittin' by on luck."

Doc laughed. "You're doing alright, Tom. This store is one of the best and biggest in the county, and if you weren't selling it, you wouldn't be stocking it." Tom waited in silence, his suspicions fully aroused. But his broad face relaxed in a bland smile as Doc continued.

"Tom, damn it, we want you to run for the school board from this district. You can win, no question about it, and the county needs you on the board. The teachers need you. But mostly, though, the children need you."

"How come, Doc? I don't know nothin' about schools. I just got six grades of learnin' myself."

"Don't let that worry you. The main qualification for a good school man is dedication and the next most important qualification is honesty. And you've got both!"

Doc waited a moment while Tom mulled those two important qualifications. On reflection, Tom suddenly realized that he was indeed both dedicated and honest, and his head wagged in agreement.

"Old Hugh Thompson is not worth a dry fizzle at anything, let alone at teaching." Twinkles giggled at this sally and Tom chuckled. "He was teaching when I started in the first grade, and was teaching mighty little, too. He's been superintendent since the end of the war and hasn't had a new idea in all that time. He hires the same old teachers every year and is letting the schoolhouses rot down. Why, if we had a livewire superintendent and a good board to back him up we could get federal money and have the WPA build good, solid school buildings all over the county. We're letting golden opportunities slip by us every day."

"What would we have to do, Doc? They's several new buildin's already been built. Got one bein' built here on Poor Fork now."

"I know about it. I helped persuade Hugh to apply for these projects. He didn't want to at first. Said nothing would come of it anyway, and besides, he said, all this spending will break up the government!" They snorted in unison.

"Rube Humble will build schoolhouses all over the county if the board of education and the fiscal court make the applications and establish the need. The need is apparent. We've got to get sound roofs over the heads of these children because we can't expect them to walk out of these hollows to freeze all day in the wintertime. We want our children to have it better than we did, Tom, now don't we?"

Tom vigorously agreed that it was so, then wondered who would make a good "live-wire" superintendent. Doc allowed that there were many fine prospects, but that none should be mentioned at this point. "Every man who has the legal qualifications imagines himself to be suitable for the job. Let 'em think so, Tom, and let 'em all be for us. They know that if Hugh Thompson's slate wins he'll keep the office. All the rest stand to gain by lining up with us."

"We'd need to raise some money, shore as the devil. You convinced me on that severance tax, and maybe we can get one levied. With WPA schoolhouses and a severance tax to give teachers a raise, we could sure enough get things to movin'.""

Now it was Doc's time to hedge. He had bought nearly a thousand acres of land from bankrupt firms and the idea of someday paying the county for the privilege of mining his own coal did not seem as attractive as it had a few years before. Doc knew that depressions, like booms, end at last and that the time would come when new companies would mine the coal another generation had lost at sheriff's auctions.

"Let's think on that one, Tom. The main thing now is to get a good slate together, and then win. When we have a solid, dependable person in the superintendent's chair, we'll find ways to get money. We'll revolutionize the schools in this county. Half the children don't go to school, mainly because there are none to go to. Half of the ones that go to school don't learn anything, mainly because the schools are so sorry. We can change all of that. We can build most of the schools we need in the next four or five years while all this relief work is still going on. We need at least two hundred teachers and thirty or forty janitors. We don't even have a truant officer, but we'll sure as hell get one! Progress like this would give educated men and women something to do. They and their folks would all appreciate the kind of improvements I'm talking about."

He paused and finished the Dr Pepper and pondered the label "10, 2 & 4, Good for Life."

"Tom, we don't have any schools worth a damn except the ones these mission women run. Time is catching up with us and conditions have to change. Somebody is going to overhaul the schools in Slaughter County, and whoever does it will get everlasting credit for the job. It will be mighty good for the economy of the county, and a man like yourself will stand to gain a lot. Gain a lot and be honest and square shooting all the time."

Tom ran. He ran on a slate with three other Democrats, George Downer from Buffalo Creek; Doc's sidekick at the hospital, Dr. Omar Ross; and Tilford's oldest son, Georgie. They brought one Republican onto the team because, as Doc allowed, "This new school law is nonpartisan in spirit, and naturally we don't want to violate the spirit of the law." To gain the kind of "balance" Doc thought necessary—four Democrats and one Republican—they went to Viper Creek and talked Rex Ballard into running. He had been a steadfast ally since the night Doc had patched up his punctured son. He spat a long stream of Ambeer, gave Doc a dram of moonshine and vowed he could get "nine out of ten votes" on Viper Creek. Doc and Twinkles ate corn bread, beans and fried pork at the Ballard cabin and went home with light hearts.

Doc put Georgie Bonham on the ticket with a small measure of reluctance, but Tilford insisted on it. "Damn it, Tom, don't be bull-headed!" his brother had demanded. "Georgie is twenty-five and has two years of college down at Mountain State. He needs something to do, and, anyway, he'll do whatever we tell him. Besides, with all these jobs and carloads of free grub, we could elect a boar hog if we wanted to."

Doc acquiesced. "Blood is thicker than water," he figured.

"We have to start using young Bonhams as they come along, and put 'em to work. The school board's not much of an office, but it'll do for a starter." Besides, the arrangement pleased Twinkles because Georgie was a favorite of hers.

Georgie was one of those characters whose personal appearance and mannerisms are so bizarre that they attract immediate attention and are referred to by mountaineers as "a sight." Georgie was a sight in more ways than one. He was about five feet three inches and slender of build. His hair was black and wavy and extremely coarse. His beard, even immediately after a fresh shave in Sie Roberts's barber chair, was sprinkled with an irrepressible blue-black stubble like a thick sprinkling of ground pepper. He cultivated a little moustache that grew outward in bristly clusters like a toothbrush that had been dipped in a black dye. He pomaded his hair in an effort to induce it to lie flat on his head, and he hopped about on outsize splayfeet. He wore a suit all the time, including a vest with a dangling gold watch chain, and was partial to dark conservative colors. He had huge teeth that despite relentless brushing were stained and yellowed like old ivory. He twitched his nose and sniffed in a manner that old Delilah Bonham once declared reminded her of "a feist pup that has smelled a mouse somewheres."

When the slate had been completed and duly announced to the public through the pages of Tim Elkins's *Mountain Courier*, Doc could not suppress his amusement. "What a school board we are going to have!" he told Twinkles. "A medical doctor, a skinflint, an illiterate, a moonshiner—and Georgie. O precious Lord, what a funny-looking board member Georgie is going to make!"

CHAPTER

13

George fulfilled his uncle's prediction and became a funny-looking board member on the first Monday in January 1937. Under the old procedure, the county's forty trustees met in the courthouse and selected a superintendent whose duty it was "to see that all laws respecting the common schools be faithfully executed." But the legislature's new law placed this duty on the board, and they assembled in the superintendent's office in the rickety frame building on "schoolhouse hill" overlooking Blacksville. Once long ago, when he was a much younger man, Hugh Thompson had dreamed of a college for Slaughter County youths, and had persuaded the county to buy fourteen acres of nearly level land on a mountain bench above the county seat. The college never materialized, but county bonds eventually financed an eight-room, two-story building with a frail-looking bell tower and another equally graceless, but larger structure, which became Blacksville Grade School. The high school had, also, a wooden gymnasium perched on wood and concrete props, rising out of a deep gully. The Depression crushed all hopes for further expansion, or even for adequate maintenance. For years the superintendent begged fiscal courts for additional funds, but schools had a low public priority and no new money was forthcoming. Then came the CWA, the WPA, and the PWA to build new schoolhouses, and NYA to aid students, but by that time Thompson was weary and, anyway, he had never been much of a wheeler-dealer. On the Saturday before the new board held its first meeting, he cleaned out the drawers of his desk, took his first-class teacher's certificate down from the wall, and went back to his steep farm on Goose Creek. He smarted under Doc's often-repeated declaration that he was a "nobody and a do-nothing" but kept his resentments to himself as he turned things over to a new administration which promised "to build a modern school system for Slaughter County." Few took note that in his own plodding way, Hugh Thompson had tried to do as much, and that his failure had not been wholly his own.

The board members promptly elected Dr. Ross as their chairman and Georgie as their secretary. The next order of business was the hiring of a superintendent, and all the teachers who had harbored ambitions for their own advancement to that august post were promptly jarred out of their reveries. The diminutive secretary, his little moustache aquiver with the new importance to which the election had elevated him, placed in nomination "a woman who harbors no other thought than to serve the people of Slaughter County, and who loves the children of the humblest coal miner almost as much as her very own."

Tom Morton seconded the nomination with remarks that glorified the nominee's husband as well. "He has worked for the people, whether they have had any money or are stone broke, and with hardly ever a thought for his own welfare. Through his efforts, hundreds and hundreds o' families have been fed and public improvements have been made in ever' precinct."

Twinkles was approved unanimously and Judge Woodrow Bonham swore her in that afternoon. Pursuant to the state constitution, she vowed that she would not use the office to promote any personal or private interest and would take care to enforce all the school laws without regard to any racial, religious or political consideration.

There were some murmurings of discontent among the voters at this unexpected turn, but Doc moved resolutely to consolidate power while circumstances so strongly favored him. With Roosevelt's reelection victory in 1936, the eleven counties in the state's mountainous eighth district had revolted against the leaden conservatism of the GOP, and, for the first time in its history, sent a Democrat to Congress. He was hawk-nosed, bald-headed Sam Mitchell, a lawyer and coal operator who lived in Plaintown, near the mouth of Indian River. Three other counties lay between Slaughter and Croghan, where the new congressman practiced law and looked after the family enterprises. Those enterprises were 12,000 acres of mountain land his father had bought with the profits of a lifetime of horse and mule trading. In Croghan County the hills stood apart and the wide bottoms grew rich crops of corn and burley tobacco. Coal royalties and professional fees had built the new congressman a huge, graceless brick house on River Street and financed his race for Congress. He advocated "fair wages for the workingman" and clamored for new federal programs to get the economy going again. But mainly he was a determined protector of the coal industry and the special privileges it had created for itself.

He was a big spender, though, with a grandiose and costly scheme to "canalize" Indian River so barges could haul out the valley's riches of coal, oil and timber—and incidentally double the value of his own holdings. Doc supported him, and Sam Mitchell's friends "at the head of the river" sold him to coal miners and relief laborers as a staunch supporter of the new President. As the population turned with growing fervor to the New Deal, Sam Mitchell's position, too, was secured "as a man Roosevelt needs to put through laws to save the country." Doc helped him, and he helped Doc.

The new superintendent put together an ambitious school construction program, and supported it with grim photographs of existing facilities and statistics reflecting the educational chaos that prevailed across the county. One weekend when the congressman was resting at home, she and Doc and Joe Carr drove in Doc's new Air-Flite Chrysler the ninety snaky miles to Plaintown and enlisted the solon's support for the proposal. "Slaughter gave me a 2,600-vote majority last time," he told Twinkles, "and I intend to pay the county back. I'll get your schoolhouses built, you can count on that. We'll take the matter all the way to the White House if necessary."

That extreme step was not necessary, however. They called Carl Rutherford and on their advice the governor recommended all the projects to the Works Progress Administration. Twinkles got her schoolhouses, but some neighboring counties were chagrined to learn that a shortage of funds necessitated curtailment of their programs even on buildings that had already been begun.

When she became superintendent, Twinkles was vivacious and firmly fleshed at forty. Tess had grown to a headstrong and tempestuous seventeen and was ready for college. Doc wanted his daughter to study medicine, but she would have none of it and declared that she intended to study psychology. Jesse J. was going to high school at Blacksville, and Twinkles was free to pour her energy into her new task. She had much of her husband's ruthlessness and cunning, and when she began to run short of either, he was always ready to supply it in full measure.

Eight new rooms were put under construction as wings to the Blacksville Grade School, and a brand-new building was started for the high school. Two new high school buildings were begun in other parts of the county, and eighteen one- and two-room structures for hard-to-reach creek communities. At Twinkles's request the fiscal court raised the school tax levy on all property in the county; with the proceeds, the Board of Education bought its first four school buses.

A trickle of young men and women had managed by much economy and labor to acquire college degrees and certificates to teach. There was a lot of "deadwood" left over from the old normal schools— men who could teach only the three Rs and even they not overly well, others who had been lax in their support of Doc's candidates, and still others who as Doc's supporters could swing only a handful of votes. All such were promptly dropped from the payrolls. The young applicants were hired and sent out to staff the new classrooms as rapidly as the WPA gangs completed them. As Doc observed to Joe Carr, "A young teacher is better than an old teacher, especially at the polls. An old man's children move away and are generally not around to vote, but a young man has his wife and parents right there at his side."

Twinkles backed her teachers to the hilt with all the books, laboratory equipment, and other aids her limited budget could supply. Sometimes she took a teacher into her confidence and revealed that she and her husband were buying a few things with their own funds, things without which the teacher's best efforts would be meaningless. The board knew virtually nothing about public education and cared less, and the superintendent was left to run things as she saw fit, with Doc's advice and counsel, of course. Jobs were scarce and hard to find and teachers were grateful for their positions, a circumstance that bound school employees together in support for their Bonham benefactors. As Twinkles was prone to explain to a young man—and his friends, relatives and wellwishers—"I scratch the back of the man who will scratch mine. My husband and I are dedicated to giving this county a first-class school system; the board needs your skills and you need the jobs. We'll work together and do the job together."

Twinkles carried in person all news of advancement and pay raises, but notices of dismissal or demotion came by mail. As the organization grew in numbers and experience, it grew also in skill, so that a flawless political machine took form within the schools. Financing was sadly short and the teaching program was primitive, but the basic structure was there, intact and loyal and ready to be fleshed out as changing times might offer new opportunities.

A new governor was elected in 1937, and he carried two-thirds of the county's precincts, most of them by large margins. He was a self-styled "country boy from the swamps in the western part of the state." He stumped the state with huge hand outstretched, a wide grin showing all his perfect white teeth and, as often as not, a guitar dangling from his neck. He spoke to crowds from the back of a pickup truck, his speeches a compound of old-time religion and pure bunk. He ridiculed the Republicans "as the worst disaster since Noah's flood" and brought crowds of relief-fed men and women to enthusiastic applause by promising "to arrest Herbert Hoover for tryin' to starve people to death, and to put 'im in jail myself, if he ever sets foot in this state." He praised FDR as "the savior of the nation just when the Republican fat cats had sold us down the river. That name, Franklin D., sounds as sweet in my ears as meat a-fryin!" he yelled, and swore that "as God bears witness, the President will have a wholehearted friend in the state capitol after I become governor." He strummed his guitar and played "There's a Gold Mine in the Sky," "Dixie," a mournful ballad or two about sinners and their brokenhearted old mothers, and "Happy Days Are Here Again!" He claimed that his grandfather had been a Choctaw Indian, and a rebel corporal and had taught him both the rebel yell and the Choctaw war whoop. He opened his mouth in a wide gape and poured forth a veritable flood of hideous sounds. He said the yell and the war whoop had seared the GOP into running for cover. "Don't be surprised," he warned, "if the next time you burn a brush pile a Republican or two runs out."

The crowds roared their approval. Apparently the people of his home county knew something about Dick "Big Red" Brady that the rest of the state had not learned, for he ran short there by an irksome ninety votes. He swept the rest of the state, though, and carried with him into the lieutenant governor's office a much less flamboyant figure, State Senator Carl Rutherford. Carl had done the organizing and fund raising, and while the crowds were listening to "Big Red," the politicians were generally locked up somewhere listening to his running mate.

Carl had planned to make the race himself and had commitments from scores of leaders. But he remembered the precedent of David's harp and as he told Doc, "I could have beat Big Red easily enough, but that guitar is too damn much for me." Anyway, Carl was still young, his progress had been steady, and he didn't want to run needless risks. Four years would soon pass and then, with the help of his friends, he would move into the governor's mansion.

So Doc and the Bonham organization swung behind Big Red Brady and his ticket. The laborers on the WPA and PWA projects, their timekeepers and foremen, the two hundred and twenty teachers and principals, hundreds of people Doc had helped with small loans or other favors—all responded nobly. The turnout was heavy and in most precincts the voting was straight. Big Red had let it be known that he was "a friend of coal, if coal is a friend to me," and the operator's association came through with ample funds in bundles of one-dollar bills to buy all the "floaters." The money was brought to Doc by Ben Fleming, who carried it in a giftwrapped shoebox. Doc told Fleming this was the best money the operators could possibly spend. "The state is broke, and there's got to be a severance tax on coal or a sales tax on everything else. This means we're going to wind up with a sales tax!"

Fleming was grateful. Hard times had lifted the diamonds from his wife's fingers, and his carefully tailored suits were no longer new. Half the corporations that remained in his association, including his own Northeast Coal Corporation, were surviving on government loans. Without the Reconstruction Finance Corporation, the entire coal industry in Slaughter County would have disappeared in weed-grown desolation at the end of abandoned rail lines. The President wanted to expand the army and navy and Sam Mitchell was on the House Military Affairs Committee. He voted for all the funds the President requested and praised the White House for its wisdom "in giving Uncle Sam a little bit bigger stick." In return, the Squire from the Hudson instructed his agencies to treat the congressman well. The congressman obliged when Doc called him and asked that he demand prompt attention to loan applications from the Indian Valley coal field. Fleming told the hard-bitten coal men of Dr. Bonham's intervention on their behalf. When the government checks began to arrive, they forthrightly forgave the doctor for the fright he had given them in his ill-advised race for county judge. Clearly he was a changed man and their friend, and when Ben Fleming hit them up for money for Doc's candidate for governor, they responded with adequate generosity. "Turnabout is fair play," Fleming counseled them, and some money from the RFC found its way into the shoebox. Enough to be sure "to put the icing on the cake," as Joe Carr phrased it. "We have already lined up ever'body who is willin' to work. The money will git all the trash votes—all the people who ain't willin' to work!"

Big Red, too, was a grateful man when Doc visited him

in his huge walnut-paneled office in the state capitol three months after he was sworn in. The guitar, his political trademark, leaned discreetly against the wall in a corner, and the governor rose from behind the huge mahogany desk, his big hand outstretched. "Doc, you old baby-ketcher you, you did it. Carl said you and Joe Carr would hand us seven out of ten votes, and it was a little better than that. Some politicians get their counties all screwed up, but you've got Old Slaughter grindin' away as smooth as silk—like a two-dollar whore who has been promised a five-dollar tip." Doc and Joe laughed and His Excellency slapped their backs and pointed to chairs.

Big Red's hair was a pale red like a faded carrot, and big freckles mottled his cheeks. His features were as craggy as the coasts of Ireland, whence his ancestors had fled during the potato famine. He was a bachelor with a colorful reputation for lechery, and as Doc studied his face, he noticed enlarging pouches beneath his eyes and a slightly bleared quality in the eyes themselves. Dick Brady was a natural on the campaign trail, Doc surmised, but he's in water too deep for him here. He calculated that the bottle would prove too much for the governor, virtually guaranteeing Carl Rutherford's succession in 1941.

Doc and Joe wanted some roads and bridges built, and they wanted some of the gravel-coated WPA roads surfaced. "Some of the people is a-chokin' plumb to death from all the dust," Joe explained.

The governor laughed, "I'm gettin' that complaint from all over the mountains. Once we get people outta the mud we gotta get 'em outta the dust. If they're not drownin' in the mud, they're smotherin' in dust!" This sally was duly appreciated by his visitors, who chuckled their agreement. The governor said the highway commissioner thought he could wring eighteen or twenty miles of blacktop per county out of his department's budget, maybe a few more than that for Slaughter.

Doc and Joe wanted a little more than roads, bridges and blacktop, however. They wanted jobs, the nineteen of them directed by the state's highway maintenance foreman out of his cluttered office in a rickety building off state highway 14, east of Blacksville.

"It's time to clean house, Governor," Doc declared. "Steve McCray has been there for ten years, and half his men are drones. They do precious little work, and when it comes time to deliver votes, they're as useless as the tits on a boar. Joe and I can take those jobs and by placing them with a little horse sense, we can pick up around 200 sure-fire votes."

"I remember Steve McCray," the governor allowed. "Met him at the state's garage when I stopped to shake hands with all the boys. He said they were all for me and they had my posters nailed up all over the place. I hate to lay off a man who supported me."

Doc sat up and drew his chair close to the desk. He looked down for a moment at his long slender fingers. "Steve is a good man, and a good Democrat. He's dependable, but he just doesn't have any clout. His wife is not even a local woman. He married her while he was in the army and brought her home with him. We need a man with a lot of kinfolks of his own and married to a woman who has a whole lot more."

"I know, I know. But what about McCray? We can't just fire a loyal Democrat, Doctor, and take away his bread in these hard times. If we do, that brought-on wife of his will starve to death."

"We won't let that happen. We've got too much relief grub in the county to let anybody starve to death, especially a Democrat," Joe assured. He and Doc had already decided that Yadd Gibbs was the man with the loyalty and other qualifications so essential for that particular position.

"My idea is to promote Steve. We can get Rube Humble to give him a job with no more work, more pay and a better title. We've got work projects going on all over the county—a new wing to the courthouse, new schoolhouses, bridges, roads. We've even gotten a big gang started building shithouses for Eleanor."

Big Red looked incredulous.

"I mean it. They're the 'sanitary toilets' that she talked Franklin D. into backing. Anyway, all these projects need a coordinator to see that no supplies or labor get wasted and that everything moves along nicely together. This would be a perfect job for Steve McCray."

The governor assented. "Handle it so there won't be any hard feelin's, then. When Humble has got it all set up and McCray has agreed to the 'promotion,' call the highway commissioner. I'll fix it for you with him so all you will need to do is tell him the name of the man you want for the job."

Doc and Joe rose to leave. They shook hands with Big Red again. "Leave it to us, Governor. McCray will be satisfied and we'll reorganize that road crew and make 'em worth their weight in votes!"

The governor had one other thing on his mind. "We got a bill through the legislature to pay pensions to the indigent aged. The old folks need some help, God knows, to help 'em out in their last years. We'll have to set up an office in each county to receive applications and determine eligibility. A couple of women can probably take care of the job. Come up with the people you need and pass their names along to Grover Fox in the Welfare Department." He winked and poked Joe playfully in the ribs so that he jumped and grunted. "Old folks vote, too, and we oughta get 'em set up to vote for their friends. It sure as hell ain't their enemies who are puttin' all this sunshine into the evenin' of their lives."

Doc had a third cousin, Jane Bonham, who was a typist and shorthand reporter. She was a tall woman, not beautiful, but decidedly handsome, with coquettish green eyes and dark hair. She was the ideal person for the job and her attributes and qualifications were duly passed along to Grover Fox. The commissioner had her come to his office for an interview, and she was hired on the spot. He called Doc to thank him for recommending such a competent person. "She's a doll," Fox observed, "and tells me she is not married, either." Then in mock seriousness, "I warn you to keep her away from the governor, Doctor. Big Red is a bachelor and some of his old lady friends tell me that he takes 'em standing up and is real rapacious. If the governor meets that woman, she'll get a raise for sure and something else besides!"

They laughed at this possibility and Doc said he would pass the word to his cousin. "She is a good politician and will find an opportunity of discussing the problems of our old-age pensioners with the chief executive."

Jane Bonham and one assistant opened an office in the cavernous old shed that had once served as the armory for Company H of the state militia. It stood a few blocks from the courthouse, and a trickle of old men and women began walking the cinder path that led to its huge door. Tilford had moved his operations into another section of the building, and Reuben Humble operated out of two newly partitioned and freshly painted rooms to the rear. The armory had become the "relief building" for Slaughter County, and from it flowed a veritable deluge of food, clothes, checks and jobs. And every person who dispensed "help" had been chosen by the camp doctor who seven years before had lain for days on a Florida beach, filled with melancholy and wondering what the future held that was worth living for.

When Doc was not operating on somebody or swabbing throats, listening to heartbeats and dispensing pills, he was doing good works that, as he occasionally observed with a show of humility and self-sacrifice, "do not pay me one single red penny." For example, Jesse Timmons came to him to complain that the county had no high school for black children. Racial segregation was strictly enforced under a state statute, and the grade schools for blacks made the modest facilities of the whites appear nothing short of palatial. Jesse had aged, a stoop had come into his shoulders and a ring of white crowned his bald head. "We is in a bad fix, Dr. Bonham. Our schools are bad—mighty, mighty bad. Our teachers jist gits about two-thirds uv a white teacher's pay and we ain't got a sign of a high school. When our younguns gits through the eight grades they gotta stop. White scholars go right on up, but ourn ain't got no place to go. It ain't right a-tall."

Doc knew Jesse had brought him a thorny problem. Most whites would object to having to pay taxes to support black schools. He could hear the outrage and murmurings now and knew that the black school would cost white votes. But the county's population was around 45,000 now, and among the multitudes who had come to dig coal were nearly 1,200 black voters. The GOP had ignored them, and the New Deal had fed them and promised them far more than it had delivered. Doc's candidates were getting up to three quarters of the ballots in the black precincts. The time had come for a grand gesture, to do something to pin down the loyalties of the blacks, and Doc was prepared to do it. He put his hand on the shrunken shoulder in its frayed coat. "Jesse, when you go to church next Sunday, invite all the colored people you can reach to come and hear you. Bring them in from all the colored precincts. Then get up in the pulpit and make an annoucement. Tell them that Tom Bonham has given you his word that they are going to have a colored high school The Slaughter County High School for Colored Students. Tell them I said the school will be built if I have to do it with my own money, and it takes every cent I have saved for the education of my own two children!"

Jesse trembled with an emotion he could not hide, and a tear rolled down each of his leathery black cheeks. Toil had made his hands almost grotesquely large at the end of slendery arms, and now the huge hands with their worn, white palms turned a battered hat round and round. A minute or two passed before he spoke. "I'll tell 'em, Dr. Bonham! I'll sho' tell 'em. I'll git the colored parents together and make the 'nouncement. And when that school opens its doors, ain't no black people goin' to forget who caused it to be built!"

Doc leaned back in his chair and told Jesse there was a lot of work to be done before any nails could be driven. "The county is out of money and will have to sell bonds to pay for it. And a bond issue has to be voted on by the people. The first thing is to see that they can and will vote "Yes" on the question. A lot of whites will be against it out of prejudice, so we'll have to have every single black turn out and vote."

He paused a moment. Jesse dried his eyes and nodded his agreement.

"You know, Jesse, a lot of the colored are unregistered. They've always been Republicans, but the Republicans never do anything for any poor people, regardless of color. Roosevelt has proved that the Democrats are the party with a heart, with a little human sympathy. That's why a lot of thinking colored people have come over and joined us. That is why they ought to register as Democrats, Jesse. The Civil War is over and Abraham Lincoln is dead. Tell them to forget about the southern Democrats and to come in and become Roosevelt Democrats!"

Doc stood up and grasped the old miner's hand. He looked deep into the brown, tear-washed eyes and smiled. "United we stand, Jesse; divided we fall! We're going to build that school and give Negro students a good education, and we're going to do it just because it's right! Let's go to work and line up all the colored leaders and register every man and woman who is old enough to vote and even a few who are just a shade too young, and let's make Democrats out of them for the same reason—because it's the right thing to do!"

The bond issue was not easy. The school board and the fiscal court presented little difficulty; they simply approved the resolution and sent the question to the voters. But the county was already deeply in debt and was paying 6 1/2 percent interest on bonds that were nearly twenty years old. The WPA could be counted on for the labor, including designing, but the county would have to buy a site and provide nearly all the materials. Then transportation costs would have to be met, a very considerable burden because students would have to be hauled in buses from a dozen scattered camps. The blacks owned virtually no land, a fact that opponents of the proposition promptly pointed out with the further observation that "whites will pay all the taxes and blacks will get all the benefits." The Republicans, roundly defeated at the last elections and discredited and without funds or patronage, took up the issue and rallied to the cause of fiscal responsibility. Arthur Hall and Jake Runyon returned from the exile into which the Democrats had pushed them and began organizing meetings to hear speakers denounce the proposal. They and a handful of ambitious young Turks—mostly teachers whose strong partisanship convinced Twinkles they would be a malevolent influence on the county's youth and were therefore jobless—began canvassing the camps. They went from house to house to tell miners, managers and merchants that the county could not afford the money, and would certainly slide into utter bankruptcy if saddled with new debts. Here, they said, was irresponsibility run rampant.

Few people paid any attention to the cant about looming governmental collapse because of overspending. This argument had worn thin from overuse. Roosevelt had been elected on a promise to reduce spending and balance the budget and had spent an entire term under a hail of charges that he was boondoggling the country into economic prostration. Doc always answered this charge with the argument that "a schoolhouse here and a debt in Washington are better than no schoolhouse and no debt. Bread and a balanced budget don't go together. You have to choose one or the other!" It was the racism that worried him, the appeal to the prejudice against blacks that lay deep in the hearts of virtually all the whites, irrespective of class or station.

To make matters worse, the coal operators quietly passed the word that they were voting "No," and urged their employees to do likewise. They were for schools, of course, but not if it meant going into debt to build them. A month before the election, Doc despaired of winning and, in his vexation, got thoroughly drunk one night. But the next morning an idea crept into his aching head, and he used it to turn the tide.

"These foolish, no-good people have no principles, just greed," he told Twinkles. "And they are going to vote for that school if we have to stomp the hell out of them to get them to do it." That afternoon a rumor began circulating among the three hundred men on the WPA road project at the head of Indian River that big cutoffs were on the way. Doc's cousin, Bert Potter, was timekeeper on the job, and he dropped the hint to a couple of men when they came to the foreman's shack to get new handles for some broken tools. It seemed, he noted, that if the federal government reduced its payrolls an awful lot of men would be out of work. It sickened him to think of the distress that would follow. Dr. Bonham was going to Washington to argue against the cuts. No doubt about it, Doc would do all he could, but the layoffs might— probably would—come anyway. The timekeeper sighed. "Doc will stick by his friends, no matter what happens. He's got a lot of influence and people who stick by him will be the last to go." He shrugged ruefully and turned back to his work at the makeshift desk.

The news of impending work reductions on the huge relief crews cropped up all over the county in the next few days, and everywhere brought the cold sweat of dread. Work in the mines was still slack—two or three days a week at three or four dollars a day. Farming was hopeless on the worn-out hills. Suddenly Doc's struggle to save the jobs became their struggle and he their champion. He disappeared for a few days, and when he turned up again, men came from all parts of the county to express concern and to thank him for his efforts to persuade the bureaucrats to leave the projects alone. Storekeepers who sold groceries and clothes to the workmen were worried, too, as were the old pensioners who had heard predictions their checks would be pared. The grim outlines of the coming catastrophe sharpened when people heard that new and much stricter eligibility rules might take half the people off the free food rolls.

Their fear and dislike of blacks dwindled before the threat of being thrust again into total economic helplessness. They thronged Democratic precinct captains to pledge loyalty. They were urged to vote "Yes" on the bond issue and they did, and Jesse Timmons got his school. Work on it was started in 1939, and when it was opened to the first scholars, Jesse Timmons prayed an inordinately long and jumbled prayer of thanksgiving. He was grateful to the God of Abraham, of course, and said so a dozen times, but he was grateful, too, to the school superintendent "who we all love" and to her husband, "our beloved friend, Dr. Bonham, who heals our sick bodies and labors to save our young folks from the affliction of ignorance. They has been our best friends, O Lord, Amen."

The payroll cuts did not come. After the election, the dire forewarnings were forgotten and more names were added to the yellow payroll sheets. New pensioners were certified for monthly checks and the lines at the food warehouses lengthened. The blacks registered almost to the last man and woman, as all public-spirited citizens should. A few skeptics remained Lincoln Republicans lost in a swarm of Roosevelt Democrats. Not all wore these labels, however. A good many followed the example of Big Dave Gray whose brother had been lynched in Alabama for trying to enroll in the county's white and only high school. When Big Dave's daughter became a freshman, he puffed a cigar for which he had traded a bottle of home brew and allowed, "From today on I'se a Bonham Democrat, pure and simple."

Doc managed another deal that added the loyalties of nearly all the miners to his list of fealties. From the opening of the first drift mouth, the operators had neglected no stratagem to keep unions and union organizers out of their works. The association maintained a blacklist, and once a name was added to it, the man could find no job digging coal in Slaughter County. Such a "radical" was ordered out of the company's house, denied a job, turned down for credit at all company stores. The United Mine Workers had tried with little success to organize the field, but the Guffey Coal Act and other laws ground out by the New Deal Congress emboldened the miners to demand decent wages and protection against arbitrary pressures from the bosses. The Communist-leaning National Miners Union made its appearance, spearheaded by dedicated fire-breathers from the old mining territories in Pennsylvania. When John L. Lewis's United Mine Workers of America sent a new batch of organizers into the county in 1936, the association organized a small army of gunmen into an outfit called the Slaughter County Coal Police and started ordering submachine guns and high-powered rifles. On a snowy day in December, some of the UMW fieldworkers were arrested for trespassing or loitering, and for "criminal syndicalism." In a cell with them was Sam Chaney, Doc's old friend who had laid aside a WPA shovel to work full time at recruiting men into the union. Joe Carr brought the news and with it the question, "How do we get 'em out without losing ever' operator in the county?"

Doc went that night to see Ben Fleming, who convened the association's directors in an emergency session. They were plainly worried by the prospect of the kind of long, costly, and disruptive warfare that had turned the huge mining county of Harlan into a bloody hell. Profits were little more than dreams for most of them, and the thought of having to negotiate with miners on the conditions of their labor rankled like a deadly poison in their reactionary souls.

Doc talked to them in the pleading and soothing tones of a swain seeking to deprive a maiden of her chastity. "Gentlemen," he cleared his throat and began. "I want us to see here tonight if we can't save this county years of bloodshed and turmoil and get on with its main business which is mining coal."

The ring of faces ranged behind veils of pipe and cigarette smoke looked dubious and sullen.

He went on. "Harlan County, Kentucky, has been in the

news for years. Men killed. Tipples burned. People put out of houses. Companies going broke to keep up a costly bunch of guards and policemen and to pay for their guns and uniforms. And all to no avail from the operators' viewpoint because Roosevelt and the government are behind the miners and they will finally organize every mine. As the Republicans have learned at the polls here in Slaughter, you can't beat the government." He laughed a little and studied the operators, who appeared extremely pessimistic.

He pulled his chair around so he could talk directly to Fleming. "Ben, the Reds are after this county and the miners are listening to them and are taking the NMU pledge. This can't be allowed to go on, and the coal association doesn't have the power to stop it."

Cavernous, hawk-eyed old Geeter Whitlaw drummed his bony fingers on the arm of his chair. In his seventy-five years, he had mined coal in three states and had organized Whitlaw Coke and Coal when he was fifty. A veritable tyrant in his town below Horse Pound Gap, he carried much influence among his colleagues. "What are you suggesting, Doc? Go ahead and cut the carbuncle!"

"I'm saying this. John L. Lewis is a Republican from Iowa. He and his gang can beat the Reds with your support, and maybe I can help out a little here and there. You fight fire with fire, and Lewis is your man. After he wins, he'll be hard to deal with, but not a circumstance compared to the troublemaking bastards from New York and Moscow who are organizing your workhands tonight while we sit here. If Lewis wins, we'll be dealing with local men, and we've had experience with handling them. But just try turning a dyed-in-the-wool Red around!" He opened his hands and shrugged.

The shaggy-browed Lewis was no stranger to the operators. He had organized some of the Slaughter County mines a decade before, but a recession had closed pits and set two miners after every job. Then their allegiance to the idea of unionism was weak; now they were determined to unite in a common effort to climb out of their misery. Geeter Whitlaw asked, "Who do you think would be Lewis's arm in this county, Doc?"

"A man you don't like very much, a firebrand you hate, as a matter of fact. He has been fired by several of you and he despises your guts. But he's no Red. Sam Chaney will run things here for John L. Sam Chaney is tough and vicious, but he likes good clothes, money, and good-looking women. Once he gets a taste of them, he'll like them a lot more. Sam can be tamed, you take my word for it. The older he gets, the easier he'll be to handle."

The conference broke up after midnight, the glum operators dour and long-faced. But there was a general, if reluctant, agreement, and the next morning at ten, Doc walked into the circuit clerk's office and signed bail bonds for the jailed organizers. As they were set free, Doc gripped Chaney's arm and told them, "Sam has been my friend a long time and his friends are my friends. This county needs a labor union, and now get the hell out of here and organize it."

The story had reached the head of the remotest creek within a day, and men flocked to take the pledge. The UMW men denounced the NMU as "atheistic and God-hating" and the fledgling Communist movement withered. When the Slaughter County locals sent their first delegation to the international convention at Indianapolis to hear John L. Lewis shout that "even Bloody Harlan will some day lie beneath the flag of UMW brotherhood," most carried money Doc had loaned them. And once there in the strange surroundings of a huge flag-bedecked auditorium, they sponsored a resolution of gratitude "to Dr. Tom Bonham, the man who got brother Sam Chaney and his fellow organizers out of jail, after the sworn lies of operators had caused them to be locked up. When the choice was between coal operators and coal miners, between coercion and freedom, between wrong and justice, Dr. Bonham was on our side."

And so, after a fashion, he was.

With every challenge faced, Doc found new confidence and fresh insights flowing into himself. The nuances of political psychology, the sure knowledge of when to punish and when to soothe, a superb deftness with both flattery and ridicule as varying circumstances required—these became by degrees his very nature. And he was supremely skilled at using at every turn the great strength of the numerous Bonhams.

CHAPTER
14

Nineteen forty was an election year, a fact Doc discussed long and earnestly with Reuben Humble. Doc also went to the state capitol and talked to the governor about it, and found Big Red much interested. Big Red had gained some weight, and his white linen suit hugged him tightly. He offered Doc a cigar, lit one for himself and asked the question millions of Democrats and Republicans were beginning to ponder. "Doctor, what does your intuition say about Roosevelt? Is the old bastard going to quit or will he surprise us an' run again?"

Doc stuck the cigar in his pocket and lit a Chesterfield. "You don't need intuition, governor, to get the answer. He loves to run things. He's ambitious as any man since Caesar. He's spent billions of dollars building up an unbeatable political machine. The country has a mighty need for relief, and relief mixes just right with politics—and he loves to provide relief! He'll run—no matter about that Republican 'no third term' bunk—and he'll win in this state and pull in with him a senator and full slate of congressmen. I'll kiss your ass if he abdicates and takes Eleanor back to the Hudson."

The governor giggled and pushed a buzzer on his desk. A young aide came in and Big Red complained of the heat.

A few minutes later a black servant brought tall, frosted mint juleps. "He really knows how to make a mint julep," the governor opined. "A little mint and a lotta bourbon."

He sipped the drink and told Doc what Doc already knew—he was going to run for senator. "Senator Blair is seventy nine," he explained. 'He's too damn old to do any good. He can't even hear hisself talk. Besides, he fell out with Roosevelt over the Supreme Court bill and the President wants him out. I'm going to tackle 'im and we'll put somebody in the Senate that an ordinary man can talk to. Take old Blair now; he spent fifteen years on the bench before he went to the Senate, and all he can think about is the Constitution, the Constitution, the damn Constitution, mornin', noon and night! Jesus Christ a'mighty, people need somethin' besides the Constitution! They need bread and jobs and pensions when they get old and broke down." He pulled long and earnestly at the julep and leaned forward, furrows wrinkling the craggy face beneath the pale red hair into a mighty grin. "In short, doctor, they need relief!"

Doc felt good as the ice cooled him and the bourbon crept outward from a warmish spot at the bottom of his stomach. After a moment of reflection, he replied.

"I want a new courthouse for Slaughter County, governor. And I want you to lay the cornerstone and make a speech, and I want more schoolhouses for my wife to fill with teachers, and two or three new road projects. I own nearly five hundred acres of coal land on Powderhorn Creek and it will be worth a fortune someday if the industry can get access to it. Most of the people on the creek are so poor they don't know how bad they're living. Little log houses, some hogs and cows and cornfields and stills—that's all they've got to their names. If I can get a road built up Powderhorn, a railroad will come in time and then the men can work in coal mines. Somebody has got to look ahead and plan, and these are things we need in Slaughter County—started soon to break the ground for next year's races. They'll help the congressman, too, and ease things all around for the whole party!"

The governor phoned Josh Wynn and they had a pleasant chat. No mention was made of jobs or projects or impending elections. Big Red mentioned, however, that "a friend of Rube Humble is here, and a good friend of mine and he wants to come by for a few minutes if you have time to see him." The overseer of all the state's far-flung federal relief operations would find time to see Tom Bonham. Doc heard the soft, urbane, deep-South voice as it directed, "Tell Dr. Bonham to come over, by all means. He is a discerning and interested citizen, and I would like to have his appraisal of our efforts in his county. We want to spend federal funds effectively, and he can give me an estimate of whether our projects are well managed."

The governor agreed, of course, and Doc spent more than an hour with Josh Wynn that afternoon. They discussed the projects that had been completed and the projects then under construction and, finally, the projects to be undertaken. They did not talk about politics in the precincts affected by all the hundreds of thousands of dollars poured into schools and roads, privies and bridges. Doc said the projects were well managed. "Reuben Humble is a godsend for Slaughter County. He gets the work done without driving the workers. Slaughter County won't ever be the same when he goes back to that place he calls Far View Farm."

At the end, Josh Wynn said he thought the new court-house could be managed, and also the roads Doc considered so important to the future development of the county's coal operations. Then he made some observations of his own. "The President is in a difficult position. He has got to run for reelection; the situation in Europe and the need to continue our domestic recovery programs rule out any thought that he might retire. And when he runs, the reactionaries will raise an unbelievable howl. It is to be hoped that the many people this administration has befriended will close ranks behind him. And not only that, Doctor, he needs Governor Brady in the Senate. Senator Blair was a great man in his day, but time and a changing world have overwhelmed him. The New Deal—and the country—need the governor in the Senate where his vote can support the President at crucial moments!"

Josh Wynn was too dignified for nicknames, so Doc did not refer to Big Red as such when he replied. "The people of Slaughter County remember the dark days of 1932 and they will not forget them at the polls. If the President gets less than 75 percent of the votes, I'll be astonished. If the governor falls 500 votes under the President's total, the Democratic Central Committee in the county can find itself a new chairman because I'll resign. Not only that, I'll see that the new senator drives a new Buick to Washington and it will be paid for out of my bank account."

Doc drove the seven-hour journey to Noreco in deep reflection on votes and voters. The rolling countryside around the state capital, with its neat farms and stately houses, turned to low ridges, then to the steep hills of the coal country. The neatness gave way to the chaos of a vast, unregulated industry set down in a sprawling backwoods. As darkness came, the headlights of his Chrysler probed like long fingers through the shadows of the three counties below Slaughter on Indian River, the beams pushing along the rows of coal camphouses through which the asphalt ribbon ran as a main street, past gaunt, sprawling tipples and giant slate dumps that towered as mountains of living fire above smoke-choked valleys. He passed strings of coke ovens and men who shoveled coal into their reeking yellow maws, and waited at crossings while the scores of groaning gondolas in the coal drags pounded through the eerie shadows toward the steel mills at Birmingham. The yellow beams picked up the wooden project signs that told of WPA and PWA post offices, roads and schools. And through it all until he reached his own driveway high above Noreco and the crags that scowled down upon it in the starlight, he pondered the people in Slaughter County's thirty-six precincts and how best to assure that the folded ballots that dropped into the sheet-metal boxes would be marked with a single x in the circle beneath the strutting rooster. He counted them over, those saved and those lost to his cause, and how he might gain the latter after all. And in his calculations, they were voters rather than patients, for the physician had been effectively supplanted by the politician.

Doc got the new courthouse for which he had bargained. The county bought a large lot down the street from the cracked and broken relic that had long housed local government, and Big Red came up from the state capital and as governor and in a strictly nonpartisan and apolitical way made a polite little talk and laid the cornerstone. It was on April Fool's Day in 1940, and after the rectangle of marble had been swung into place and a preacher or two had prayed that the rising walls would house a long and resolute pursuit of justice, the crowd went down the street to the old courthouse and the governor made a rip-roaring political speech.

He stood on the top step under the peeling columns of a building marked with the bullets of feuds and civil war, the foul reek of decay and neglect seeping out its doors. The streets were blocked off by barricades as WPA project AK789A1 strove to replace layers of cinders and haphazard stretches of stones and bricks with eight inches of steel-reinforced concrete. Dust swirled up in the dry spring winds and stung eyes and cheeks. It was Saturday, and the mines were not working, and bosses and timekeepers on the relief jobs had urged the men to come to town for the ceremony. A couple of federal officials spoke at the corner-stone laying and drew polite applause for their efforts, but they vanished before Big Red got down to business at the door of the old courthouse.

The governor was introduced by Joe Carr, whose terms in the state legislature had given him a measure of hillbilly confidence and aplomb to go with his insatiable appetite and vast belly. He said he had been mighty proud to work with the governor on projects that were getting the state out of the mud, the children into schools and meat into the empty kettles of working people. Joe brought a gargantuan guffaw when he described the "Hoover starvation days" and avowed that he "liked to have starved to death before Roosevelt got in."

Big Red Brady had been raised rough and mean in a low-roofed pole cabin. His tenant-farming father drank too much and was a ne'er-do-well, and his mother wore herself out at the washboards and in the tobacco rows and conceiving and bringing forth sixteen children. Food had never been abundant and money was almost unknown. The red-headed boy had been agile and strong and had gone through the state university on a basketball scholarship. He had been a fair law student, but a great hand with the girls. He got one of them pregnant in his senior year but, notwithstanding his affection for the flesh, had avoided the snares of matrimony. He hated poverty with a passion, and some observant reporters had disclosed that he never missed an opportunity to line his pockets with as much money as circumstances allowed. Not all of the loot that came his way was honestly acquired, a fact that bothered Big Red not at all. "If the Good Lord didn't want me to get that money," he allowed, "he wouldn't have put it where I could lay my hands on it!"

In Blacksville, he began with a story that explained why he was a Democrat. "My paw was a coal miner," he lied, "just like most of you men are, or have been. We lived out on a farm and raised everything Paw didn't buy at the commissary. Maw made our clothes at her old sewin machine. We had an old cow named 'Flossy,' and ever single year she had a calf and would give plenty of milk for the whole family to drink. Then Paw would sell the calf and take the money and buy each one of us younguns a pair of brogan shoes to wear to school in the winter. So things went along real good all the time Woodrow Wilson was President. Paw had plenty of work, and we had all we needed to eat, good shoes to wear and more milk than we could drink!"

He looked down at the expectant crowd, his face solemn,

his arms outstretched in an all-embracing gesture. Then his arms fell to his side, his shoulders slumped and he shook his head as if overwhelmed with disbelief. "Then the Republicans got into the White House and old Flossy never would let a bull get in ten feet of her. She went dry and stayed dry. We had to go to school barefooted and drink water. The old man lost his job, and I had to run for something to keep the whole family from starving to death!"

The crowd went wild and stamped, clapped and hollered. The men stood pressed together by the hundreds, in blue denim overalls and long-billed caps and floppy hats, their shirt collars unbuttoned. Here and there a sad-faced woman listened impassively or suckled a baby at a bare breast.

Big Red's voice took on a confidential tone. "That went on till 1933. Hard times on the farm, hard times in the mines, hard times at the dinner table. Then Franklin Delano Roosevelt got elected and was sworn in. Old Flossy changed her mind and took a shine to old Bart Bingham's Jersey bull. She had twin calves and started giving more milk than ever. The Brady family put on shoes again and registered Democratic, and praise God, friends, they are goin' to stay Democratic! They've had enough of dry cows, bare feet and empty bellies under Republican presidents."

The crowd roared its approval and Big Red was obviously having a wonderful time. Doc leaned against one of the rotting pillars that struggled to support the decrepit portico and laughed and applauded with the rest of the crowd. He admired the governor as an artful campaigner and smiled at a remark Big Red had once made at a state nominating convention. "Running for a public office is like chasing women. Sometime's it's more fun to hunt . . ."

The candidate went on. He described FDR's efforts to save the country from the wreckage of the Hoover Depression. Roosevelt was trying to save the industrialist and the industrial worker, the farmer and the merchant, the schoolchild and the schoolteacher, "The New Deal is trying to give you a hand with a king or an ace in it," he shouted. "The Republicans want to give all the winning cards to the Mellons and the Rockefellers!"

He began to batter his opponent, the venerable Ambrose Blair, who had already served eighteen years in the Senate and was its acknowledged expert on constitutional law. "He's a good old man and knows all about the Constitution," he roared, "but what did the Constitution do for you in the Hoover days? You couldn't eat it when you were hungry or drink it when you were dry, or wrap up in it when you were cold, and it won't be worth a cobbler's tack to you in the future if you don't have a job and money to buy groceries! The truth is, my friends, the Constitution ain't worth a lead slug if the people who run the country don't have soft hearts!"

He stopped and wiped his brow. "My opponent loves high society and the company of fancy lawyers in striped pants from big offices on Wall Street. He gets dressed up in a black suit and starched shirt and goes to a party somewhere nearly ever' single night. And he sits there and drinks French wine and eats caviar and talks about the Constitution, the pore old Constitution—while people like you good men and women here today are lucky to have coffee and beans." He pulled an envelope from his pocket and held up a clipping from a newspaper. The crowd could not see what was on the paper, but Big Red explained, "This is a picture of my opponent. It was cut out of the *Washington Post* and shows him at a party given by some fat cat or other. And he's shovelin' in the caviar! Now, friends, do you know what caviar is? It's a jelly made outta fish eggs from Russia! Did anybody here ever hear about that before? Fish eggs! Jellied fish eggs! Fish eggs and crackers from Russia!"

Again he reached outward in a symbolic embrace that took in the whole crowd. He leaned forward for a moment in an expectant silence while his listeners waited, every eye upon the strong Irish features beneath the shock of wavy, red hair. Then he exploded in a finale that brought sustained whoops, hollers and whistles. "Let's send a country boy up to the Senate from this state—somebody who will tell the Russians to keep their fish eggs, and who will eat a plateful of ham and biscuits for breakfast and then go out and get the work done for the peepul!"

He plunged into the crowd, shaking hands left and right, patting shoulders and embracing with convivial hugs scores who said he had made a great speech and that they were for him. The Black Marks, the band from Slaughter County Colored High School, struck up a slightly off-key rendition of "Hail, Hail, the Gang's All Here," and Doc's handsome cousin, Jane Bonham, was so carried away that she hugged the candidate in return and kissed him on the cheek.

After the governor had "worked the crowd" Doc snatched him away and carried him to the stone house on the hill overlooking Noreco. There Twinkles and a cook she had borrowed from the King Coal Hotel fed him fried chicken and other delicacies dear to his southern heart. Then, as Doc had previously arranged, carloads of Democratic precinct captains and workers began to arrive for personal introductions and chats. They were all there at one time or another in the afternoon, as well as another hundred or so men and women who had distinguished themselves as persons of influence in their neighborhoods. Big Red assured them that he believed "the man who raises the corn ought to eat the corn," and that patronage ought to get to those good Democrats who fight the good fight and persevere to the end.

He told a group of "crossover" Republicans, though, that no man would be discriminated against for partisan reasons. "We love all our friends, regardless of the name of the political tree that shades their houses." Some blacks came, shuffling and ill at ease, to say they hoped he would support the President's anti-lynching bill, and he vowed that he would. "I believe in equal protection of the law for blacks, whites and Chinamen!" And Sam Chaney and his loyal union chiefs got a promise of support for a federal coal mine safety law and legislation against transporting strikebreakers in interstate commerce. I know what it is to labor for my bread, and organized labor will find me on the side of the worker against the corporations, the poor against the rich." Again he lied, "After all, I was raised by a union coal miner and will never forget the principles he taught me!"

Then, after the precinct officers and other "leading Democrats," the delegations of dissident Republicans, the blacks and the union miners, had all shaken the candidate's hand and filed down the stone steps and disappeared into the gathering night, Ben Fleming came with nearly a score of his coal operators. Things had improved immensely for their companies and a measure of their old jauntiness and self-assurance had returned. The federal pump priming had had its impact, and both the army and navy were taking on men and new weapons so that the coal mines that had survived the ghastly debacle of the early thirties now found themselves titillated by orders for egg, block, and stoker fuel. They were hiring a few men occasionally, and though John L. Lewis was pitiless in his exaction of higher wages and shorter hours, still, as Doc had anticipated, he was no Red and the Commie threat had passed. So now they came in new suits and with expensive black cigars clamped between their teeth. They patted Twinkles affectionately as they filed into the huge living room and were all gaiety and mirth as corpulent Arthur Baslin of Moosehead Coal and Coke set up a bar on the cherry dining room sideboard and began to dispense iced Coke, Old Bardstown, Canadian Club and Cutty Sark. Jane Bonham came up from the welfare office to help with the festivities, and Big Red met and talked with the men who ran the Slaughter County Coal Operators Association. He nursed his bourbon well, and listened to their complaints and displayed a quick grasp of their problems. He stood in the middle of the living room with the operators about him in a huge and close circle, and, amid the heady fragrance of whiskey and blue wisps of cigar smoke, listened carefully and well as Ben Fleming explained the main cause of unease in the nation's reviving softcoal industry.

Fleming's hair had turned gray and his face had wrinkled, but he was as neat and sharply tailored as when Doc, a neophyte physician, had first met him a score of years before. His gray eyes still penetrated, and he continued to manage well most of the situations he encountered. With a white handkerchief in the breast pocket of his tweed jacket, he stood with his arms crossed, sipping a glass which contained scarcely enough Scotch to color the soda water with which it was mixed.

"The New Deal saved the country from collapse and probably from civil war," he said. "The coal industry has opposed much that the President has done and sometimes, as businessmen, we have strongly disagreed with both goals and methods. But notwithstanding, Roosevelt saved us from ruin and nationalization, and we are grateful for that. We are grateful to him and to the Democratic party, and we acknowledge it."

Some of the operators frowned slightly at this opening, but none ventured a comment. Fleming went on. "The RFC loans have enabled us to buy machines and modernize our mines. They have made it possible to hold our companies together. We have learned to live with union labor and a tangle of new regulations. We have adapted to the changes, but we think the time has come to go slow for a while."

This brought nods and murmurs of approval. "We think the New Deal has gone far enough in its social and economic reforms. We don't need any more strikes. Government ought to make it plain to labor that it is not supporting any more militant demands against industry. In short, what we urge is that government become impartial again in labor and management disputes, and even allow the pendulum to swing back a little to do justice to the companies."

The conversation continued and the governor agreed. He thought the President had taken on some dubious advisers, "some mighty far-out lefties." He would hear both sides, of course, and do what he thought was right on the issues as they might come up, but he recognized the importance of coal to the state's economy and would protect it. "The people who invest their hard-earned dollars to open mines and give people jobs are entitled to a decent profit without a lot of harassment and I'll stand up for them in the United States Senate."

The operators were pleased with the meeting, and when Doc got around to mentioning the subject of campaign expenses, they drew envelopes from their pockets and left them on the table in the entranceway. When they were gone, the governor's campaign chest was richer by $14,000—considerably more than his annual salary—and Dick Brady glowed and tingled with satisfaction at a day well spent in the fantastic industrial outback that was Slaughter County.

He had a good night coming up, too. He was tired and after the last of Ben Fleming's colleagues had shaken his hand and disappeared into the night's darkness, he drank freely of the bourbon, and a little after eleven Doc prescribed a good night's sleep and showed him to an upstairs bedroom. Jane Bonham, too, spent the night at Doc's invitation and soon retired. Doc drove down the hill to the hospital to look in on some patients he had left in the care of Dr. Ross since the day before. When he came back, the house was in darkness.

Dick Brady had served three years of his term as governor when he resigned to go to Washington as a newly elected senator. Carl Rutherford moved from the obscure lieutenant governor's office by the senate chamber into the huge suite of the chief executive. Doc wrote him a congratulatory letter, saying that from their first meeting he had never doubted his visitor's goal or that it would be reached. In reply, the new governor expressed gratitude to the doctor for his years of friendship, counsel and encouragement. He said that he felt a special sympathy for mountain people because of their kindness to him on many occasions and vowed that his administration would seek new ways to aid them. "I share your determination to see that the aged, the sick, the disabled, the widowed and the orphaned are cared for. We will seek constantly for new ways of making state government the servant and benefactor of the people."

Big Red kept his promise and took Jane Bonham to Washington with him, where she bacame an important part of his life. She worked as a receptionist in his office and managed the administrative details with a cool competence that became the envy of many another senator. Their apartments were in the same building and on the same floor and quite close together.

Doc found another cousin, a schoolteacher named J. Fred Hampton, to take over Jane's old duties at the state welfare office. The new courthouse was dedicated in 1941 by Governor Rutherford, who was pleased to take time out from his campaign for a full term in the governor's office. The Public Works Administration built an impressive new post office at Blacksville, and Twinkles had several new two- and three-room schoolhouses under way at the end of the year. Even the blindest and most partisan could see that Tom Bonham's connections were bringing a marvelous flow of blessings to Slaughter County. Then, on an otherwise tranquil Sunday, the Japanese Naval Air Force upset many American warships and apple carts.

CHAPTER

15

For several years a rectangular wooden frame had been nailed to the battered, weatherboarded wall of the Noreco post office. Juno Markham was the postmaster, a good Democrat and Doc's fourth cousin. The kinship was on Doc's mother's side, and Juno had lost a leg when a roof crashed down through a thicket of pine, hickory and white oak timbers and pinned his foot against a steel track rail. Doc had gone into the mine with some ether and morphine and a bag of surgical tools, the car swaying wildly as it rattled at top speed along the dank, eerie tunnel. Doc and a foreman had worked as an operating team, amputating the crushed limb, tying off the gushing arteries and lifting the blood-soaked Juno onto the man car for the bone-jarring ride to the mine mouth. When he got well, Doc called Juno's qualifications to the attention of Sam Mitchell, and the congressman mentioned the vacant postmastership at Noreco to an assistant postmaster general, and Juno took his new cork leg to the oaken desk in the long room between the recreation hall and the commissary. And there, in addition to handing out letters and parcels to the good people of Noreco, he kept a succession of illustrated posters tacked in the wooden frame beside the post office door.

In the thirties, they exhorted people to support the national recovery programs. One showed a benign, gigantic Uncle Sam standing behind and supporting a farmer, an automobile assembler, a coal miner and a trio of businessmen in blue suits and white shirts. Stretching to the rear were patches of plowed fields, busy factories with smoking chimneys and an office with secretaries, typewriters and uncluttered desks. A legend in tall white letters read, "NRA means working together for Economic Recovery."

When time and the wind and the merciless fingers of children reduced that one to tatters, Juno brought out another. Again, there was a stern but kindly Uncle Sam staring down with Jovian majesty, this time on a range of bills verdant with forest. On the foreground ruddy-faced youths with broad smiles and rows of healthy white teeth wielded shovels to plant trees and clear fire trails. The caption appealed to sallow, undernourished lads and their hard-pressed parents. "Join CCC—Good Food, Good Pay, Good Work!"

On December 7, 1941, a poster extolled the virtues of the Works Progress Administration. Within a fortnight, it was down and a new one proclaimed a vastly different mood. A steel-helmeted and exceedingly brutal-looking Nazi soldier with a Mauser rifle strapped across his shoulder stared his evil gaze into the eyes of Juno Markham's postal patrons each time they went for a letter or stamps. A stubble of blue-black beard darkened the jaw and chin, and coarse hairs grew thick and ugly on the hand that grasped the Mauser. A buck-toothed Japanese sergeant with a machine gun and hand grenades loomed behind him in the burst of a rising sun that sent its rays across the shattered walls of a ruined, corpse-strewn Chinese city. An Italian infantryman stood between them, his bayonet dripping blood, his jack-booted foot on the naked, upturned breasts of an Ethiopian woman. The legend leaped at Juno's patrons: "Only YOU can save the world from them!"

With unbelievable swiftness, America went to war, and Slaughter County's two great gifts to the war effort were men and coal. Outraged by the Pearl Harbor effrontery, resigned to the certainty of the draft in any event, with nothing to do at home and seeking relief from boredom in the glamor of a uniform, the young men poured out of the camps and hollows to the recruiting stations. Nearly two thousand of the county's youths were in service when it began, and within six months another two thousand were gone.

For those who stayed the preoccupation was with coal. Another poster went up on the other side of Juno Markham's door. It portrayed Uncle Sam in the garb of a coal miner shoveling huge black lumps toward a frightened Hitler, and proclaimed: "Coal is power and power will bring victory!" All at once the shrunken industrial muscle of the nation vibrated into life and coal had to be found for troop trains and freight engines, electricity plants, steel mills and defense factories. All these markets swelled prodigiously like voracious babes that grow to be voracious adults, and their hunger could be quenched only with coal. As the tipples began clattering full time along Indian River, Doc thought much of the hundreds of acres of coal land for which he had sacrificed to buy when the demand was small and the price was low.

The demand for lumber kept pace with the expanding coal market and Doc's land was cloaked with huge trees. The splendid chestnuts had died of an Asian fungus blight and stood only as brown dead shafts, and selective cutting in earlier days had taken out some of the prime white oaks and tulip trees. But still the forest was there waiting for the saw and ax, and in May 1942, Bonham Coal and Timber Company was incorporated. Doc transferred title to his timber to the corporation in return for half the stock. He paid in another $40,000 and sold the remaining shares in three blocs for $20,000 each to three gentlemen whom he esteemed and whose concern could be of inestimable value in promoting the fortunes of the new enterprise—Congressman Sam Mitchell, Senator Richard Brady and Governor Carl Rutherford. Big Red was broke, of course, and had to borrow his part of the capital, but all three knew a good thing when they saw it. As the congressman observed when they met in a hotel room at the state capital for the first stockholders' meeting, "We owe it to the country to get this operation going. We would be unpatriotic, even un-American, if we passed up this chance to put that coal and wood where they are needed."

All agreed with this patriotic sentiment, but agreed on another point as well. The coal Doc owned lay in seams ranging from five to seven feet thick. There was none better anywhere in Appalachia—and Appalachian coals were the best in the world. But before a tipple could run its streams of clattering lumps into strings of railway gondolas, it had to be built. Crews of competent miners had to be rounded up and foremen had to be found who could keep men profitably busy in a labor market certain to grow increasingly tight as the war advanced. Already stern federal regulations governed the allocation of steel rails for sidetracks and the diesel engines, electric drills, mechanical undercutters, and the joy loaders that would make production both quick and profitable. And another war measure fixed the price at which the output could be sold, limited the profit per ton and specified the customer to whom it could be shipped. The National Solid Fuels Administration and the Office of Price Administration were but two of the agencies with which a wartime operator would have to deal, and Doc calculated his associates would be able to speed bureaucratic action in those bottlenecks which were already vexing other companies in the Slaughter County field.

Doc's first action was a master stroke. Walter Martin was Julie's son and Doc's nephew, and he had studied to be a mining engineer. Hard times had forced him out of college and into the mines before he finished his third year, but he had a steady competence and firmness that appealed to Ben Fleming, and within a few years he was chief foreman of Northeast Coal Corporation's three hundred miners. Fleming intended to make him superintendent of all the operations when Roscoe Leach retired, an appealing prospect Doc dashed with a gift of fifty shares in Bonham Coal and Timber and an option to buy more as the company prospered. Doc set the new superintendent's salary at $300 a month, with assurances of raises when coal began coming from the hill. "It looks like the coal business is going to be good for a long time, Walt, and we'd rather pay the money to you than to the tax collectors." With Doc's help, Walt lined up a crew of forty-three miners and two bosses to help the superintendent. While the massive oak and locust timbers were being bolted together into a tall, ungainly tipple, the railroad company workmen laid the sidetrack around the foot of the hill and along a narrow creek bottom where Old John-of-All had once burnt off the wild cane to make way for corn. The tipple stood at the mouth of a hollow on Finn's Fork, and the drift mouth was dug into the hill a hundred yards above it in a thicket of dark green laurel. The dirt and rock from the excavation were trammed past the end of the point and dumped amid a grove of black oaks and was the beginning of a mound that would soon swell with daily accretions of slate from the top of the coal vein and sand rock from the five-inch "parting." The sear was visible to the teachers at the settlement school and some of them complained to Doc that the dump was marring the beauty of the green hill. Doc and Twinkles looked at the scarred slope and altered view brought by the tipple, headhouse and sprinkling of crude lesser buildings, and agreed that the prospect from their spacious front porch would never be the same again. "The teachers are a little too worried about the green hill," Doc allowed. "After all, there are two kinds of green, and green bills are as pretty as green hills any day, especially when there is a war on."

But even with Walter Martin's supervision and Doc's best efforts at finding miners of that rare type who would not get drunk on weekends and miss work on Mondays, the new mine was slow in getting underway. One difficulty lay in the immense demand for coal that had sent a swarm of investors into the Appalachians to open scores of new mines and the adding of extra shifts at all the old portals. Suddenly a new joy undercutter was beyond price; drilling machines and mechanical loaders were far more eagerly sought after than the late model "frozen" and unsalable automobiles gathering dust in the display windows. But Carl and Big Red made some telephone calls that were helpful, and in August two flatcars of machinery that otherwise would have gone to Matt Richardson's Diamond Coal Company on Crooked Creek were diverted instead to the new siding, where Finn's Fork flowed into Indian River. The indignant Richardson was told that the Solid Fuels Administration had ordered the switch, and he swore at the bureaucrats and their bungling ways instead of at the operation that benefited from their directive.

When the tunnel was a hundred yards long, Doc and Twinkles and young Jesse J. went to inspect it. The track that curved around the hill from the headhouse slashed like twin steel rapiers into the yawning hole framed with black locust posts and sawed oak crossbeams. The vein was so thick that Twinkles could walk upright, and Doc and his son—now eighteen and ready for college—could walk with only a slight stoop. At the face, the cutting machine was tearing at the coal with a gigantic whirring arm, ripping a ten-inch gash just above the slate floor that extended deep into the suspended face. The machine stopped as the visitors approached, and they peered through billowing clouds of gritty black dusk toward the shadowed faces of the miners who greeted them with much pleasure and jocularity. Twinkles recognized the voice of old Steve Banion's son, Clark, and when the beam of another lamp swung around she could make out the Irish pug nose with sparkling green eyes now ringed with coal dust. "They say a woman is bad luck in a coal mine," he laughed, "but that wouldn't apply to the school superintendent. She ain't brought nothin' but good luck to this county so far."

The other men joined in the banter and one of them handed Doc his lamp so he could inspect the coal more closely and run his fingertips along the jagged edge of the rib and see the blue-black carbon glittering in the beam of the light. Walt unfolded a ruler and extended it from floor to top—five feet, eight and a quarter inches. The seam was dry with no water seeping out of the roof or sides, and the top was hard sandstone that stayed tightly in place. "The parting is low, Doc," Walt explained, tapping his fingers against an area near the bottom where for a few inches black turned to a lusterless gray, "and we get practically all of it out with the cutter. We're not goin' to have much need for slate pickers."

Doc did some mental calculations. An acre-foot of such mineral would contain 1,500 recoverable tons at a bare minimum. This meant 9,000 tons to the acre and the entire tract—the old Bonham territory that had once belonged to all the heirs of his father, William—contained 482 acres of such coal in the Grey Elk vein alone. There were more than three and a half million tons and the company was paying Doc a royalty of 25 cents on each one taken out, a prospective $900,000 if the war and the coal boom lasted. And that morning the headlines had told of massive German thrusts into the Caucasus and of Japanese plans to round up the last isolated guerrilla forces still resisting in the Philippines. Then there would be Doc's share of the profits after the coal was sold. The Office of Price Administration had limited the company to a profit of 54 cents a ton, which paid out as dividends should net him at least 27 cents—a tidy additional $900,000. Doc gasped at the implications and licked black dust from his lips as he thought of those other tracts he had bought at sheriff's foreclosure sales in the thirties when everybody else had thought the coal business was dead forever and he would never get back his hard-earned money. He had put $50,000 into those purchases when they were all added up, and he had mortgaged his home and pledged his life insurance policies to buy 296 more acres when the misnamed Lucky Strike Coal Company was auctioned off to raise a few thousand dollars for its despairing creditors. As they walked back to the blinding brightness of daylight, Walt was speaking of sump pumps, drainage hose and copper trolley wire for the electric locomotive, but Doc was thinking of Matt Richardson's proposal to lease that coal for a new mine. The old name would be resurrected under Richardson's proposition and Doc would get a quarter a ton from Lucky Strike, and, as partner, a fourth of the net. Richardson said U.S. Steel would take every pound of their production—he already had assurances of that—and the giant steel company would help them find machinery and bank credit. Here was another prospective $600,000, and though Tom Bonham was never one to count his chickens before they hatched, he suddenly became very conscious of the heavy new wartime tax levies and they seemed terribly unjust and harsh.

In truth, though, the war years were not harsh ones in the doctor's life. As a physician, he was able to obtain a new Dodge sedan in 1942 and to replace it with another two years later. The strict rationing of tires, oil and gasoline which swept nearly everyone else off the roads kept physicians adequately supplied with all three so that Doc and his family were able to drive the cars as needed. The relief programs had all been phased out and relegated to history by the end of 1943, and their "workhands" had been drawn into the mines or enticed into war industries in Baltimore and Detroit. Rube Humble had dusted off his reserve captain's commission and gone off to a training camp in Georgia. However, Doc and Twinkles continued to perform in the public interest, and when the Office of Price Administration inquired of the senators and congressmen for likely personnel to supervise rationing and price controls in the myriad counties of the state, they, in turn, inquired of Doc, and Doc consulted with his wife. The county supervisor, in particular, had to be a man of competence: honest, fair and dependable. The agency stressed that a breakdown of price controls and the rise of a huge black market would plunge the country into runaway inflation. No hanky-panky could be tolerated; the man must be dependable and his four or five subordinates must be cut from the same cloth.

Doc did not hesitate to name Tilford, whose long service at the relief and WPA offices had accustomed him to federal procedures and requirements. The end of relief dispensation had left Tilford unemployed, and he took the job with alacrity, and with the help of Doc and Twinkles, put together a staff that would win citations for excellence of performance when it, too, passed into history in 1946. Notwithstanding such dedication to duty, Doc was sometimes able to obtain a few extra ration stamps for a friend whose shoes had worn out or who hungered for an extra slice or two of ham or bacon. In addition to keeping his brother gainfully employed and holding the line against price gouging, Doc's connection with the supervisor brought a strengthening of his ties with the coal operators. Tilford could justify many favors to them as aids to the war effort. The coal had to be kept rolling and tires, gasoline, oil, nails, bolts, screws, and a multitude of other things were indispensable to their operations, and Doc generally gained goodwill from each little extra dispensation. It might have been noted that the truckers who began bringing coal from the mushrooming "truck mines" to the Bonham tipple never suffered unduly from the irksome delays imposed by worn-out equipment.

So many Slaughter County men were in service when the war began that casualties were always high. The yellow envelopes from the War Department piled up in the Western Union office in Blacksville, and the telegraph company hired Lee Gilliam, a one-armed veteran of San Juan Hill, to deliver them. As the war wore on, the white-maned, one-time sergeant became a messenger of death, whose appearance along a winding creek road or in a smoky coal camp made hearts stand still. Twinkles worried about Jesse Boy, as she had called him since he began tugging at her hem at eleven months—and Doc shared her alarm. In the spring of 1942, he entered the state university and enrolled in the ASTP the Army Student Training Program. A year later, though, the army's manpower requirements had become insatiable, and the students were called to active duty. There were a few weeks of basic training in an infantry camp in Mississippi, during which time Doc and Twinkles went to see Sam Mitchell about the threat to their son and heir. The congressman had been in the House for seven years and was ranking majority member of the Military Affairs Committee. He had faithfully upheld the chairman in his unswerving support of the generals when they asked for more, and had some due bills at the Pentagon.

He seldom requested anything of a general, but when he did, it received, to say the very least, careful attention. When he asked that Private Jesse J. Bonham be admitted to Officers Candidate School and assigned to the Quartermaster General's Department as a procurement and inventory officer, it was done. Jesse Boy served out the last two years of global struggle supervising a hectic and crowded warehouse on a New Jersey dock. The work was never particularly interesting, but it was not particularly dangerous, either. Between Pearl Harbor and the last charge on Okinawa, Lee Gilliam delivered 383 of his mournful messages, and no fewer than 71 of them gave notice that a young Bonham had died in the cause of freedom. When it was over, Doc's son came home entire and unscratched, trim and straight in the natty green jacket and pink trousers of a quartermaster captain, and all who saw him were pleased to note that he, too, had served his country even as their own sons had done.

After demobilization in November 1945, Doc set him up in business with Joe Carr—and with himself as a silent participant in the venture. Joe had wrangled a lease from Eastern Coal and Land Company on several hundred acres of practically virgin land on the Clear Fork of Dead Man Creek, and the railroad company had extended a sidetrack for two miles to open the territory to mining. Joe had no intention of operating a mine of his own, but subleased the land in small tracts to "truck miners." These were ambitious coal diggers who managed to go into business for themselves with a few employees, a few bank cars and some obsolete steel track rails and a truck or two to haul the "mine-run" coal from the simple bin at the mine mouth to a railroad "ramp" or loading dock. Such a minuscule operator could dig about a hundred tons a day and enough of them could fill a long coal drag. By the end of the war, dozens of these little operations were swelling Slaughter County's contribution to victory and the postwar boom required even more of the fuel. Bonham and Carr, Inc., built a dock along a spur that jutted off the new sidetrack. Trucks could be unloaded into a hopper that chuted the fuel down the hill into the waiting gondolas. The immense snorting, smoky locomotives of the Appalachian and Northern—"the coal road"—could shove a string of sixty empty cars onto the new spur; and by May 1946 more than two score frightfully ugly little mines were sending coal across the scales onto the huge oaken ramp where a hoist lifted the front end of the truck and sent its cargo roaring into a railroad car. Clouds of the dust escaped and turned nearby trees a melancholy black. The excavating of the numerous little mine openings with their accompanying muck dumps turned Clear Fork yellow with mud, and its deep waterholes and schools of black bass promptly vanished.

Joe and the ex-captain—now simply "Jesse J." once again—paid the operators $5 a ton and sold it for $6.15. As the voracious requirements of the Marshall Plan and domestic boom pushed hard against the straining coal industry these prices climbed, but the spread never narrowed. On a good day, Joe and Jesse grossed $3,000. There was the payroll of five men at fifteen dollars each, plus a few other items, and repayment of the $71,000 at 6 percent the enterprise had borrowed from Doc. But in June 1947, the debt was fully paid and swarms of whining Ford and Studebaker trucks lined up at their premises and Doc, Jesse Boy and Joe were netting $14,000 a week, which they divided as dividends every three months.

It was a much different proposition for the truck mine operators. Each of them had to pay eight or ten miners, buy costly explosives and electricity, hire a bookkeeper and someone to make his tax returns, and pay a trucker to haul his coal to the ramp. He had to pay Joe Carr 30 cents a ton as royalty—20 cents of which Joe sent on to Eastern Coal and Land in Philadelphia. Then there were Workmen's Compensation Insurance premiums and all sorts of shortages and breakdowns, accidents and costly foulups. If the operator was lucky, he cleared 40 cents a ton and netted $250 in a good week. Still it was a heady situation, with overwhelming temptation to speculate and plunge and sink the savings of yesterday and the profits of the present on new and bigger ventures in a fuel market that would never, never cease to grow.

In 1947 Doc, Twinkles, Joe Carr, Ben Fleming, and a few others organized the Slaughter County Bank and Trust Company. They housed it in a nondescript new brick and concrete block building near the courthouse, and while they were at it, built a pleasant suite upstairs which they rented to the school board for the superintendent's office at $150 a month. The directors of the Miners' Bank of Blacksville were aggrieved by the formidable new competition and watched in frustration as their own deposits began melting away.

Nineteen forty-eight brought several notable developments. In March U.S. Senator Morse Flinchum died in a traffic accident at a Washington intersection. It was 2:00 A.M., and the senator had just left a party at which he had been the very soul of conviviality. Unfortunately, he proceeded to drive his car in the wrong direction on a one-way street and encountered an oil truck. There was an outpouring of laudatory statements for the deceased and expressions of grief and loss. No mention was made of his notorious weakness for bourbon and his prolonged absences from all legislative activities. After Carl Rutherford had headed the delegation of official mourners at the graveside ceremony in the decedent's hometown, the governor came back to his desk and three days later handed his resignation to the secretary of state.

Lieutenant Governor Albert Forbes proceeded to move the cautious personality of a one-time juvenile court judge into the big brown leather chair under the gubernatorial seal. The new chief executive told a news conference he would dedicate his time in the office to prison reforms, improvements of the courts, and expansion of public assistance programs "to rout hunger and cruel want from the state." He would be "a fighter for people, in the lowlands and the highlands," and would "strive to fulfill the people's yearnings for a truly modern and effective school system at all levels." The youngish Forbes drew favorable responses from editorial writers and columnists, for few doubted his sincere desire to be a progressive and liberal influence in shaping the state's future. Two days later, he appointed his mentor and old friend Carl Rutherford to the U.S. Senate "to fill the vacancy created by the untimely death of the Honorable Morse Flinchum." Carl was the essence of humility as he accepted the trust and vowed to "toil unceasingly in fulfillment of the great tasks so ably advanced by a great senator, a great Democrat, a great American and a great citizen of this, his beloved state."

When he ran for reelection as governor in 1946, Rutherford had looked around for an urban personality with the luster of a reformer about him. This was necessary because newspapers and radio commentators had begun carping that the Rutherford administration was a wool hat affair that ignored the problems of towns and cities. "Tobacco, coal and timber," one editorial had shrilled, "run the state and the people—particularly urban people—are taxed and then ignored." Carl pulled the teeth of these critical gentry by adding to his ticket the youngish lawyer who as judge and alderman had fought with commendable diligence for better treatment of juvenile offenders and an overhaul of the cumbersome machinery of state government. As for Forbes, he was delighted to find himself projected onto a winning ticket and won without really understanding just how. He was adept enough at ward politics in a city of 400,000, but operations in precincts strung along the flat, steamy river bottoms in the west and in the cramped valleys of the eastern hills were beyond his comprehension, and he simply gave his gratitude and support to rural politicians like the Bonhams in Slaughter County whose know-how had delivered the margin of victory. Doc instinctively mistrusted Forbes as an impractical do-gooder, but naturally omitted to say so in the warm congratulatory letter he mailed to the governor a day or two after his accession.

Carl joined Dick "Big Red" Brady in Washington, and with his characteristic painstaking attention to detail, began the task of building for himself an important niche in the Washington establishment. He championed the tobacco farmers and coal companies whose production accounted for most of the state's cash income and was ever alert to support a dam, road or drainage project. Doc and Twinkles called and expressed their pleasure with his appointment, and delighted him mightily with the news that Bonham Coal and Timber had declared a special dividend in his honor.

In that year, too, Jesse Boy went back to college after a four-year absence. A year later he entered the law school. Doc had always wanted a son to walk in the footsteps of William Bonham and to realize the ambition of a judgeship, on which Twinkles had set her sights. The law student promptly found himself a wife among the coeds and moved her into his apartment. The lovely young lady was the envy of her peers because her husband bought her a new red Pontiac convertible and always possessed enough money for whatever else was needed. This puzzled many students because at the time of the nuptials, the groom's home county was much in the news as the setting of stark hunger, destitution and wretchedness. In fact, Jesse Boy had done quite well in a financial way. Despite the oppressive taxes his father so often decried, the twenty-four-year-old ex-quartermaster captain had stowed more than $200,000 away in stocks and municipal bonds and a savings account and owned a desirable stretch of land or two besides. Joe Carr had long since risen out of poverty and could now clothe his huge girth in firstclass wool. Doc persuaded him to spend some of the money in a successful race for the state senate in 1947, and in January of the following year, Joe moved to a desk in an obscure corner of the "upper" chamber. Joe never made a speech, but never missed anything that was going on either,

and collected lists of IOUs which he steadfastly used in support of administration measures. Both "Ole Carl" and the
younger and sometimes idealistic Forbes relied upon his
judgment and counsel.

They were grateful to Joe, and Joe was infinitely more
grateful to Doc whose loans and banknote endorsements had
made possible his venture into the coal business in the first
place.

For three years after the Japanese surrender, the coal
boom soared and swelled like a mighty tide and the heady
wine of quick riches swept through the mountains. Its course
was not without interruptions though, most of them decreed
by John L. Lewis, who called numerous and vexatious strikes
in an effort to drag mine safety legislation out of an indiffer-
ent Congress, and to wrench an industry-supported health
and welfare fund from outraged and fiercely resisting operators. Each time a strike was called under the cry "no contract,
no work," Doc signed the new contract promptly for Bonham
Coal and Timber and sent his miners back to the pits. In the
climate of the times and with the union's iron grip on all the
country's producing fields, Doc perceived the inevitability of
ultimate victory for the UMW, and while other corporations
went through paralyzed and profitless weeks, his company's
coal went to the frantic "spot market"—the power and steel
firms who were short of fuel and faced total shutdown without new supplies. Such a seller's market sometimes doubled
the price in a fortnight, and long before July 1948 the slate
dump above Fort Bonham was a towering manmade mountain. Impressive, too, was the wealth Doc and his still-comely
wife had laid up, for as summer came on that year, their

stocks, bonds, land and other holdings were worth, by a cautious estimate, at least two million dollars.

But Doc and Joe became uneasy as prices and orders declined in May and June. In July, the miners would take a ten day paid vacation and as a rule the thawing of the Great Lakes and the reopened steel trade combined with the impending July work stoppage to make June a month of much activity. But in 1948, the reverse occurred and Doc took time from his surgery, politics, and business to read the signs. The railroads were replacing their coal-burning locomotives with diesel-powered engines and reopened mines in Europe slackened exports. Huge federally sponsored pipelines were delivering gigantic flows of gas from Texas and Louisiana for heating buildings in the cold and populous East. Doc remembered the collapse of 1929 and retrenched. His money went into stocks—banks, insurance, automobiles, communications, drugs, building materials, oil and gas—and he got ready for a time when his tipple and machines would rust and rot in another long spell of idleness. He had lived a long time without the easy money that flowed from coal royalties, mines and ramps and could do so again. When a steamy July overtook Indian Valley, Doc's enterprises were safely debt-free. He had passed up opportunities to plunge into enlarged operations and greater profits though, the truth to tell, he had often cursed himself for the caution that held him to a safer course.

But his caution made him the envy of other operators in the weeks that followed the end of the miners' vacation. The Indian River field had come into production late, and its production had been needed in those periods when other

coalfields closer to the cities and their mills and factories could not fill the demands. Now, suddenly, those nearer and older producers could supply all the coal the nation required, and for Slaughter and the counties around it there was economic debacle. For many operations, there were no orders whatever. For others, some orders came but the price was halved. Too, the buyers became extremely finicky about quality; if shipments contained bits of dirt and rock or proved to be a little high in ash or sulfur, penalties were withheld from payment at the end of the month. The "middlemen" in Cincinnati and Chicago ceased to answer the frantic calls from their suppliers. For six years, the hustle of boom, profit and importance had pervaded Slaughter County, sucking thousands of new people into its bulging county seat and coal towns, and along its winding creeks. In 1945, the census bureau issued an estimate that 63,000 people lived within its borders, and Twinkles and her staff above the new bank struggled with classrooms crammed with 50 or 60 pupils.

Suddenly, all was reversed as 1948 repeated the ruin of 1929. The once-coveted black mineral lay undisturbed in the hills. The new diesel locomotives of the Appalachian and Northern burned petroleum from Arabia and pushed strings of empty cars onto silent sidetracks where they waited beneath locked ramps and deserted tipples. The work sirens on the commissaries and scrip offices ceased to sound, and the men began gathering in huge bands, scrubbed and in their best clothes, at recreation buildings and union halls to discuss the jarring turn of events. At the beginning, there was no panic, though. Both operators and miners thought the situation would be only temporary. The country needed coal, of course, couldn't run without it as a matter of fact. In a little while, things would pick up and get going again and prosperity would come back. Not boom, maybe, but good times. In the meantime a few days of loafing wouldn't hurt anybody. A man could go fishing or just sleep.

But Doc was not so optimistic. He took Twinkles to visit Jesse Jackson at the law school and then drove on to the state capital. They talked to Governor Forbes about the ominous economic developments and said huge amounts of relief would soon be required. The governor was astonished by their narrative and their somber estimates, and sent them over to see the commissioner of economic security. The commissioner said funds were short. Doc said, "Up our way relief is soon going to be a bigger business than coal mining about five times bigger." The commissioner hoped the mines would soon go back to work. "A job is a wonderful morale booster!" he smiled.

Doc had no argument with this splendid sentiment. "Grub is good for morale, too," he replied. "Tell the governor that regardless of the shape of his budget, the relief trains are going to have to run. Otherwise, a lot of good Democrats will starve to death, and we really don't have any of them to spare!"

CHAPTER
16

In the years after the coal bubble burst, the G.I. Bill of
Rights was a tremendous help to Doc and Twinkles and all
who labored with them to make Slaughter County a better
place in which to live. Without it, trained men and women
could not have been found to staff the multiplying agencies
that struggled to preserve order in the deepening chaos of
the county's wrecked economy.

When hard times struck, thousands got up and left. They
were the best human protoplasm in the county. They included most of the foreign-born who joined relatives in
Newark, New York and Jersey City, miners who had come
in from other states during the war and were without lasting
ties to the region, the young blacks who headed for Chicago,
and most significantly of all, perhaps, the thousands of war
veterans who had learned to live beyond the deep folds of
the hollows and their dusty camps and who had no intention
of stagnating in idleness just because the place was home.
They sold out or abandoned their possessions, loaded wives
and children in cars and headed for the cities—a small wave
on a vast demographic tide rushing from the American land
into the nation's industrial centers. They stayed, and the
young, the gifted and the energetic flowed after them as one

wave pursues another along a beach. The 1950 census showed 49,000 inhabitants, and the population was stamped with the flavor of dependency, passivity, and old age.

Governor Forbes first acted to extend unemployment compensation benefits for twenty extra weeks. His economic advisers assured him that by then Appalachia's coals would be indispensable again and full employment would return. A special session of the legislature appropriated the money and adjourned in a mere five days, adjourned and forgot the trouble in the hills as completely as if it had never been called to their attention. Nor was this surprising, because the coal country was only a small part of a state that had many parts and varied interests, and most of the parts were prosperous. And being prosperous, the people were heedless and little noted the endless flood of tax dollars that disappeared annually from their own communities to subsidize the hill-girt valleys with the quaint old-time names along the eastern reaches of their "commonwealth."

But not withstanding, the vast emigration that carried coal miners and their families to twenty states, other multitudes stayed behind—the timid who feared the pressure of city ways, the sick and the crippled whom employment officers rejected, the shiftless who didn't want to work anyway, and some who just liked the mountains with their familiar crags and sharp, laurel-draped shoulders, and doubted that life in another setting would be worthwhile. These remained, and as the birth rate indicated and Doc once described it to an amused Governor Forbes, "They all like sex. They just read that one part of the Bible where it says to multiply and replenish the earth, and immediately quit and got busy."

But the twenty weeks passed, and the coal business did not revive. The scores of little mine operators whose tiny wooden bins and chutes flecked the hillside turned their trucks back to the dealers and joined the migration to other climes. By the end of the year, a new wave of bankruptcies swept through the companies whose coal had powered the Great Arsenal of Democracy, and their machinery was dragged from a tunnel and piled up in rusty stacks at prominent crossroads where, their creditors hoped, a buyer would purchase them. The machines that were so valuable in 1944 were unneeded junk in the glutted coal market of 1949, and no buyers came. Doc and Twinkles rejoiced that their bank had had the good sense to invest its money in federal bonds and in a suburban housing development far from the hills where it was safe from the economic earthquake now battering its older rival, the Miners' Bank of Blacksville. The worthies who sat on that institution's board of directors boasted that their money financed Slaughter County's prosperity. "We invest at home!" was their slogan, with the consequence that when Doc called his own directors to order on a November night in 1949 he chortled, "So they invest at home, do they? Well, let 'em go broke at home, too!" This sally brought little murmurs of approval from the men around the table. Ticky Charlie said he had checked at the circuit clerk's office to see how many foreclosure suits their competitor had filed and allowed, "One thing is certain, they may not have much money left over there to loan out, but if a man happens to need 'em, he ought to be able to rent a carload of picks and shovels and a lot of old camphouses real cheap."

A few years earlier, Twinkles had bought a store building in Blacksville from the heirs of old Dave Simpson and had renovated it and partitioned it into offices which she had rented to the state's Department of Economic Security. She and Doc had helped the commissioner keep a small staff of competent "fieldworkers" who could, as Doc hoped, "recognize a blind man when they see one." As a matter of fact, nearly all of them were his kin by either blood or marriage, and they recognized no fewer than 83 men and women in the county who were sightless and eligible for pensions. They found meritorious the applications of 3,800 old men and women who had passed their sixty-fifth year and whose pauperization made them eligible for small pensions. Then, in the wake of expanded generosity in Washington's marble halls, there came AFDC—Aid for Dependent Children—a special program of public assistance designed to get food, clothing and shelter to persons under eighteen whose parents had died or disappeared.

After the legislation was approved, Doc took Twinkles away from her duties at the office of the school board, and they drove to the state capital to see the commissioner. The thousands of needy children jammed into Slaughter County presented an opportunity to be both political and benevolent. Strict federal laws ruled out politics. The Hatch Act applied to all who supervised the spending of U.S. funds, and severe penalties were inflicted on personnel who sought to influence the vote of any "client" benefiting from public assistance funds. To violate such laws could be disastrous, with its horrifying publicity and attendant fines and prison sentences. But as Doc sat down in a deep leather chair across the glass-topped desk from Commissioner Horton Winslow, he had every intention of garnering benefits while avoiding disaster.

Doc nursed a grudging respect for Governor Forbes as a man of genuine compassion for the down-and-out and whose Governmental Reorganization Act was his greatest pride. The governor wanted efficient administration of the state's affairs, and Horton Winslow was part of his pledge to provide public services without waste or any lack of concern for human needs. The commissioner was thirty-six, a New Hampshire man and a graduate of Dartmouth. He was a dedicated professional who took seriously the governor's promises that the commissioner would run his important agency without political interference from any quarter. "Make your department the best-run state welfare agency in the country!" he told Winslow when the appointment was announced.

The commissioner was determined to do just that as he settled his family into a house a mile from the statehouse dome. But he was a stranger in a strange land and so had to seek advice, and Doc had come down from the hills to offer some.

Twinkles broke in sometimes to help Doc as he brought the commissioner up to date on matters along Indian River. He described his own origins in poverty and violence, his education in a mission-supported school, and his years of work as a coal-camp doctor. As an operator, he had employed the poor and had done his utmost to make their working places safe and their lives pleasant. Twinkles told about her work as a teacher and superintendent and of the decades she had dedicated to giving the sons and daughters of needy mountaineers the education that could lift them out of want and dependency. Then they gave examples of hunger in mountain children, of pupils so listless from malnutrition they could scarcely stay awake, let alone learn. Both hoped the state would set up a program to get aid to the suffering children to all of them, and quickly—and that honest, sympathetic people would administer the effort. They supported the commissioner's announced determination to hire no hacks, to staff the county offices with solid professionals. "The children must have help," Doc said with a sad expression and a shake of his head, "and nothing could hurt them more than a scandal growing out of corruption and wrangling or mismanagement."

All that was said was clearly true and the commissioner was duly impressed. He drew on his pipe and explained some of his problems. The state had more than a hundred counties and careful testing and personal interviews were necessary before new personnel could be hired. After all, they were hired for keeps and as civil servants could not be fired without a substantial showing of incompetence or misconduct. "We're trying to keep the bad apples out of our barrels," he said, to which Doc and Twinkles fervently agreed, "We are ready to move in Slaughter as soon as we can find the right person as director of the AFDC section. Do you, with your long background of experience in the county, have anyone in mind whom you would like to recommend?"

As a matter of fact, Doc did have such a person in mind and he described her. She was Millie Roberts, age twenty-nine, and a former WAC sergeant who had spent a year overseas during the war. She had gone to college under the G.I. Bill of Rights and had majored in education but with considerable work in psychology and sociology. "She has brains," Doc summed up, "she knows the county and is willing to work." Then after a little pause, "She has integrity and compassion, too."

Neither Doc nor Twinkles misled the commissioner, though they omitted to point out that Millie Roberts was a registered Democrat whose maiden name had been Bonham. She was Wash's daughter, and Wash was JP in the county's remote district along the high mountain country where the state and Slaughter County jammed up against Tennessee. Hundreds of Melungeons lived there on broad, flat mesas from which the oaks had been cleared and which were dappled now with shacks and cabins and fields of corn. They were dirt poor and Wash Bonham, who had made what his neighbors regarded as a fortune with the stave mill he operated at the foot of Barlow Mountain on Dry Creek, was the only man in the precinct with any money. He had spent enough of it to get his children through high school and a couple of them through college, and a judicious use of his own and Doc's money, combined with the favors he was able to do for his neighbors, gave him a hammerlock on Dry Creek's votes and an easy dominance in the five other precincts in his magisterial district. Wash knew the wise and cunning uses of largesse among a poor and ignorant people, and his daughter had grown to womanhood amid elections, perpetual scheming after votes, the dispensing of favors and rewards and, when required, the administering of punishments. She had seen her father's eyes turn hard and icy cold as he refused to make a small loan or recommend a man for a job. "You know," he would say as he turned away, "one good turn deserves another, and it's mighty hard for me to help a man who wouldn't help me when he had a chance."

Her determination to put Dry Creek behind her forever, her deference toward authority and a capacity to dominate lesser personalities, brought promotions, and she ended three years in the army air force as a master sergeant with a letter of commendation from General H. H. Arnold. Doc told the commissioner about the general's letter, but omitted the other details about her background.

Andy Roberts was a football coach at one of Twinkles' high schools. He was no intellectual giant, but as the superintendent told her board when he was hired, "A man doesn't have to know too much to be a coach." In any event, he knew enough to make the most of the fortuitous circumstances that had made Millie Bonham his wife. One week to the day after Doc and the school superintendent had discussed the situation with Commissioner Winslow, Andy drove his wife the 230 tortuous miles to the state capital and had a milkshake at a corner drugstore while his wife went through an hour-long interview with the commissioner and a couple of his aides. The session was a complete success, for Millie could be both charming and commanding. Winslow had been an air force captain, and he saw at once that the ex-WAC was the woman for the job in Slaughter County. A letter went out over his signature that told Dr. and Mrs. Bonham of his gratitude for their concern and for having called the new appointee to his attention. "Under Mrs. Roberts' supervision," he wrote, "we should be able to set up an excellent program to aid dependent children during the present economic troubles in the county you both love so much."

Millie did the good job Doc had foretold for her, though

she had to have assistants from time to time as the caseload steadily increased. And as such helpers were needed, Doc recommended them to her, and she passed the names on to the commissioner, and they were hired. Each was grateful for the boost into a position that paid a fair salary and offered job security in a time when jobs were scarce. Grateful, too, were the men and women who came to see Doc at the hospital and Twinkles at her office and described the hunger that plagued their children and asked for help. Over and over they told of a lack of jobs or of a day's work now and then in low coal and for trifling pay. There was shame mixed with the tenseness in their faces, and their plea nearly always ended on the same note: "It don't matter too much for me if I live or starve to death, but I sure would like to git some help for my kids." And Doc and Twinkles listened patiently and promised to help insofar as their limited influence could reach. And whether they made the promised call to Millie Roberts or got busy and forgot it, the result was the same because virtually all the applicants were eligible under the law. In time, the small but precious monthly checks began to arrive, and meat could be cooked with the beans and some milk could be bought to go with the bread. The promises were remembered.

In Governor Forbes' second term, in 1954, the legislature took advantage of an earlier congressional enactment and provided a new category of public assistance—aid to the totally and permanently disabled. Members of the new generation were found with the degrees in education and sociology that were required to staff the multiplying desks. And the commissioner asked Doc to take time from his busy practice and examine the applicants and certify as disabled those men and women who "under approved criteria suffer from such impairment of mind or body as prevents them from performing any substantial amount of gainful labor or otherwise to earn a livelihood." Doc agreed—as he replied—"to accept the responsibility out of a sense of public duty," and suggested that his associate of many years, Dr. Omar Ross, be retained as his "backup physician" to examine those doubtful cases where a finding of disability required reexamination lest deadbeats and fakers gain access to the public purse. The arrangement was approved, and the state sent down a stack of forms, one of which was to be filled out on each applicant referred to the physicians. The questions were 26 in number, with half a page for additional comments on the applicant's condition. A modest fee of $5 per examination was paid by the state, but as Doc told Commissioner Winslow, the money was not a consideration with him in undertaking to do the work. He would have shouldered the task simply as a physician and citizen "to try conscientiously to see that the sick and the crippled do not starve and that chiselers do not avoid work."

By the inception of ATPD, most of the jobless in Slaughter County had exhausted every thinkable prospect for self-support. They had worked at mines for wages that dwindled to the starvation level, then ceased altogether when the pits closed. They had formed partnerships with other miners and "gangworked" a section until the profits became too insignificant to divide. They had pounded the torrid pavement of distant cities, working as janitors and street sweepers until economic fluctuations snatched even these lean vines from their grasp. Back home, they had eaten from a bean kettle financed with little more than hope and shreds of charity. They were physically and mentally depleted and reacted instantly and affirmatively to the news that a man could draw a monthly check just for being totally and permanently disabled.

They soon learned, too, the procedures by which their applications were investigated by a fieldworker, received the rubber stamp of approval at the director's desk and were forwarded to the "main big office" at the state capital for final approval. If the man or woman was an established friend of Tom Bonham, he was in pretty good shape, but a record of antipathy to Bonham candidates could result in a finding of "no disability" or "not totally disabled," and if a beneficiary wandered from the path and became unfriendly after his claim had been approved, then, lo, it could come to pass that a "routine reexamination" was ordered. Such a session with the physician sometimes produced findings of recovery and notations of "applicant is now able to work without risk to his health."

In 1952, the Bonhams' daughter came home from the state university with a master's degree from the College of Education and an engagement ring from a campus idol, "Slim Jimmy" Long. Slim Jimmy was most appropriately nicknamed, and his six feet seven inches enabled him to toss ball after ball through the basketball net with a consummate ease that made fans roar their approval. Roaring and chanting with the others on cold evenings when Slim Jimmy was laying them in was Tess, a well-developed, beautiful young woman. Jimmy heard someone say that the gorgeous creature had a rich father who was a doctor, coal mine operator and politician, so he investigated and found that the report was true in all of its particulars. When she brought the good-natured basketballer to Noreco for a visit and to tell her parents about their wedding plans, Doc was incredulous, to use the mildest term that could be applied to his reactions. After he and Twinkles went to bed that night, he raved his disapproval. "He's a regular jumping jack. Why his neck is as long as a pool stick, and those hands! Christ a-mighty, he could reach up and knock squirrels out of the top of a hickory tree!"

Twinkles tried to calm him. The man loved their daughter, and Tess was crazy about him. They'd make a fine pair and, besides, they were not married yet. The whole thing might blow over. Tessie was high-spirited and might find someone she liked better.

But Doc was pessimistic. "She'll marry him, alright," he affirmed with a sad waggle of his head. "She's got a marrying gleam in her eyes. And their children will be regular human giraffes. Imagine having giraffes for grandchildren!"

The marriage came off as scheduled, at a Baptist church on the edge of the campus. The newlyweds honeymooned in New Orleans for a while and then came back to Slaughter County a month before the school term commenced in September. At Twinkles' request, the board hired Tess as her assistant—"the superintendent's job has gotten so big one person can't do all the work, and I think my daughter is well qualified to assist me"—and jumped at a chance to hire much-admired "Slim Jimmy" Long as head basketball coach for Blacksville High School. Doc's bank loaned them money to build a long, brick-veneered ranch-style house halfway between Noreco and Blacksville and to stuff it with expensive and pretentious new furniture and vast expanses of carpeting.

As a matter of fact, things worked out superlatively all around. Slim Jimmy was an excellent coach and the pupils admired him with unmixed fervor. Their parents knew nothing about the state university, except that it had a good basketball team, and Twinkles was admired and honored for having brought such a famous person to the crowded little high school campus. His teams learned little algebra, history or chemistry, but played demonic basketball so that a row of gold-plated trophy cups began lining up on a shelf in the principal's office. Only an occasional complaint was heard and that to the effect that the huge hands that had so startled his father-in-law occasionally found their way down to pat the firm bottom of one of the senior girls—a practice that upset more parents than students. Doc was not unmindful of the popularity of his ungainly son-in-law and hoped it would last. After all, as coaches aged and thickened, they and their teams tended to slow, and new slots had to be found for them.

Jesse J. got his law degree the next year, and at the ripe age of twenty-seven, hung his shingle outside three rooms next to the Slaughter County Bank and Trust Company. Old Jep Callihan had been the bank's lawyer since it was chartered, but his selection from among the dozen local lawyers had been carefully calculated. He would practice only a few years, at most, and Doc and Twinkles intended to turn that plum over to their son as soon as they had a counselor of their own in the family. Jesse had been a diligent B student, never good enough to get on the staff of the law journal, but never in danger of flunking out, either. He was careful, soft-spoken, plodding, a keen observer, and blessed with a good memory. When Jep Callihan said he was too old to handle the work any longer, the retainer went to the new lawyer, as did such other clients as a host of Bonham supporters across the county could send to him. His practice grew steadily but unspectacularly as coal companies, the railroad, an oil and gas company in search of leases, and a state agency or two found his advice and services to their liking. In jury trials, it was hard to get a panel together without at least a few of his kinsmen on it, and, in any event, a desire to curry favor with the powerful Bonham machine could usually gain him at least a hung jury even when the evidence was against him. From such situations reputations are built, and within a couple of years, it was generally known across the county that if one had a hard case he had better line up young Jess Bonham as his lawyer.

The next year Governor Forbes pushed through the legislature a bill Doc and Twinkles strongly supported. It was styled the Educational Foundation Act of 1954 and was intended to establish a decent basic or minimum level of educational quality beneath which no school would be allowed to sink. It would consolidate schools and house them in modern one-story buildings with ample grounds, raise the standards of teachers by sending them back to college and recruiting new teachers with college degrees, update libraries and laboratories and finance fleets of new buses. All this sparkled with the bright light of a new day dawning, but it smelled, also, of patronage, with scores of new jobs and increased pay for the old. At last, Twinkles' long years of self-sacrificing endeavor in behalf of Slaughter County's young-sters was about to pay off and she could build the kind of school system she and they so richly deserved.

When the legislature was considering the Educational Foundation Act, the governor suggested that Jerry Grimes, the senator who chaired the joint committee, call Slaughter County's superintendent as a witness. His letter pointed out that Mrs. Bonham was very popular in her county, was singlemindedly dedicated to the cause of education and had held her own school system together during the darkest days of the war when draft boards and war industries were me-thodically robbing classrooms of teachers. "Her insights could prove of immense value to the joint committee," the governor concluded.

Forbes had quietly promoted the proposal throughout his first term and had been reelected mainly on the strength of it. "The people are the state's greatest resource" was his administration's unofficial slogan, emblazoned on letterheads and agency walls, and the words came to life in laws setting up mental health clinics, providing college scholarships and loans for poor students and, now, the "keystone" itself. The governor had groomed Jerry Grimes to spearhead the legis-lation and hoped the young senator would acquire enough luster in the process to make it to the governor's mansion as Forbes's successor.

Grimes was a freckled redhead of forty, an irrepressible optimist and liberal whose political career had begun when he was elected president of his distillery workers' local union. Whiskey was a big industry in the state's largest city, and the distillers, vatmasters, warehousemen, bottlers and labelers had sent their happy colleague to the state senate. He managed to be "prolabor without being anti-business," and the owners liked him because he worked hard for labor peace and to prevent strikes. He had once been a teacher himself and so had a link to the state's 26,000 teachers and administrators. His drawbacks lay in those two noble defects of the Irish: he drank too much of the bottled-in-bond his colleagues turned out, and he believed the good Lord had set the swarms of pretty clerks and typists in the capital for his own personal edification. "Miss Mossie," the governor's secretary, tittered as she related the latest of seduction and downfall, and warned that only the militia and a full-scale state of emergency could save the others. Miss Mossie was a fifty-six-year-old spinster, and her efficiency was indispensable to the governor who found much to amuse him in the gossip she collected like a human radar. 'It's hard for a girl to keep her panties on around that Irishman," she grinned.

"The ladies are enfranchised, too," the governor rejoined, "and among the loved and the hopeful, there lie many votes!"

Grimes and his ten committee members heard Twinkles in complete silence and with profound respect. For two hours, she described her long struggle to provide the best of teaching to the boys and girls of her impoverished county. She told about the isolated camps clustered in deep valleys far from the county seat, the advantages the governor's road program was bringing, the scattered schools, the underpaid and overworked teachers, the slender libraries and laboratories, the labors of mission teachers to uplift and inspire, and finally, the shockingly high dropout rate that had produced an illiteracy level of nearly a third. She concluded with, "My husband and I have devoted a lifetime to mountain youths and to their parents. We have taken advantage of every state and federal program to improve the schools upon which their future depends—and the federal efforts, in particular, have often been quite generous. And we have dipped into our modest personal resources on countless occasions when public funds have fallen short. For many years as superintendent, I have lived and breathed and wept with the unmet needs of mountain students—and it has been a losing battle! Illiteracy reigns in unnumbered families. Chilly drafts blow through dilapidated classrooms. Teachers live in poverty and bitterness, unable to buy the simplest amenities for their families. Untaught and poorly taught thousands drift away to other cities, to a life they have been in no way prepared to live."

Then, her voice thick with emotion, she closed her testimony with, "The Educational Foundation Law will mean, in time, a good solid education for every boy and girl—everywhere in the state! It will mean, eventually, an end to ignorance, dependency and relief—everywhere in the state! It will mean a new era of progress, prosperity and well-being everywhere in the state! The dollar cost will be trifling compared to the results it will achieve. Pass it, gentlemen, pass it, and earn the everlasting gratitude of all who love our commonwealth!"

The committee was fulsome in its praise, and the members encircled her to shake her hand and express gratitude for her presentation. And they reported the bill favorably, and the assembly passed the ninety-three-page law with only seven "Nays." They then proceeded to frighten Doc within an inch of his life with a wholly unexpected development.

After all, dollar costs too were involved, millions of dollars a year to begin with and scores of millions a year as the program gathered momentum. And the same legislators had to find the millions or leave the brave promises unfulfilled and 26,000 angry teachers breathing down their necks. So, to Doc's vast chagrin, twenty-two house members introduced a bill to raise $20,000,000 annually with a levy of the kind he had once so foolishly advanced—a severance tax on minerals taken out of the state's hills and plains.

Their arguments were impressive, as Doc's had been twenty years before. Gas and oil wells flowed in the broad river valleys to the west. Giant quarries in the green hills shook with explosions and sent trainloads of talc and limestone to many markets. At Iron Gate Gap, where three states joined in a tangle of laurel and oak and plunging waterfalls, hundreds of thousands of tons of iron ore were dynamited from the hills each year. There were clays for bricks and porcelains, sand and gravel for construction, mica, fluor spar and lead. All these would be taxed in their prosperity, as would coal in its depression. The tax would apply at 3 percent of market value, and its proponents argued that every ton or barrel should leave the cost of a few bricks behind for a new schoolhouse—two hundred million new bricks a year. As for coal, it was cyclical and far from dead, and the economists who advised the legislators said it would revive and boom again in a few years. In the days of his youth, these arguments had sounded on Doc's own tongue, but that was in other years and circumstances, and now he found them bitter as gall. And as for Jack Weston, the leader of the severance tax bloc, he was "an obnoxious little jerk."

Indeed, the coal industry was far from dead, and it roused itself from New York and Pittsburgh to the remotest tipples at Flax Patch and Dankey to fight Weston's legislation. Its lobbyists joined forces with whole cohorts from oil, gas and quarries and from the iron, rail, bargeline and electric power interests. They mustered hosts of their employees, wholesalers, retail merchants, bankers, and county and municipal politicians. Doc himself brought down a sturdy delegation to wave a huge sign that begged "Don't slaughter Slaughter County—kill the severance tax instead!"

The lobbyists brought money too for expensive dinners and whiskey and women for the solons, and gifts for their reelection funds—and to help finance Jerry Grimes' campaign for governor—in the event he proved himself to be a true friend of business. Doc and Twinkles put $10,000 into the "kitty," and Grimes yielded and decided to support Joe Carr's alternative proposal, a 4 percent general retail sales tax on everything from beans and aspirin to coffins. Forbes preferred the severance tax as incomparably more just and equitable, but could see no hope of electing a friendly governor in the 1956 election if the vast power of the mineral lobbies opposed him. The governor's capitulation allowed the legislature to finance the grand new era with a tax on everything a citizen used—as Jerry Grimes phrased it—"from erection to resurrection, from womb to tomb!"

There were loopholes, though. Doc and Joe Carr and a few leaders of the state coal association conferred and came up with a brief amendment to the new revenue act. It was designed, according to its preamble, to assure that the depressed coal industry was not placed at a disadvantage in national markets by having to shoulder "unreasonable and undue burdens." It exempted from the sales tax all machinery, explosives, tools and general supplies used in "the mining process." Jack Weston denounced the proposal as an outrage and disgrace, but it was adopted, and Doc and the other lobbyists who had hurried to the capital vanished from the marble halls.

When the legislature adjourned a week later in mid-March, Doc and Twinkles looked back on it and on their lobbying efforts with satisfaction. A new two-cent levy per gallon of gasoline would get a wave of rural road construction going, with several much-needed projects in Slaughter County. The school law meant more of everything for Twinkles to dispense—more of everything from chalk to salaries. Their affinity with the governor's chosen man was now very close, indeed, and as a final measure of good fortune, the thick black ledges of coal that still lay in their lands could be mined as of old without a lot of new taxes to nibble a body to death.

And after all, the new levies were eminently fair. Good citizenship required everyone to pay at least some taxes to support his government, otherwise he would have no personal stake in it, and now all alike, from the humblest pensioner to the proudest magnate, would pay as he consumed—and be much the better citizen for it, too.

CHAPTER

17

The 1950s were lean times in the hills, but, ironically, the grinding depression caused the Bonhams and their political machine to wax ever more fat and powerful. The same conditions that brought grief to so many mountaineers enhanced the Bonham position at every turn.

Within four years after the Educational Foundation Law was passed, the amount of money spent by the state for its public schools more than doubled. Millions of dollars poured into the belt of Appalachian coal counties in a spirited effort to make their classrooms equal in quality to those in the cities and in those fabulous limestone-rich agricultural counties where the farms stretched lush and verdant around pillared mansions. And Doc and Twinkles used the money skillfully and ruthlessly to elect and reelect board members who would do their bidding and to discard and crush those who questioned or sought to obstruct. Then, their power base buttressed and secured, they used the new funds to improve the schools in accordance with the legislative mandate.

A team came up from the state department of education and assisted Twinkles to survey the county's needs for buildings and to develop a "comprehensive plan." It was agreed that nine new elementary and four high schools were needed, and that the rickety structures that had housed so many decades of pupils should be abandoned and demolished.

Rex Ballard had never wavered in his loyalty to the man whose scalpel had saved the life of his son, and consequently many other favors and advantages had come his way. Young Ballards taught school and drove school buses, and Kittle Head Jake's girl, Mable, was principal at Viper Creek. Once when Jake himself was indicted for owning and operating a moonshine still, Doc pulled some wires with the U.S. District Attorney and saved the old man from the penitentiary. Doc and Twinkles saw to it that when Rex Ballard promised a man a job on the road crew or as a school janitor, the job came through. Long ago, the oft-beaten Republican leaders had read Ballard out of the party as a turncoat and Judas, so in 1949 he led nearly a score of his kin into the courthouse and switched their formal allegiance and registration to the Democrats.

He was stooped now beneath seventy-five years, and the once-round paunch had vanished from beneath the bib of his overalls. A seven-acre stretch of bottom land lay near his home, and Doc and Twinkles declared it to be ideally suited for the Viper Creek Elementary School—the first to be built under the foundation law. Old Rex agreed without reservation—he said he had always hoped to see a real fine school on that land someday. It would be mighty good for the people to get the scholars out of the little drafty shacks in the hollers and gathered up in big gangs where a teacher could have a chance to do some good. "Yessirree," said Rex Ballard, "I held onto that land and kept houses from being built on it because it was such a natural place for a school!"

But how much, he inquired of Twinkles with his eyes narrowing cautiously, did she think the land was worth? "No matter how much a man wants to help out the schools, he can't afford to give his land away. A body has to have a fair price."

Twinkles and Doc had discussed this topic in advance and had an answer ready. They knew it had been used for growing corn or sorghum cane since their friend bought it forty years before. At that time, he had bought 250 acres for $1,550. Bottom land on Viper Creek, twenty miles from Blacksville and with a diminishing population, was worth about $100 to the acre—if a buyer could be found. Old Rex had reported to the county tax commissioner under oath that the whole farm was reasonably worth $5,000, and it was taxed accordingly. But in twenty years, the Ballards had never failed to deliver solid majorities in their precinct. Bob Ballard had served on Twinkles's board for two four-year terms and one term as a justice of the peace. As a member of the fiscal court, he always voted for Bonham policies. Now his son Chester was a member of the school board and was counted on to preserve Twinkles' control against the endless machinations of Republicans who would have liked to capture control of the schools, turn back the clock and end progress. Besides, Rex was old and a little extra money—money from a "capital outlay" fund the sales tax was steadily swelling—would assure his independence. So Twinkles' answer was a comfort to Rex and his narrowed eyes relaxed.

"There's not too much good land around here, Rex, and you've held this tract a long time waiting for the county to provide this community with the kind of school it needs. You've got a lot of land, but the part we want is the very heart of your farm. So I'm willing to ask the Board to pay you a thousand dollars an acre—seven thousand dollars altogether."

The school building rose where Old Rex's plow mule had scratched long furrows for the corn planter—a low L-shaped, red-brick affair with absolutely no claim to architectural distinction, but with an auditorium, gymnasium, lunchroom, kitchen, library, science lab, nine classrooms, and a small office for the principal, Old Rex's grandson, Bob. People drove out from all parts of the county to see the modern marvel, to commend Twinkles for her achievement in building it, and to urge that similar facilities be provided for their own communities. And Twinkles and Doc heard their requests and promised to do their best. As the superintendent told a delegation from Crane Creek, "The people are demanding modern, consolidated schools, and when the people speak, we in this office hear no other voice!"

Doc and Twinkles did not quite meet their planned schedule of a new consolidated elementary or high school each year, but 1960 found them with two completed and two more a-building. The governor recommended Ace Engineering Company—a firm in which he owned a few shares of stock—as being particularly adept at designing schoolhouses, and it took on Slaughter County's architectural tasks. A bland sameness characterized its works, but no one complained about the aesthetics. The buildings were spacious and clean, airy and well lit, and each had its gym and sports field, so nothing more could be desired. Invariably, when a building was completed, grateful parents spread a banquet in the new cafeteria and extolled the superintendent and her husband for the dedication and work that made the new symbol of educational progress a reality. And, also invariably, Twinkles replied in a short speech in which no mention was made of Governor Forbes' long struggle for the legislation and the revenue to implement it. Instead, she spoke of Slaughter as the best county in the state, of the pure Anglo-Saxon blood of mountain children, and how she deemed it an immense honor to work—even at a low salary and for long, wearisome hours—for such a place and people.

But salaries didn't stay as low as they had been. Twinkles was paid $6,000 a year when the county alone financed its schools, but her salary was doubled in 1955 after the first of the new funds arrived. And Tess was paid $11,000 as assistant superintendent. Then, as the new program fleshed out, a raft of other administrative posts were created, each with a desk and an ample paycheck. There was a director of transportation, a director of sports and athletics, a dietitian who was known as the director of lunchrooms and nutrition, a chief librarian, a coordinator of state and county programs, and a director of custodial operations and maintenance. Each of these posts was filled with a loyal ally of the Bonhams.

In 1956, Dwight Eisenhower reluctantly concluded that "private sector" jobs were never going to materialize for the hosts of ragged one-time miners who huddled in the nation's coalfields. The Department of Agriculture held immense stores of surplus foods which it could not sell, so it was decided to give the stuff away. Under the federal plan, meal, flour, meat, peanut butter, cheese, butter, dried milk and canned fruits would be delivered to the states for distribution to the needy. Governor Jerry Grimes moved with alacrity to accept

Washington's offer and turned to local officials to implement "on a fair and lawful basis a program of food relief to the poor."

It was about 3 o'clock in the afternoon, and Doc was relaxing after a day of seeing patients when the cheerful voice of "Duck Dingus," the governor's chief administrative aide, came over the telephone. After a few pleasantries, he outlined the federal food program as authorized by the White House, and said that Governor Grimes wanted to discuss some aspects of the matter with Doc.

Grimes' voice was resonant as a well-tuned fiddle. "Doc, you old dragon, what are you doing up there in your den? Devouring Republicans? Well, hell, you must be scarin' 'em out of the county at least, because the population keeps on goin' down!"

Doc agreed. "We've done pretty well within our limited means," he conceded, "and we've managed to get it, so a Republican finds it mighty hard to make a living up here unless he is sort of tamelike, and cooperates with us Democrats. We keep a few, though, mostly for seed, but they're what that lawyer son of mine calls 'Republicans by sufferance'."

The governor dissolved at this sally and vowed to incorporate the term in a speech he planned to make before the state Democratic Committee. In a more serious vein, Doc warned that Republicans were tricky and deceptive like an old bear that plays possum. "When you think he's dead, he comes back to life and swats you."

The governor said he needed help. He thought perhaps Doc and his friends in Slaughter County could do the state administration a great service, do much good for a lot of people and maybe get some political mileage for themselves in the process.

"The President has ordered the Department of Agriculture to ship food commodities to the state for distribution to the poor in the coal counties. They will be given to the state at no cost, but the state must see that they are distributed fairly to the people who need them—and in conformity with federal law. Absolutely no hanky-panky! Now, I don't want to set up a great big elaborate and costly state agency to pass out the commodities; I hope the counties can do that with the state serving simply as a kind of legal conduit to carry the shipments from the federal to local hands. What I'm wonderin' now, Doc, is just what you see as the best way to handle the job at the local level up there in your county."

Doc's mind ran rapidly over a number of possibilities, but the fiscal court offered the best way to get the job done. His nephew, Woodrow Bonham, was serving his fourth term as county judge and chairman of the court. The other members were the eight justices of the peace—three illiterates and five who could read passably well. Six of the JPs were his allies and had been elected with his help, though one of them was a Republican who represented a small district around the upper reaches of Eagle Creek. Bill Day and Lige Simpson were mavericks and unreliable. Doc thought the best system would allow the court to make up lists of eligibles and certify them to the state from month to month. Each JP would receive applications and compile a list in his district and submit it to the entire court. The court, as a whole, would strike or add names as justice required. The two unreliables could thus be circumvented, and credit for the relief dispensations could go where credit was due—to the farsighted men and women in the Bonham political organization who issued the eligibility vouchers. Food could be funneled to thousands of hungry mouths, and those stubborn holdouts who persisted in opposing Bonham candidates could be softened up with a wee bit of judiciously managed deprivation.

Doc explained his thoughts, and the advantages of his plan. The magistrates and county judge were ready and available, and by placing the job in their hands, the cost of setting up an entirely new office could be avoided. The JPs knew their districts in detail and could keep chiselers and deadbeats off the rolls. In cases of doubt, the full court by majority vote could assure fair hearings. The court could hire a competent man and a few helpers to store the food and hand it out to the people. There was a vacant warehouse at Blacksville that could be rented for storage. A single clerk could keep the necessary records. "By this means," he concluded, "costs could be kept down to a bearable level and fairness could be assured for everybody involved. And there'd be no reason why the federals ought not to be satisfied with the arrangement. After all, we're dealing with a Republican administration and Ike wouldn't like it a-tall if we fed the Democrats and let the Republicans go around with their guts growling."

This last observation delighted the governor again, and his big laugh came over the wire so joyously that Doc held the receiver away from his ear. The scheme, too, pleased Grimes, and he promised to discuss it with the attorney general. If he raised no legal objections, the governor would call County Judge Woodrow Bonham and propose the plan to him. When the court approved it, the first carloads of food would be dispatched by rail from Chicago and Des Moines.

The governor said he would suggest the same Plan to his friends in Kilgore, Devlin, Stoner, Croghan, and other coal counties. "If it works in Slaughter, it ought to work in the rest of the coal fields," Grimes allowed, and Doc assured him there would be no problems. "It will be helpful all around because strong, healthy, well-fed voters are easier to get to the polls." The governor thought the observation was unassailable and vowed to come to Noreco for a visit. "And, Doc," he added as an afterthought, "tell our friends on the fiscal court to stress the state side of this program and to play down the federal side of it. Stress that 'Eisen-hoover' caused the hard times and that state and county Democrats are providing the relief." Doc assured him the game would be played no other way.

That afternoon Doc called on Woodrow Bonham, and the two went for a long leisurely ride along narrow, winding State Highway 17, the outmoded ribbon of blacktop that wound like a writhing serpent from the state line at the head of Indian River westward to the last range of hills. They stopped and visited with some of the JPs, including "Sugar Bill" Day, who served the good people of District 5, and whose nickname was derived from a stretch he had once served in a federal pen for making moonshine and the piles of empty sugar sacks revenue officers had found at his still. They took him with them to the home of his colleague, "Stiller Lige" Simpson, who had suffered a similar misfortune at the hands of federal agents back in the twenties. The four of them stopped in a shady place by the roadside and talked about the governor's desire to get food to the people. They talked, too, about the practicalities of the situation and the qualifications of the man who would see to the actual distribution after eligibility was certified. Doc cautioned, "We don't want to get 'em in and then have some sourpuss at the warehouse make 'em mad. That would leave us in worse shape than if the stuff had never been sent here in the first place."

The wisdom of this observation was apparent and the four reflected a moment in silence. Then Doc thought of and suggested a man marvelously qualified for the job. He looked at Simpson and asked the one-time con about his son-in-law, Tink Preston. "He is a man everybody likes. He's not got an enemy in the county. He served a term on the school board a few years ago and knows his way around at the polls and in the courthouse. He has a family and could use the pay and is just a little bit of kin to me on my mother's side. He is a man we can all get along with, and I hope the court will offer him the job."

As he sat with his eyes closed waiting for Stiller Lige's reaction, Judge Bonham gave no hint that he and his uncle had already discussed Tink Preston's suitability as director of commodity foods distribution. Stiller Lige was the court's sole GOP member, and his conversion would smooth things in the future. They hoped to tame and capture him by this gambit, for Tink Preston was not only a son-in-law of Stiller Lige, he was also a nephew of Sugar Bill. And Sugar Bill had loaned his nephew a thousand dollars back when coal was booming, and there was money to be made in truck mines. Coal stopped booming and so did Tink and the debt had never been repaid. "The county could pay a pretty fair salary, and Tink could settle up some old debts that have worried him mightily for several years," Doc added as a cincher.

Both of the JPs were delighted with the suggestion, and when they stopped at Sugar Bill's place, he insisted that they come in for supper. Supper was corn pone, green beans, ham and coffee, and they ate in a spirit of goodwill that told Doc the county judge would have no further troubles with Sugar Bill. As Doc piled dark sourwood honey on a piece of corn bread and stuffed it into his mouth, he calculated that Sugar Bill could bring at least 35 votes into line and vote them for Bonham candidates in the next county election—and that election was only one year away. Those votes had nearly always been hostile in the past, and their capture was cause enough to evoke a bit of self-congratulation.

Tink Preston got the job at the next fiscal court meeting. His pay was $400 a month, and at the end of the first month, Sugar Bill collected a hundred-dollar payment on the long-delinquent loan. Stiller Lige was relieved of the troublesome burden of having to lend financial aid to a daughter and son-in-law and their six children. All eight JPs glowed with importance as they heard pleas for food and filled in and signed—or "marked"—the yellow food vouchers. Doc and Twinkles made calls that hastened or delayed a few requests as circumstances justified, and lines of ragged, self-conscious people were deeply grateful for the huge bags and boxes of food they carried away from Tink's warehouse. The director was so warm and outgoing and worked so hard to put people at ease that he became a veritable hero of the ragged wretches who lived by the free groceries. Soon Doc began to hear rumors that his protege had become a mighty popular man and would make a hell of a fine candidate for jailer or sheriff.

Within two years, half the people in Slaughter County held food vouchers, and a good many others were added unofficially. About once a month, Tink loaded the trunk of his Studebaker with a splendid assortment of food staples and a little later spread them on the huge table inside the screened back porch of Doc's house. Doc never once asked him to do it, but he didn't forbid it either, and the gifts were both delicious and wholesome. Doc allowed there was no point in buying groceries when they could be gotten free and besides, as he told Tink with overwhelming logic, "I'm about the only man who gets the stuff who pays any taxes to buy it in the first place. If the government is going to feed a pauper who hasn't worked a day in four or five years, it sure as hell ought to feed a taxpayer who works every day from nine to five thirty!"

Not everyone was happy, though. Merchants complained about their unsold groceries, and Doc promised to try to find some way to help them. But this promise was empty, and Doc knew it, for the eaters outnumbered the sellers and the latter would simply have to suffer.

Jerry Grimes brought another bit of long-overdue progress to the state when he persuaded the legislature to provide for "a model, humane system of probation and parole." When felons had shown evidence of rehabilitation, there was no earthly justification for keeping them in cells or on penal farms, he argued. They should, instead, be released under the supervision of a parole officer who could look in on them from time to time, help keep them away from sinister influ-

ences and steer them toward good citizenship. Doc saw much justice in this constructive philosophy and recommended his nephew and namesake, Tom B. Lacey, for the job. Tom B. was Mahala's son, a full-fledged graduate of Mountain State Teachers College and a splendid young man. He proved to be a good investigator and could sense both criminality and political disloyalty with a single sniff. His reports to the circuit judge could bring a man release and a return to his home or a trip to the cells of the reformatory. And an adverse report to the parole board could bring an end to freedom already granted.

Tom B. was a good man to know, and Doc and Twinkles knew him, a circumstance that brought many a worried supplicant to their doors. Doc and Twinkles tended to be merciful so that after juries had returned verdicts and sentences had been typed into massive judgment books, recommendations often went up to spell freedom and another chance. They had to be and were discreet, for they could only advise the men who advised the court. But His Honor was Doc's old friend, Daniel Boone Dickson, and he knew the workings of the game and all its nuances. Besides, he was a passable circuit judge and had been especially helpful to Jesse J., and he and Doc had already discussed the vacancy on the state's supreme court which would occur in 1960.

Judge David Day had served in that office for three eight-year terms, representing twenty counties with an integrity and dignity that made him unbeatable at the polls. But a combination of age and failing eyesight had brought a mid-term announcement that he would not seek reelection. Doc promptly took Daniel Boone to Washington for a conference with Big Red and Carl, and to the state capital for a talk with Jerry Grimes. Doc calculated that with a clean sweep in Slaughter County and the votes the state organization and his own connections could line up elsewhere, Judge Dickson could be built into a winner. And Doc craved a friendly, dependable and understanding judge on the state's court of last resort. From time to time, voters proved rebellious, and margins of victory were slim, and occasionally there was the bitterness of defeat. In such situations, election contests in the courts could prove marvelously effective in weeding out troublemakers and ingrates.

There were a dozen statutory grounds for which a school board member could be removed from office. There were nearly as many "corrupt practices" which could bar a winning candidate from claiming his office in the first place. But to debar or remove a Bonham adversary required friendly courts and reasonable judges. Doc and Twinkles believed they could capture both circuit and appellate benches in 1960. In that year, Daniel Boone could be quietly elevated to the state's supreme court, and onto the circuit bench they could then propel their own flesh, blood and name, Attorney Jesse Jackson Bonham.

Probations and paroles proved to be excellent weapons in the political arsenal. Men and women, who were too proud to ask his help for themselves, swallowed their pride and sought it unabashedly when some ill-advised act brought a son or daughter within the shadow of the state pen. The device dovetailed perfectly into the burgeoning mechanism that fed and hired, planned, built and maintained so much of the county's life. The apparatus of relief was so ubiquitous that when a flash flood lashed Indian Valley in 1958 and ravaged the wretched homes of several thousand people, the American Red Cross turned with perfect aplomb to that same organization. Nothing could have been more natural than the call that came to the superintendent of schools from New York. The gentleman expressed the concern of the Red Cross and pledged its assistance to abate the suffering. He had learned about Mrs. Bonham from someone at the governor's office and so knew that she was beloved by the people, had served them more than two decades, was devoted to their service and worked selflessly to see that while money was not wasted, suffering people were not turned away unaided. The directors were especially delighted to find a local personage of such integrity and so strategically placed through whose hands and heart they could work. So $175,000 worth of desperately needed supplies were handed out—by employees of the school board. And practically every recipient assumed that Dr. Tom Bonham and his wife had induced the vast relief agency to concern itself with the stricken little county so far down in the hills, and the expressions of gratitude were directed to them rather than to the numberless donors whose generosity made the dispensations possible.

The fifties brought a steady extension of Doc's influence into every aspect of the private sector of the county's economy, also. The coal men looked to him as their shield because of his close ties to the congressman and both of the senators, and his strong effort in the fight to ward off a severance tax. The UMW men in the shrunken locals still came to him for counsel, which he freely gave.

Thirty-three supervisory workers in a brand-new eco-

nomic security building in Blacksville smiled their appreciation when they encountered him on the street. Every official
in the county courthouse acknowledged that the "Bonham
vote" had boosted them into office or had discouraged expensive and wearying challenges. Every man who worked
for the state department of highways had been hired after
Doc signed his application—certifying as a private and dis-
interested citizen that he knew the applicant to be a man of
"good character and integrity, and qualified for the position
sought." Scores of convicted felons knew the nightly joys of
conjugal love instead of the stifling horror of a prison cell
because of a good word from Tom Bonham.

Preachers whose dwindling congregations threatened
them with starvation stayed on and ate—because of occasional gifts from Doc who, though no churchgoer himself,
was nonetheless deemed a man of religion, "a God-inspired
man." The game warden who hunted the idle men who hunted
the rabbits and squirrels, the mine inspectors, the doctor and
nurse in the health department and the sanitarian who made
a spectacularly unsuccessful effort to enforce sanitation laws,
even old Joe Morley, the dog warden, sent Dr. and Mrs.
Bonham Yuletide greetings each December and used every
other opportunity to appear thankful and loyal. And most
thankful and loyal of all were the thirteen thousand men,
women, and children who drew state welfare checks each
month and ate welfare grub each day. The highly coveted
federal patronage had long since passed into Doc's care and
two-thirds of the county's thirty-three postmasters had been
appointed after Doc recommended them to Carl, Big Red and
Sam Mitchell. And they, in turn, called their qualifications to

the attention of the White House. In 1957, five of Doc's friends moved onto the board of directors of the county's soil conservation district and subsequently all projects to build dams, straighten and dredge creeks, dig farm ponds, reforest hills and drain swamps were approved a mite faster if farmers first mentioned the applications to the party's county chairman and induced him to nudge the men in the conservation office at Blacksville.

But Doc's wealth and sway did not bring him unalloyed happiness. The same interval that brought almost total consolidation of his power brought problems that nagged like daggers in his flesh.

In the first place, he turned fifty-five in 1950, and the robust good health of youth never survives such a milestone. Doc had always possessed tireless energy and a good appetite, and when he set his head upon the pillow, he was capable of sleep and restoration. And he was always a weight watcher, carefully limiting his food to his needs. These qualities preserved his appetite for feminine flesh so that Twinkles was grateful she was five years younger than he. But with the 1950s, came an inevitable slowing down, and with it, profound self-doubts.

At first he paid little attention to the white hairs that dotted the black growth above his ears, and used nail scissors to snip them out. But one morning, when he prepared to shave, he was quite astonished to observe that his temples were gray, indeed, almost white. And when he studied it closer, the face that peered back at him was different, a face that had aged and altered while the brain behind it was engrossed with other things.

The forehead had crept up and back and the hair had thinned. Small pouches hung beneath the eyes where once the flesh had lain smooth and firm. Lines creased the forehead and the flesh beneath the chin was elongated into a kind of empty wattle pouch. When he stepped onto the scales, the needle pointed to its accustomed place, but his middle was enlarged into an unsightly sag beneath a sunken chest and flabby arms. White hairs bristled along the tops of his shoulders and in a tuft at the base of his neck. It was a demoralizing spectacle and a distasteful one.

He put on a new suit that morning and dragged at his belly to suck it within its old confines, but he left the bathroom a shaken man.

And the old fire that moved him to seek his wife every night subsided with, or because of, the realization that he was growing old. When he made love to the still-winsome woman with whom he had shared so much, he sometimes had to imagine her to be someone else—someone young and salacious—before he could bring himself to the act at all. And the bouts with young whores he sometimes encountered on political or business forays to the state capital or some other city were approached with trepidation and lessening frequency. As he confessed to his old confidant, Joe Carr, "I'm like an old hog rifle: I shoot hard but load slow."

The demoralization that came with age and creaking joints brought concern for another matter: succession. Twinkles would have to retire as superintendent at sixty-five. State law required it, and in the meantime, Tess had to learn all the ropes and develop the capacity to hold her mother's organization together, refine it further and steadily enlarge it as opportunities permitted. He perceived that in politics, as in biology, when one ceases to grow, he begins to die. And Jesse Jackson, now balding and sagging in an unfortunate manner, must be eased into that judgeship with reins of power held securely and wielded discreetly. Could such a division of power between brother and sister be made to last or would they fall into feuds between themselves and dissipate the power and influence their parents had toiled to secure for them, and which by right ought to be directed only against Republicans, and against ingrates and rebels within their own party? Could they be trusted to choose and support the right men in the all-important gubernatorial races and in the battles certain to ensue when Carl and Big Red died or retired? Doc worried much about such matters as John Fitzgerald Kennedy ushered in a new era for the people who ran things in Slaughter County.

CHAPTER
18

From the beginning, Doc didn't like John Kennedy one whit. He was too young and stylishly dressed, too self-confident and urbane. Besides, he was a city man and Doc instinctively distrusted the cities with their teeming blacks and pushing, obstreperous minorities demanding power and recognition. Doc didn't like Kennedy's religion, either, because the church could influence men sometimes even beyond the reach of the state, or party or money, and such influence, being alien to Doc's background and experience, appeared sinister and fearsome.

He felt much more comfortable with Lyndon Johnson, the tall homey Texan who was Senate Majority Leader, and he shared Carl and Big Red's desire that the state's delegation to the Democratic convention go instructed to vote for LBJ. Doc didn't care about participating in the convention personally—for years he had refused to serve as a delegate, though his interest in electing those who did serve was always keen—but in 1960 he arranged for Jesse Jackson to head the Sixth District delegation. It would be a fine experience for the judicial candidate and give him an opportunity to meet other up-and-coming Democrats from across the country. The state convention was a cut-and-dried affair which the governor dominated throughout, and at Sam Mitchell's personal request, Tessie B. Long was named as a delegate also. He told the delegate selection committee that "no young person in the state has demonstrated a keener concern for public affairs, especially in the field of education. I guess she comes by it naturally from her mother who has spent a quarter of a century in devoted service to mountain people."

Naturally, Doc and Twinkles were pleased to have both their children participate in the selection of their party's standard-bearer, and they watched the proceedings on television for many hours in quest of an occasional glimpse of them when the camera poked along the rows of delegates. Several times they came into view for a few seconds, Jesse J. bland and attentive, his sister alert, commanding and generally surrounded by admiring listeners. Beautifully dressed, Old John-of-All's great-great-great-granddaughter stood out as one of the loveliest spectacles on the convention floor, and her parents noted that the television crews seemed to share their predilection. But 1960 was not LBJ's year.

Tess caught the drift of the wind early and at a caucus made an impassioned plea that the delegation swing its support to Kennedy. This was not done, but her action was noted by Kennedy staffers. After the ticket was put together and party unity restored, a JFK aide called to express the nominee's gratitude and to say that as a result of his electioneering in the West Virginia primary, Senator Kennedy "feels an especial concern for Appalachian mountain people." When she came home and told about all that had happened, both of her parents were proud of her, but Doc hedged a little with the reservation that he was afraid Kennedy was a young smart aleck. Nevertheless, with all his strengths and shortcomings, Kennedy moved into the White House the next January and Carl moved up in seniority on committees that dealt with public works and appropriations. In the same month, Doc was able to bring good news to his own household and to his three friends in Washington by pointing out that long-quiescent Bonham Coal and Timber Company had begun stirring to life once more. Whether the new President's pledge to "get the country moving again" had anything to do with the occurrence was uncertain, but in any event, the coal market began to perk up and coal brokers took rooms in Blacksville's little Top Hat Motel.

But as the revival of the market after Pearl Harbor brought forms drastically different from those of the industry when it was new, so the revival of 1961 was unlike those of earlier days. Jay and Roy Carson came down from Detroit to get into the strip-mining business and made their way to the huge stone house above Noreco. They were Canadians who brokered coal for steel and utility companies, and as the economy began to expand with the arrival of the new decade, they decided there was more money to be made in mining the fuel than in finding markets for someone else's output. They drove down to Blacksville in Jay's milk-white Lincoln Continental and stopped at the Slaughter County Bank and Trust Company to inquire about coal lands they might be able to lease. Ticky Charlie listened, his left eye and cheek twitching in a manner that thoroughly disconcerted his callers. But their inquiry was fruitful because he called his uncle, and within an hour, they were enjoying a cool glass of iced water and prime bourbon on Doc's deep shaded porch.

They could see the tottering tipple with its rusty machinery and huge slate dump and listened appreciatively as Doc described his company's activities from 1942 to 1948. In those six years, nearly two million tons had come out of the hills, tons of sparkling carbon that was rich in energy and nearly free of sulfur. Doc pointed to the ridges that wound up Finn's Fork and, from the mouth of that tributary, up Indian River a mile above the little cluster of buildings on the campus of Indian River Institute.

"The nearer coal has been mined out of the center of the hill," he explained, "except for a barrier pillar about a hundred feet wide at the outcrop, but the heads of the hollows have never been touched and there are millions of tons there still to be mined." The Canadians sat together in a wide wicker swing suspended from the ceiling and looked across the valley. The hills had been logged intensively during the war for saw timber and mine props, but a new growth of hickory, oak, gum, and tulip trees had sprung up, cloaking the cleared fields and spreading to fill the gaps left where the old giants had come down. Even the gray slate heap had green tufts sticking out of it where pines and sycamores had put down roots in the decomposing shale. The sun was setting in a gap where Old John-of-All had once paused to look down into the valley where the wandering and long-forgotten T. Finn had left his name. It lit up the crags and pinnacles on Stone Coal Ridge and Great Laurel Mountain, and pointed a few last glinting rays into the sinuous hollows of Bonham's Branch, leaving in gray-blue shadow the valley down which Isham had led his family and his slaves so long ago. Now a train whistle blew from the same depths as a locomotive made up

a drag for the wearisome haul to Detroit or Chicago. It was a wild scene, a land far more pregnant with vitality than the cooler valleys and hills of Canada, and the brothers marveled that the marks of so much violence could have healed so much in a mere dozen years.

The track that curved around the twisting hill from the sagging tipple to the collapsed portal was brown with rust and the sixty two-ton steel cars that stood upon it had moved not an inch in the last decade. Doc told how during the war electric motor cars had kept the trains of heaped-up cars rattling out of the hills around the clock. "Three shifts a day in 1944," he reminisced. "Walter Martin was the best mine superintendent I ever saw. Put safety first all the time and got good steady work out of his men. He really made money for me and my company back in those days." Doc's eyes took on a dreamy luster as he remembered so many things; then, a little wistfully, "He went out of here with 20,000 other people in the fifties. He's in Cleveland now, a night watchman in a warehouse—a mighty sad comedown for a first-rate mining man."

The Carsons shook their heads and Ray said, "That kind of mining is just about a thing of the past; it's just simply out of date and too costly. Still a body can't help but feel sorry for the miners who don't know any other line of work and get dropped when the changeover comes." The sun dropped behind the tall cliff called David and Herod's Rock on the head of Dead Man Creek and instantly there was a slight cooling of the summery temperature. Jay gestured toward the old mine works. "What we have in mind, Doctor, is not deep mines. They're too expensive and too slow to start up. We plan to strip. In those territories that were mined during the war, we would face up a terrace on the outside of the hill and auger the outcrop. That way, we could recover for you nearly all the coal that your foreman and his workhands just couldn't get. Then, where no mining has already been done, we would do contour strip mining. I guess we could highwall those ridges to sixty feet and make a bench eighty to a hundred feet wide—maybe a hundred and twenty-five. Then we could auger it, too. By doing that on both sides of the hill, we can just about get the whole seam." His eyes swept to the crags.

"Now that high seam, the old Finn vein sixty or seventy feet from the top, has never been touched. It's too near the crest to be deep mined anyway. In that situation, we would simply take off the whole overburden and lift out the coal with shovels and conveyors. This is the way to get coal nowadays—a few men, some machines and trucks, low overhead and a good quick profit. Even in today's market, and as slow as things are, we could pay you a royalty of thirty-five cents a ton, and there is still a fortune waiting in those old hills. We can all make a good thing out of it. TVA or some of the other utilities will take the coal, but they will insist on holding the price down. Stripping and augering are the only way the coal can be mined at a competitive price against oil and the atom. If we don't strip, oil and atomic plants will be built and the coal will lie here in the hills of Slaughter County forever, doing you and the rest of the people no good whatever."

He fell silent and Doc pondered what he had heard. He visualized the change that the proposal would bring to the hills—deep and wide gashes blasted and gouged along the steep slopes at the coal veins, the tops of the ridges removed entirely, the vast amounts of rubble tumbled down the hills to crush and bury trees, bushes, ferns and wild flowers. "It would ruin the land," he said. "The creeks would fill up with mud; not a water hole would be left for fish. It would totally destroy everything!" He shook his head. "It would drive the rest of the people out too, I guess." He remembered the tradition of Margaret Strother Bonham's oft-repeated admonition: "Take good care of the land and the land will take good care of you."

"Not necessarily, Doctor," Jay Carson interposed. "We would sow grass on the flats and spoil banks and you will be surprised how much of it will grow. In another twenty years the trees will start coming back. It will look bald at the beginning, but as you doctors know so well, time heals even the deepest cuts and bruises."

Doc said he would think it over, and the Carsons went back to Blacksville. Doc called Jesse J. and Tess, and they came out for a conference. Twinkles was worried about what such a mine would do to the view from their front porch, but her objections were feeble. As Jesse J. put it, "It would be downright criminal to leave the coal in the ground just to hold up the hill and make a pretty view when somebody is willing to pay thirty-five cents a ton for it." Tess agreed emphatically, but Doc was not willing to part with his treasure for a mere royalty. He wanted in on the operation itself, with a slice of the profits from the sales.

Mountain Movers, Inc., was formed two weeks later, with the Carsons holding half the stock and the rest held by Doc and Twinkles and their two aspiring offspring. Bonham Coal and Timber leased its holdings to the new firm, and the stockholders in Washington were pleased with the arrangements and wondered when the first dividend checks might be paid. Doc calculated it would be three or four months, and Carl could not restrain his enthusiasm. "Public service is not very profitable," he reminded them, "and a little bit of extra cash would really warm my heart!"

The first of the bulldozers arrived a month later, then air compressors and a drilling machine. The new company set the dozers to work on the Handshoe Branch of Finns Fork, and the crash and snap of toppling timber resounded like the crackle of musketry all the way to Noreco. Two weeks later, the immense auger sent its 72-inch bits slamming into the naked black face of the coal seam. A fleet of trucks, their engines moaning to restrain thirty-ton loads on the steep, narrow haulroads, started the fuel on its way to the Tennessee Valley Authority's gigantic furnaces.

For its part, Bonham Coal and Timber put a crew to work restoring the rotted coal dock and sliding new black oak ties under the rusty railroad spur. New shaker screens and sizing machinery replaced the weathered junk that had worked so faithfully for the Great Arsenal of Democracy. It all cost $70,000, and Doc advanced the money as a loan, but the corporation collected twenty cents on each ton loaded across its facilities, and the first trainload that went clanking down Indian River left $300 in the corporate till. Royalties on the coal came to another $470, and when Doc telephoned the news to the solons they were jubilant. "For a company that has lain dead for twelve years, old Bonham Coal and Timber is showing a hell of a lot of life," Doc told his henchmen as they sat with glasses of bourbon in Big Red's office for a conference call.

"Coal is like Lazarus, doctor," Sam Mitchell boomed. "When it's dead as hell, it comes back to life. The world can't live without coal!" Doc clucked his agreement, and the operation took its name from the congressman's remark. The five miles of blasting and dozing that flayed and decapitated the hills along Finn's Fork was called Lazarus Mine No. 1. As the slopes sank beneath twenty feet of "outspoil" (mud, shattered rocks and slabs of ashen-gray slate) and the creek ran thick with silt, it was apparent that this Lazarus, at least, would rise no more.

Helen Boyd's schools had survived her demise of old age in 1950, and Doc was one of hundreds of former students who were present at her funeral at the Knob Fork School. The corporation she had set up found Naomi Howard to preside as its chairman, and the Knob Fork and Indian River institutes took on new life. She, too, was an indefatigable fund-raiser and benefited from the youthfulness of a mere thirty-three years. She brought charm and good looks and a Bryn Mawr education to the stultification and exhaustion of the coal country, found new teachers, raised salaries, improved buildings, widened curricula and began talking of "a new era of outreach and uplift." A childless multimillionaire in Manhattan yielded to her blandishments and doubled the endowment fund so that some new scholarships began bringing additional children in from the remote hinterlands along the roadless upper stretches of Big Laurel Ridge where Twinkles' buses could never penetrate.

Neither Doc nor Twinkles took kindly to this new round of activities. For years, Twinkles had thought of the institutes as competitors—educational interlopers whose time had passed and should now have the good grace to die. She grumbled that the public schools were so strengthened by the Educational Foundation Act that such "charity schools" were anachronisms. Where once they were welcomed as volunteers lifting part of the burden from impoverished public schools, they were changed by time into challengers. Doc and Twinkles were comfortable with teachers spawned in Slaughter County hollows and educated at Mountain State, and they suspected that the people at the institutes with their degrees from distant universities held all of them in secret derision. Certain it was that outsiders failed to esteem the superintendent of schools and her husband as highly and as openly as their money and positions merited.

Hugh Cooper followed Naomi Howard to Slaughter County, giving up a brief professorship at UCLA to do so. He held a Ph.D. in botany and took a brutal salary cut to live in the midst of Appalachia's ancient woodland. He dreamed of updating E. Lucy Braun's great treatise on the deciduous forest of eastern North America and brought impeccable qualifications to the principal's office on Indian River. Within a year, he had organized courses and seminars dealing with the fabulous variety of flora. Over and over he told students, "Learn all you can about the world, but begin with the hills and trees you've lived with all your life!"

Within six months after the arrival of the Carson brothers, a half-dozen other stripping companies were at work, the vast splotches of rock and mud lacing the face of the county like some gigantic pox. There was some muted grumbling elsewhere, but the reaction at the two little mission schools was outraged and, in Doc's opinion, outrageous.

Its first manifestation took the form of a letter to the editor of the *Herald-Courier*, the state's biggest newspaper. A half million subscribers read Hugh Cooper's notice that strip mining had suddenly swept into the hills and was ruining entire mountain ranges. He described the "dismembered hills and obliterated forests left in the wake of an industrial scourge," and predicted that rains would choke the streams with mud from the spoil banks and cause widespread and deadly floods. The coalfields were so extensive, he declared, that stripping might well ravage a half-dozen counties at the headwaters of the state's most important river. He castigated strippers as men who would destroy their own country for lucre. "Hitler could have visited no worse destruction on Indian Valley if he had won the war!" he concluded.

Doc was furious, and his wrath grew to boundless dimensions when classes were organized on "Our Appalachian Environment" in which the ill effects of strip mining were emphasized. Cooper, Naomi Howard, and some other teachers invited people to public meetings where the stripping was protested and a petition asking that such mining be stopped was mailed to the governor. Jerry Grimes was not about to get into a fight with the Bonham tribe over so small a detail as a few expiring mountains and promptly forgot the matter. The editor of the *Herald-Courier* did not, however, and within a few weeks the Sunday magazine section described the stripping in horrifying detail and illustrated the story with more than a dozen large color photographs. One of them showed Naomi Howard on a spoil bank, her beautiful face contrasting strangely with the hideous backdrop, and quoted her as saying, "In the mountains Coal and Poverty have always been linked together. If it is not stopped, stripping will assure that destruction will always go hand in hand with the other two."

There was a flurry of other letters to the editor, a dozen or more from all over the state. State Representative Jack Weston called for an investigation which the governor said was unnecessary and would cost too much. The matter was soon forgotten, and the bulldozers and lurching powershovels continued their inexorable progress from hill to hill. Doc's household profited nicely, and on December 20, a Christmas dividend was declared and checks for $20,000 were mailed to Senators Carl Rutherford and Richard Brady and Congressman Samuel P. Mitchell. But not one of them forgot the "troublemakers" whose complaints had set off the minor tempest in the first place, and Doc's old alma mater soon found itself under as much pressure as the trees that daily collapsed beneath the treads of his Caterpillars. "We'll teach those damned meddlers a lesson," Doc swore to Twinkles. "They'll learn that in Slaughter County people put coal mining ahead of a little bit of scenery."

Doc called his co-partners in Washington and enlisted their aid in a matter he was about to take up with Governor Jerry Grimes and the state superintendent of schools, "Happy Dan" Toler. He wanted the state department of education to investigate the institutes, find their standards in teaching and physical plant inadequate under state standards for private schools, and cancel their authority to operate. Doc took Jesse J. and Twinkles to see Happy Dan and assured him, "Why those crummy buildings are decrepit old firetraps, and the teachers are a bunch of socialists and general failures who couldn't make it at home and are now preying on mountain people for a living."

Twinkles agreed and said most county school administrators shared her opinion that such institutes were obsolete and should be closed. Dan remembered that he had carried Slaughter County by 4,800 votes and was not about to argue the point. Besides, he, too, had once been a superintendent in a rural county and felt a deep distaste of his own for educational interlopers.

In fact, his nickname grew out of those earlier years and an incident that happened one evening when he went to a tiny high school to hand diplomas to the twenty graduates. He had drunk too much Jack Daniels Sour Mash Whiskey, and the climax of his speech brought his downfall. He was emphasizing the advantages of education, with his voice a bit thick and a slight lurch to his gait. "Education has made me happy!" he shouted. "Education will make you happy." He leaned forward, his hands on his knees, then suddenly straightening, "Education will make the whole world happy—" The last effort was accompanied by a violent wave of his arms and a half-pint whiskey flask catapulted out of an inner coat pocket onto the black-robed lap of the startled valedictorian.

The voters laughed and forgave him for the episode but never forgot it. His opponent in the race for state superintendent dredged up the incident and throughout the campaign

called him "Little Half-Pint," but Dan won anyway and reveled in the task of spending the biggest school budget in the
state's history—and far more money than was appropriated
to any other agency. So it came about that in March, a team
of "quality evaluators" arrived at the institutes to study their
performance. In the past, such surveys had produced high
marks and letters of commendation, but this year things were
different. In May, a letter took note of numerous "grave shortcomings" and gave notice that the schools Helen Boyd had
founded were both superfluous and "qualitatively insuffi-
cient," and would have to terminate all educational functions
with the end of the current term. There was a considerable
little firestorm of protest against the "bureaucratic decree,"
and much of it was directed against Doc and Twinkles, but
they sat tight and ignored the hubbub. "When that rat's nest
has been cleaned out, the rats will soon be forgotten," Joe
Carr counseled.

Hugh Cooper and Naomi Howard tried one last desperate gamble to save matters for the twenty-one teachers to
whom the institutes were both a home and a cherished calling. They flew to Vermont and visited a nursing home where
a hundred men and women dwelt in the pain and futility of
old age. And a week later, June Markham laid on Doc's desk
a letter that startled him as soon as he saw the handwriting
across the envelope. Infirmity had cramped the letters, but
the marks of Rose Quilan's pen portrayed a spirit that was
still strong and full of remembrance.

*"My Dear Dr. Bonham, I am nearly ninety now, and for
five years have been confined to my room by the illnesses of
age, but I have never ceased to remember my wonderful years*

amid the wild beauty of Indian Valley and the many people who treated me with so much kindness. And of all the hundreds of students it has been my pleasure to know and teach, young Thomas Jefferson Bonham is remembered most often and with most pride.

She went on to relate that she had kept up with his career in medicine and politics through the pages of the *Mountain Courier*, to which she had continued to subscribe nearly forty years after her departure from Slaughter County. She was pleased to learn that so many of the old fields had gone back to trees again, and noted that "those hills are best suited for woodland and naturally support a fantastically rich web of life." She had been profoundly disturbed to read about the ravages of strip mining, "a practice that kills land for its coal and is comparable to killing a man for the money in his pockets." She had been told that landslides from the immense mining cuts were likely to encroach on the Indian River campus and hoped this would not be permitted to occur. Then, to her dismay, she had learned that the institutes were to be closed. She was in touch with a number of people on the campuses—all of whom were bright, impressionable, honest and dedicated—and she sincerely hoped they would be allowed to stay in the hills and continue their work.

She appealed to her one-time student to use his immense influence to save them. "Your mother," she concluded, "once told me about your great-grandmother, who came up to the hills from Georgia. She loved the land and urged her children to care for it and preserve it. She said many times, 'Take good care of the land and the land will take good care of you.' That is the feeling so strongly held by the young men and women who now carry on the work Helen Boyd began. "They need your help in taking care of the land. They know that the strengths and joys of Appalachian mountain life, its aspirations and its very culture, all will perish if the land is battered into ruin by men who love money and power too much." She wished him many more healthy years of useful service and said good news from Slaughter County would do her more good than all the medicines her physicians could prescribe.

Doc sat at the battered oaken desk to which he had first come as a young man when the desk itself was still bright and new. Behind their steel-rimmed glasses, his eyes narrowed and smoldered as he reread the three pages. Then they wandered to the ancient leather medical valise, its corners worn through and the golden lettering of his name long since obliterated. His mind probed back through the years to his father dead in the dust, his days in Rose Quinlan's classroom, the years of toil, luck and cunning that had brought him wealth and power. Through a dirty window, he could see on a distant hill a long apron of mud stretching hundreds of feet below the ghastly bench of a strip mine. Then he grunted with distaste, and the surgeon's long fingers, now mottled with advancing age, crumpled the sheets into a tight little ball and flung them into a wastebasket.

He never answered Rose Quinlan's letter, and he never relented in his bitterness toward Hugh Cooper, Naomi Howard, and "their nosy buddies" at Indian River and Knob Fork. The institutes died under the decree of the department of education, but they would have perished in any event because the gifts that supported them dried up with magical speed in the face of an official report that their offerings were "so substandard as to pose a positive threat to the educational requirements of mountain boys and girls." The doors remained closed when a new school term began in September, and the teachers drifted away. Several of them, including Cooper and Howard, sought positions elsewhere in the mountains, but Twinkles called her colleagues in other counties and reported the shortcomings and ingratitude of the mission school people, and their applications were promptly rejected.

After fifty years, the joint venture launched by Helen Boyd, Delilah Free Bonham, and Rose Quinlan gave up the ghost. A mantle of decay fell over the wooden buildings, and packs of children from the camps vandalized them. One or two burned in spectacular midnight fires, and the directors who inherited the mess strove frantically to sell the property and pay off some small remaining debts. The county school board did not need it and no one else had any conceivable use for the land and buildings. Doc eventually bought the Indian River campus for a few thousand dollars "just out of sentimental reasons," as he phrased it, "and to show some measure of gratitude to the little school that did so much for me." But on Knob Fork weeds replaced the grass, and young hickories and poplars pushed up along the walks and sagging porches. Owls took over the abandoned structures Melungeon workmen had once hammered and fitted together. The dormitories rotted and lurched, and the grandchildren of those workmen rode buses ten miles to a shiny new installation the school board had of its own free will and accord resolved to name "The Thomas Bonham Elementary School." In offering the resolution, board member Jody Gibbs pointed out that Doc was his cousin and had spent a lifetime working for the folks of Knob Fork. "He was there when a lot of us were born and pulled us into the world. He got the state to build us a highway, and he backed the building of this school-house a hundred percent. If they ever wuz a man this community ought to honor, it's Tom Bonham!"

As the old passed away, the new came on in all parts of Slaughter County. The courthouse Big Red had dedicated a score of years earlier had known little paint and few repairs—the county treasury had simply never been able to afford them. So young Dave Baker, the county attorney and a good friend of Doc's, conferred with Judge Woodrow Bonham about the problem. They talked to Doc about it also, and he was enthusiastic about their project. The Federal Accelerated Public Works Program was underway and Ferpy Jordon, the mayor of Blacksville, was laboring in the toils of a federal bureaucracy that was building his town a new city hall and a sewer and water system to match. Ferpy was Doc's fifth cousin. Doc had loaned him money to go to an embalmer's school and he and Charlie's son, Jakie, had set up a funeral home a couple of blocks from the courthouse on another loan. He was a tireless promoter and loved to tell Rotarians about his generous plans for "a new Blacksville." His activities were good for business and good for Blacksville, and in 1963, the wrecker's ball crashed into the walls Harry Hopkins's WPA workers had cemented together.

The old courthouse was clearly outmoded—too small, without air-conditioning, architecturally unprepossessing—so it came down and in 1965, in the middle of a hot campaign to elect his successor, outgoing Governor Jerry Grimes came up to dedicate a brand-new temple of justice. It was built of red brick and lined with Doric pillars in front and rear. The massive building was electrically heated and pulsed in hot weather with soundless air-conditioning. The governor spoke tenderly of the good people of Slaughter County who "under the dedicated leadership of Dr. Tom Bonham and his wonderful, warm-hearted wife—and so many others like Judge Bonham, County Attorney Baker and Mayor Jordon, who are privileged to be both their kinsmen and co-workers—have struggled so successfully to bring progress and lasting solid benefits to the mountain region."

Bix Jennings Carlisle was a youngish man with all the right connections for political advancement. He was a 1954 graduate of Harvard Law School and had worked for two years as an assistant U.S. District Attorney in Washington. Carl Rutherford got him the job as special counsel for the Subversives Control Commission, and he established a sound reputation as a fiery Communist hunter. When he came back home to practice law, his firm specialized in appeals to the state's highest court and its clients included coal, oil, gas, railroad and utilities companies. He looked a little like Senator Edward Kennedy, and the president of Appalachian and Northern thought he would make an excellent governor. When Jerry Grimes was reelected in 1961, he appointed Bix to head the department of highways. The commissioner visited all parts of the state on inspection and speaking tours and was a great favorite as a speaker before Lions, Rotarians and Chambers of Commerce. He loved to be introduced to an audience as "a man of careful and sound instincts who believes this country's problems can and will be solved in reasonable time and at reasonable cost—within our present system of government."

But 1965 was not a good year for Bix J. Carlisle. Jack Weston, the obstreperous tax reformer, ran on a pledge to "put the tax bills where the money is, break the power of the corrupt county and city machines and put the power and the benefits back in the hands of the people where they belong." Nobody took Weston seriously at first. He had little money while Bix was abundantly financed, and he reminded people of problems they wanted to forget or ignore. But the murder of John Kennedy had caused fresh stirrings in the country, and the state had not escaped them. The new and enlarged campuses were crowded with thousands of students and the exodus that had drained rural counties had shifted much political power to the cities. Weston appealed to emerging new alliances, and Jerry Grimes became a harried man as alarming reports and estimates filtered in from the wards and their perplexed mayors. To Doc and Twinkles, the challenger was a Red radical whom they abhorred and who failed to visit them even once in the course of the campaign. He lost all the Indian River counties and the Slaughter County margin was spectacular—5,812 in favor of Carlisle. But the cities and the fast-growing industrial areas in the west were a different matter, and he won the primary by a modest 9,300 votes.

The upset of the intricate political machine Carl Rutherford, Big Red and so many others had so carefully assembled compelled them to reappraise a nearly forgotten man Lucas Finney, the Republican nominee. He had left a circuit judgeship to seek an uncontested nomination on the theory that the time was ripe for a mammoth Democratic split. He was right on target, and a month after Carlisle's defeat, his backers began shifting to Finney. He was a drab, cautious soul who just wanted to be governor for a while, and Doc told some dubious Democrats, "He is a man we can live with for four years, then we'll get rid of 'im. Take my word for it, folks—a tame Republican will be a hell of a lot easier to live with than a wild Democrat!"

The bolt was an unqualified success. Lucas Finney presided over the destinies of the state so serenely that the Democratic legislature never once threatened to impeach him, or even to investigate his appointees to see if they were guilty of fraud, theft and other like misconduct. In fact, he was so grateful to the Democrats who elected him that he and they got along marvelously well to the end, and, in Slaughter County for example, all went on as it had before. The governor perceived that the state employees who worked there were competent, qualified and dedicated people whom there was no need to fire. A few Republicans were added to the payroll from time to time, but they were quiet souls anxious to keep their jobs and wise enough to know 1965 was most unlikely to be repeated in 1969.

CHAPTER
19

The 1960s were hard years for Doc. He was too old, and the world was changing so fast he could not keep up with half that was going on. The big color televisions in his bedroom and living room brought all the problems and difficulties of the world under his roof to plague him nearly as much as they did the visibly sinking LBJ. The power base he had been building and extending for more than three decades was strengthened and refined to the point where he was virtually unchallenged at any point, but the electronic tube disclosed harried men at the White House grappling with vexations they could neither comprehend nor master, and he frequently felt as overwhelmed and futile as they appeared.

Jesse Jackson was duly elected circuit judge in 1960 by a margin that warmed his parents' souls. The people performed marvelously, and from the Wild Pigeon Roost Cliffs at the head of Indian River to the "doubles" of Stone Coal Ridge and southward to the county line beyond Knob Fork, the ballots poured in a torrent—and 81 percent of them were marked for Jesse J.! The men who owned and managed the coal camps were for him because they thought he would take his father's advice at crucial moments and judge the affairs of men in a manner not unfavorable to the rights of property.

Miners who wrested coal from the earth for a living said laboring men had never had better friends than the Bonhams. Eleven thousand people lived and ate because relief checks came once a month to their doors, and few and far between were those old enough to vote who failed to back Doc Bonham's son. A few hundred had to be bought and paid for like any other service rendered one man by another and they were taken care of by the "chain ballot." Doc feared and dreaded voting machines like the plague, and by 1960, Slaughter was the only county in the state that had never bought a one. There was no way to run chain voting on a machine, and when Bonham money went to a man or woman, Doc wanted a Bonham worker to mark the ballot on the outside of the polls and a dependable election officer on the inside to see it safely deposited in the box. It required careful preparation and discreet handling, but Bonham workers were never short of these qualities, and Doc figured all the "trash votes" went to Jesse J. He doubted that "a single vote-selling vagrant" in Slaughter County escaped.

Doc felt good about this, and when Twinkles retired from the superintendent's office three years later, he liked the way it, too, was handled. The schoolteachers bought her a sterling silver punch bowl with no fewer than twenty cups. All bore the monogram "B" and a coat of arms somebody dug up out of heraldic records and imputed to the Bonhams by an ancient and royal decree. The bowl was inscribed "Presented to Supt. Irene Bonham by Slaughter County teachers in grateful remembrance of her many kindnesses to them." There were other gifts, too, and "Happy Dan" came up to make a speech and say education was losing its clearest voice and strongest arm. She would not retire completely though, he said, because he would continue to seek her advice in planning further progress for schools all across the state.

Then the board elected her daughter to carry on the tasks Twinkles was compelled to lay down. Tess was a joy, handling the work with her mother's old skill and finesse and with a smoothness born of long experience in her mother's shadow. Jesse J. was another matter, though, because he frequently came to his parents with furrowed brow and burdened heart to seek their aid on some troubling point of law where the litigants were both old Bonham supporters and were about equal in political influence. And when the pressure of work and troublesome decisions piled up, he tended to drink too much and stay home with his wife, Ruby, and their clutch of brats. He and Ruby would hit the bottle together, and Jesse would come back to his office with a hangover and blackish circles under his eyes. This weakness troubled Doc mightily, for how could a man run a county and hold onto the reins of power others would constantly strive to snatch away if alcohol was his refuge? Tessie was a different story, there was not a doubt about that. She had produced two babies (neither of which, incidentally, turned out to look like a giraffe) with scarcely a day's absence from her work and with a hauteur that was marvelous. When troubles beset her, she attacked them in cold blood, keeping her own counsel so completely that even Slim Jimmy rarely had an inkling of what was afoot. And Doc had to concede to himself that her political instincts had proved virtually flawless at every turn.

Doc left the hospital the year his son became circuit judge

and almost—but not quite—gave up his profession. He looked back on a lifetime that had known only one vacation, and one morning the work he had pursued so long suddenly turned into a chore without challenge or interest. Fifteen years earlier, he had bought the building and its contents from Northeast Coal and Iron, and he offered them to Omar Ross for the same amount of money. But Dr. Ross was moving to Florida, so the hospital was simply emptied of patients and boarded up. Like so many things in Slaughter County, it rotted beside a street on which fewer and fewer people walked, its paint peeling, the glass eyes of its dirt-caked windows staring dully back at all who glanced at its trash-strewn porch. Ferpy Jordon, Jesse J., Tess and Woodrow Bonham got busy on an application for Hill-Burton funds to build a new county hospital to replace the old coal-camp facilities Doc and a handful of his vintage colleagues had operated.

Doc disliked the idea as he disliked the new doctors coming out of the medical schools. Their "group practice" ideas and everlasting emphasis on specialization ran counter to his old-time conviction that they had a personal and unavoidable responsibility to know their patients, and out of that knowledge to diagnose and treat their ailments. Doc mistrusted machines, squiggly lines drawn by electronic monitors to tell what was going on inside a heart, and batteries of tests administered by people he derisively called "flunkies." He preferred the old way of sitting down with a sick man, studying him minutely, hearing the sounds of flowing blood as they came gurgling up to him through his stethoscope, measuring his blood pressure, correlating complaints with all he heard and saw and then moving on to a decision and cure. The new healers were too impersonal, too prone to let things and technicians shield them from their patients, too reluctant to get really deeply involved with their patients' pains and problems. They quit too early in the day, would not make a house call, wanted too many vacations. Doc didn't want such characters brought into Slaughter County, but he kept his misgivings to himself because, after all, no new physician had settled in the county for more than twenty years. There was no other way, and he knew it. Thus the application for the hospital was approved and the money came down from Washington, and the work began.

The College of Medicine at the state university was very helpful, and when the gleaming steel, glass and aluminum facility with its ninety beds opened, there was a staff of seven young doctors, three of whom were, to Doc's vast disgust, Filipinos and Puerto Ricans. Within there was a startling array of diagnostic and treatment devices—everything from X-ray and electrocardiogram machines to laboratories and therapy centers—and the Chicago architect who had envisioned it all showed it off to the county medical society with understandable pride and boundless enthusiasm. Doc stood at the door to one of the huge surgeries and looked at the glittering chrome table under the domed Plexiglas skylight, and its banks of sterilizers, monitors, portable X-ray projectors, dialysis machines and cabinets of implements.

His mind sped back through the decades to the distant day when Ben Fleming showed him through the little hospital on Indian River, and Doc wondered at the youthful pleasure that had thrilled him so much. He relived some of the battles he had fought there against the agony of gunshot wounds, gangrene, trauma suffered in collapsed tunnels and by fiery explosions, the plagues of smallpox, diphtheria, whooping cough, polio, and meningitis, the wracking misery of cancer. He had battled there alone, and later with Omar Ross, to aid and counsel, and with not much else except hunch, intuition and cunning. He shook hands with the young doctors and listened with half an ear to their explanations, and as they talked, he marveled that he had won so many victories. In this sparkling, alien world of the new medicine, he suddenly felt forlorn and even insignificant, and his shoulders sagged like the deep lines that grooved his face.

But the fiscal court, too, remembered Doc's battles on Indian River and the countless nights when he left his bed to carry his medicine bag and his skills to suffering flesh and blood. The JPs remembered also how the powerful Bonham machine had chosen them and boosted them into office. So Refrow Day made a motion that was seconded by Joe Carr's son Denver. All the JPs thought it was a capital idea and approved it, and in time, a huge sign on the corner of the hospital grounds proclaimed: "Dr. Tom J. Bonham Memorial Community Hospital." And there were his name and a likeness of his face cast in an inch-thick bronze plate on the wall near the main entrance.

So many things were going on in the world of medicine that keeping up with even a significant part of them was a Herculean task and Doc was not inclined to take on any such labors. He left the healing up to the young men and their clicking and whirring machines, except for a tiny office he maintained in a discreet brick building on a little flat twenty yards from his house. There he continued to see a few old friends who had been his patients for many years—and a steady trickle of welfare patients clutching their printed forms. These Doc examined with all his old attention to detail, carefully hearing their dolorous accounts of misery and disability and never omitting to inquire into their backgrounds, voting habits and blood and marriage relationships. He knew the older people, all of them and instantly, but the younger ones had to be identified, catalogued and figured out. He no longer needed the fees—ten dollars instead of the original five—but wanted people to continue in the knowledge that where public assistance was concerned, they were sick or well according to his findings.

And there were numberless other things to see about. Teachers and would-be teachers came to enlist his help and Twinkles', sometimes for positions and sometimes for promotions. Men and women jostled for slots in political races, reciting past support of Bonham candidates and laying claims for favors in return. A lot of Doc's old reliable stalwarts were quitting the game or giving up the ghost, and new men of doubtful loyalty had to be sifted through. It was all time consuming, but he and Twinkles had friends in every precinct whose advice on such matters could be depended on and who constituted an excellent surveillance apparatus. Besides, Tess knew all the young bucks and fillies and in the final analysis it was generally she who made the decisions.

Some time back in the fifties, Ben Fleming went off to a nursing home and died; after a few years of floundering about, the Slaughter County Coal Operators Association elected Doc their president. He used the association's money and prestige with ruthless efficiency, fighting pernicious taxes some fool legislator was always proposing and pushing to preserve benefits already enjoyed. He noted with satisfaction that in 1962, 74 percent of the royalties received for coal taken out of his land on Indian River and Powderhorn Creek was tax-exempt as long-term investments and depletion allowances. More than half the mining in Slaughter County was from strip jobs now, and there were bird-brained critics springing up all over the state to complain about the "environmental desecration" and demand an end of the business.

Outrageous beyond belief was the behavior of eleven young VISTA workers who were sent down like a swarm of chattering locusts from an abomination called the Office of Economic Opportunity in Washington. Not one of them sought his advice or that of any elected official who could have set them on a straight and sensible course at the beginning. Instead, they scattered out into the poorest, most dilapidated camps and started preaching that the "establishment" was the people's enemy. They told people the county was in the hands of a political dictatorship that was in league with the coal operators and was stealing them blind. They claimed the Appalachian land was rich and that the people were poor because their state and county governments had betrayed them—selling them "down the river like coffles of slaves," one young rogue insolently phrased it at a meeting. Demand your rights, they insisted. Break the grip of the welfare autocracy and rule your own affairs. Doc was furious with Sam Mitchell and the senators for letting such pests be loosed on the county and at his insistence they quickly demanded their recall. After a few midnight dynamite bombs went off in their yards and some .45 slugs tore through their windows,

Sargent Shriver's young Volunteers in Service to America were reassigned, as Doc wearily allowed, "to worry the flesh off somebody else's bones!"

So many of Doc's old friends had died or were about to that it was just about impossible to keep up with all of them. And when one passed on and Doc went around to pay his respects and say a few words to the widow and children, he was startled to see that most of the descendants had come back from other states, Ohio mostly, but Michigan, Indiana and Florida, too. People Doc remembered as little tykes their parents had once brought to him with the afflictions of childhood were now middle-aged with broods of their own. When Steve Dominic passed on, Doc found that all his offspring were residents of Detroit and one of them at least, Tony the oldest, had done exceedingly well in the plumbing business. He arrived in a blue Cadillac and after the funeral spent a day showing his wife and carload of disbelieving children about the old place where he had grown up before the war.

Then Tom Morton dropped off, and Doc missed the thump of his peg leg as he pounded over from Poor Fork to discuss some need or problem. George Donner's wife called to say he was feeling bad and wondered if Doc might be able to drive out to his house to see about him, but he died of heart failure before Doc could get to Ewalt on Buffalo Creek. Jesse Timmons died of old age, and a multitude of blacks gathered to assure him a splendid funeral at the African Church of the Living God of Prophecy. These and others left blanks in Doc's organization, but new faces and figures moved in, most of whom talked to the judge and superintendent before they got around to discussing matters with him.

Joe Carr's omnivorous appetite caught up with him at sixty-five, and he was fenced in with a hopeless array of ailments and breakdowns—diabetes, kidney insufficiency, and heart failure. When it was much too late to do any good, he went on a crash diet that peeled off forty pounds, then died one morning in the fancy intensive care room at Bonham Memorial. Joe left a goodly sum to his grieving family, and Denver moved in with commendable skill to get most of it for himself and to exert his father's old political influence. Doc liked Denver as a chip off the old block, and he could always count on him for the cautious, carefully considered and generally successful politicking of his father. Still, Doc missed Joe, too, and sat for a long time in sad reflection when the news came that he was no more.

Twinkles went one morning in a manner that should have left Doc shattered and grieving, but much to his own astonishment did not. After she turned her office over to Tess and came home for the rest all agreed she had so richly earned, she took much pleasure in the small flower garden she had planted by the stone steps. The soil was black, fertile and sweet with lime, and in a year or two, her dahlias and chrysanthemums, roses, and daffodils were superb. One June morning she went out early to stir the soil around a plant heavy with huge white roses. Doc read his paper with its maddening account of a Democratic President who could make neither peace nor war and was ruining the country with inflation and trade deficits. He heard the door close as Twinkles came in and went back to their bedroom. An hour later, he laid the paper aside and went to tell her about something he had read. He found her lying on the bed, her eyes closed and apparently asleep. But Doc's eyes told him in an instant that she was dead, and a touch of her waist confirmed it.

Ferpy Jordon did a marvelous job of embalming her body, and Tess and Jesse J. selected a magnificent walnut coffin. Doc had always avoided churches, while carefully pointing out to preachers and deacons that deep inside he was a most truly God-fearing man. His donations washed away their doubts, and his wife's occasional Sunday visits to Blacksville Methodist gave them both a moiety or more of religious respectability. Her funeral was conducted by the Reverend David McCoy, and the church was filled for a day and a half by throngs of people who came to sign the register of "Friends Who Called" and to show their sorrow. Gifts of flowers were banked everywhere, and their cloying perfume lay heavy in the aisle. The people came from every part of the county— the camps and "hollers" and hills—and a shoe box full of cards attested to the sense of loss felt by former students, teachers, and administrators who had served Slaughter County under her tutelage. "Georgie" drove all the way up from his new home in Florida to greet his old friends who had enabled him to make a small fortune selling whiskey in his state-licensed stores, and to remark over and over that "Uncle Tom and Aunt Irene" had made him what he was. Without them, he declared, "I wouldn't be nuthin'."

A delegation from the state department of education attended the services and affirmed the eminence she had achieved as teacher and exemplar. The minister's voice was shaky as he pointed to the immense floral wreaths from the state's senators and congressmen and read their telegrams of tribute and sympathy.

Some of her relatives came up from her home county of James and went away astonished by the many and varied achievements of their kinswoman. She was buried on a green knoll two miles below Blacksville in the Green Gardens Perpetual Care Cemetery she and her husband and Ferpy Jordon had incorporated a couple of years before. With its concrete Christ beckoning at the gate, it had turned out to be a pretty fair business proposition, and Doc dipped into his robust bank account to provide a white marble shaft to mark her place of repose. It was by all odds an impressive piece of work and unlikely ever to be surpassed in those grounds for either size, elegance or cost. In addition to her name and the span of her years, the stone related:

Matchless wife, loving mother, dedicated and selfless public servant—she served her family, friends, county and country with devotion and was universally cherished in both life and death.

Twinkles had been at Doc's side for forty years, and he had accepted and relied upon her as one of like mind. With the zest of a Bonham, he had made love to her well and often until time cooled and jaded her, and he recalled with passion those earlier years when they had slept in a close embrace, her warm breath and perfect breasts and legs close against his own. She had never failed him in anything, and her competence and tirelessness had finely crafted the political machine by which Slaughter County was ruled. In moments of sickness or discouragement, she had been there, quick to sympathize and console. Everyone knew they were a devoted and compatible couple. Still—and this was amazing to Doc as he went through the ordeal of wake, funeral and burial—he was little moved by her loss. He felt detached and unconcerned, as when some stranger had died in his old hospital at Noreco. As a matter of fact, while the preacher played out the final words of his funeral sermon, Doc was calculating the significance of the new gas well Trident Oil had just brought in on the little flat a hundred yards above old Fort Bonham.

Trident Oil was actually run by a wildcatter, J. C. (for Julius Caesar) Huckleberry, a character as unlikely as his name. He was an Oklahoman and a Choctaw who had made and lost a couple of fortunes since 1930. He once had an overpowering weakness for blond women, but time had cured that, clearing his mind for more essential tasks. Among his other attributes was an instinct for land that contained oil and gas, and that instinct brought him to Indian River. He had seen maps of the "dome" that centered around the mouth of Finn's Fork and doubted the conventional wisdom of geologists that held that old fractures in the earth's crust had permitted the gaseous and liquid hydrocarbons to escape. Someone connected with Phillips 66—another Indian, he sometimes hinted—bankrolled the well that Doc authorized, with a proviso that if oil or gas were discovered, a well would be sunk on the Powderhorn Creek land within a year. Doc was to get 12 1/2 percent of the product, "if any," at the well head and other wells would be drilled if the first proved successful.

Huckleberry set up his rig, opened a fifth of Ancient Age and began drilling. At 5,900 feet there was a roar and a flood

of gas and oil blasted the bit from the hole and sent the rig tumbling down the hill. When the hole was capped after a tumultuous week, thousands of barrels of oil had drenched the slopes and the well registered a gas pressure flowing at a rate of 24,000,000 cubic feet per day. Huckleberry named the well after a whore he had once known in St. Louis, "Samantha Discovery Hole No. 1," and Slaughter County's fame spread within hours to the uttermost limits of that strange, circumscribed and rambunctious world in which men live by their drilling rigs and shrewd guesses. Gas prices were rising, and Doc's royalties were certain to be at least eight hundred dollars daily—nearly six hundred of them tax exempt. Pipelines would have to be laid to carry the stuff away, and more wells would have to be drilled, but the field was vast, no doubt of that. And Doc's land lay at the crest of the field, according to J.C. It was along these lines that Doc meditated as the preacher uttered a final prayer and sent the mourners off to the cemetery.

Doc was lonesome in the big house without Twinkles, and both Jesse J. and Tess urged him to close the place and move in with them. But the gray stone immensity was a part of Doc, and he would not leave the thick walls and deep porches, the huge chimneys and heavy roof of red terra-cotta tiles. So he and they set to work to find a housekeeper who could keep it clean and prepare his meals. One of them came up with Ruby Madden, one of those nearly faceless camp people who counted mostly as numbers in elections and on welfare rolls. Her husband, Joshie, had been killed in a slate fall in the mine at Noreco, leaving her with a baby and nothing else. She lived in the camp on a public assistance check of $109 a month for the child's support. She had worked for a while in a restaurant in Hamilton and as a cleaning woman in a motel. She jumped at the chance to move her seven-year-old Minnie from the frail four-room shack to the Bonham house from which rich and powerful people had run the county for so many years. Doc paid her well, and Millie Roberts never got around to terminating her AFDC check. With Doc buying the food and taking care of all the other costs of the household, she rejoiced in the good fortune that had lifted her daughter and herself out of poverty in dismal, rotting Noreco.

She was an excellent housekeeper and a passable cook, and Doc had no cause for discontent. Minnie caught the school bus each morning, and Doc began to enjoy the arrangement that brought the sound of a child's voice to his home again. Time and the tides of worldly affairs had made sexual enjoyment little more than a memory for him, but one morning Doc got to thinking about Ruby and decided she had definite possibilities. She was forty and had never been beautiful, but on the other hand she was not ugly either. She was a bit flat in the chest, perhaps, but her legs and hips were quite nice and her disposition was pleasant. Doc pondered the matter all day, even while he was talking about coal, oil, gas and politics to a succession of visitors, and as night came on and he sat on the broad porch to enjoy the cool evening air, he called his housekeeper to him and forthrightly propositioned her. She giggled, then frowned and said she didn't want to do anything like that, but Doc patted her hips and was insistent. She went to her room to get her daughter ready for bed and to consider the matter. Her wages and AFDC amounted to more than $400 a month, and there was no overhead. She had much to lose and nothing to gain by being difficult, so she bathed, and when Doc turned off his light and went to bed, he heard her footsteps on the hall carpet. She entered, and the door clicked shut behind her. She sat on the edge of the bed unmoving for a few moments, and Doc's heart began pounding with much of the same excitement a strange woman could arouse in him thirty years earlier. He reached out and took her arm, and she slipped between the sheets, hesitant and uncertain. After a moment, he kissed her and began stroking her body. He induced her to take off her pajamas, and he reveled in the joy of having a naked and youngish woman by his side again.

Doc's seventy years and a touch of prostatitis and arthritis had by no means sapped him, and he enjoyed his session with her immensely. She responded enthusiastically, and when they had finished she loosed a long and pleasing sigh. Later she stood up in the moonlight and pulled her pajamas on again and padded silently back to her room. Doc found the bed altogether too big without her, and she came regularly each night after Minnie was asleep. Doc soon found himself relishing her two or three times a week. It was a great restorative for him, that and escape from the pressures of the hospital, so that he turned with the zest of a second youth to money-making and politics. Jesse J. and Tess suspected that something was up and warned against starting a new family, but Doc only snorted. He knew a thing or two and had no intention of getting himself caught in a trap like that.

And it was an incredibly busy time for him. There were so many and such varied things to attend to and worry about, and such an outlandish number of things to go wrong.

In the first place, so many people had left the farms and towns all across the state and piled up in the cities that the old power structure of the Democratic party was being drastically reshaped. Some counties that once contained 20,000 people now had no more than four or five thousand. All the coal counties and the hardscrabble knob country had been especially hard hit, and Doc's old friends everywhere were losing power and prestige with the people at the top. They could win elections at home, but they represented less and less of the party when they attended caucuses and conventions. Twinkles' youngest brother, Jack, was sheriff down in James, as his father had once been long ago, but he called Doc to complain that he couldn't even get an appointment with the governor. And at the same time, the cities were being transformed by rising educational levels and living standards so that the urban politicans were increasingly young, urbane, and even Kennedyish.

They did not talk Doc's language or sympathize with rural viewpoints, and a wide gulf was opening between the relatively liberal city men and the conservative rural leaders. They were always talking about "reform and revitalization" of the party and of the state government, "with broader grassroots participation," the closing of tax "loopholes" and of a new concern for resource conservation. They even proposed to consolidate counties so as to reduce the total number by half, make judges and a number of other officials appointive rather than elective, and reorganize the new state school system so as to tighten state control over expenditures and policies. The idea of a severance tax kept knocking around and gathering support, and some idiot was roaming over the state talking about "the rape of the mountains" by strip miners and calling for laws against it. He was a lawyer from someplace or other and had once addressed several thousand people who, according to the *Herald-Courier*, "listened attentively and applauded frequently." The things he proposed could cost Doc thousands of dollars monthly, and Doc was astonished and outraged when he read that the entire legislative delegation of the state's second largest city had breakfasted with him and listened to his spiel.

He was Newt Deskins, a son of old Will Deskins of Croghan County. Doc knew Will well and no solider, more dependable man ever lived, and yet here was his son leaving his law office to go gallivanting around trying to arouse people to hate an important industry and outlaw it. Furthermore, he never failed to make a pitch for a severance tax of a quarter a ton on all coal! He mystified Doc with his conduct and made it necessary for the coal people to gather one Sunday afternoon at a Holiday Inn a few blocks from the state capital and discuss the implications of it all. The Carsons and half a hundred others met with rail, electric power, and steel company representatives and wrangled all day about the best course of action to take. Doc suggested—and his advice was ultimately followed—that no public reaction was the best, but that a chest of a couple of hundred thousand dollars should be gotten together without delay for the benefit of sensible candidates in the next election of state legislators.

He had scarcely gotten back home and into bed with Ruby Madden again when trouble exploded under his very nose. On Powderhorn Creek where Mountain Movers, Inc., was disassembling a long, snaky ridge Doc had bought at a sheriff's sale in 1932, people became alarmed about the vast amounts of mud sliding from the hills and choking the streams. Three hundred of them petitioned the legislature and the governor to stop "this threat to our community," and led by Doc's friend, Sollie Potter, they came to Doc and pleaded with him to put an end to the operation. Sollie's round face and popeyes gleamed with earnestness as he finished, "You know, Doc, this is mighty rainy country around here and we've had some awful flash floods in past years. Even back then with the creeks all clear and the mountains in brush and timber, as many as eight or ten people have got drownded in one night. Now we're really scared of what will happen with the mountain sides all covered up with loose mud and ever' creek bed choked with it four or five feet deep."

Doc lied to Sollie in a stark and straightforward Machiavellian fashion.

"You know, Sollie, I had had no experience with strip mining when I leased my land on Powderhorn to be stripped. If I had known it would tear it up so much, I would have never signed the lease." He opened his hands and dropped them to his side in a gesture of helpless futility. "But the lease has been signed and is recorded, and I am bound by it. I can't do anything to stop the stripping now, Sollie. I'm as helpless in that respect as you are."

The situation got nightmarish. A band of men and women, most of them old and in the frayed clothing of poverty, undertook to stop Mountain Movers when its workmen started blasting away the vast, pitted, domelike crags called the Dove Rock which the famed naturalist, John James Audubon, had once visited to study and paint the passenger pigeons that swarmed about it in Old Isham's day. The company sued for an injunction which Judge Bonham issued after carefully declaring to a packed courtroom that he was most reluctant to do so, but he could not avoid it as part of his duty under the law. Doc called the governor's office and said he was afraid some of the more excitable young people along the creek might get rash and kill some of the company's employees, and the next morning, eleven state policemen arrived at dawn, red lights flashing ominously on top of their cruisers. When they got out of their cars, the cops carried an arsenal of high-powered rifles, machine guns and automatic shotguns, and the cowed and overawed people scattered to their flimsy little houses. All day long, explosions thundered along the hillcrests, and through the valleys gigantic fragments of sandstone crashed and bounded down the slopes. When the troopers went back to other tasks, Jack Weston came to see the situation and told a press conference that he was appalled by "a conscienceless, vicious rape of the land." However, the newspapers were headlining the passage of LBJ's Appalachian Regional Development Act—under which nearly 80 percent of appropriated funds would be spent for roads and took little note of events happening near the heart of the range the act was designed to save.

A fortnight later, at sunset, immense black clouds gathered above the ridges and thunder and lightning foretold a storm of shattering dimensions. And the storm came in a nightlong cloudburst that sent torrents of water smashing against the rubble. The mud, broken stone, and smashed timber were carried into the creek to form a barricade that resisted for a few minutes the tremendous weight gathering behind it. Then, with a splintering roar, the mound disintegrated and the rubble and water rolled like a juggernaut down the meandering length of Powderhorn Creek. The little houses were lifted up, then flung down and crushed, and the next morning at dawn, Denver Carr knocked on Doc's door to tell him that twenty-seven people were drowned.

"Fourteen houses were plumb washed away, Doc," he avowed, "and a whole lot more people than that may be drownded when we learn the whole story!"

Doc acted at once. He filled his old valise with medicines, stuck his stethoscope and a thermometer in his pocket and went to the scene. But he did not go before he called the governor, Carl Rutherford and Big Red to report the catastrophe and ask for public funds. Then he called Tessie and had her telephone the story to the American Red Cross. When he and Denver Carr started to the stricken community, the lumbering machinery that would send money, food, clothing and shelter had already begun clanking slowly and ponderously into action.

The devastation was indescribable, and Doc worked as hard for the sick, injured and homeless as in any of the old mine disasters that had scourged the county when he was young. He loaned money to some and gave small sums to others, and charged no one for any professional service. The county road crew and men from the state highway department cleaned up the rubble, burning the broken trees and the heaps of planks that had once been houses. The mud and stone was graded into fills and seeded with grass. The White

House and both senators sent representatives to sympathize and pledge help—and the help came in the form of twenty gleaming mobile homes. The people in economic security were magnificent, increasing old welfare allotments and hurriedly approving new ones. Doc called on coal operators and merchants for donations to a relief fund which paid Ferpy Jordon's hefty funeral bills and gave survivors a few hundred dollars each for new furniture and new cars. Doc led the little delegation who delivered the checks, and they were a welcome supplement to the assistance the Red Cross was able to provide. The agency was quite generous though, funneling its benefits through an office they got together with the co-operation of Tess's assistants. Athletic director Jimmy Long volunteered to head it. When the project was finished, he received a citation from ARC headquarters that commended him for his "generous gifts of time and energy in succor of the unfortunate victims of the Powderhorn Creek disaster."

On the whole, it was all handled well, and the griefstricken people were soon snugly settled in their new wood and steel rectangles. Dozens of people told Doc how much they appreciated the help he gave them, and scores of letters and phone calls came from Dayton, Hamilton, Chicago and Detroit to express thanks for favors done their relatives. Sollie Potter summed it up well in late summer when he brought Doc a gift of sparkling fresh vegetables from his garden and said, "Doc, we would all have been ruined teetotally if it hadn't been for you, and the help you wuz able to get us. The people out on Powderhorn Creek will appreciate it as long as you or your children live."

Doc was warmed by this expression of gratitude, but he

was indignant when a group retained Newt Deskins to file a suit for damages against Mountain Movers, Inc. The company's lawyer filed a pleading, asserting that the storm was an act of God and unforeseeable, and after a show of deep and sincere sympathy for the plaintiffs, Judge Jesse Bonham announced that the law being what it was, he felt duty bound to dismiss the complaint. The Supreme Court of Appeals, with Daniel Boone Dickson writing the opinion, upheld the circuit judge a few months later and the tragic incident was closed except for the constant agitating and editorializing in the press. The *Herald-Courier* was especially vitriolic, and Jack Weston declared that he would run for governor again and, if elected, would move to outlaw all strip mining for coal.

To make matters worse, Sam Mitchell became senile and had to retire in 1966. Doc wanted Jesse J. to make the race, but the governor was committed to a young state attorney from Stoner County. With strong backing from the party organization and the coal industry's endorsement, he won handily. Then, to Doc's dismay, he had no more than arrived in Washington when he announced his support for "resource conservation," federal legislation to preserve the quality of water in the country's streams and a new federal mining code "to make U.S. coal mines the safest in the world." He wound up his declaration with an assertion that mountain people must be dealt a better hand of cards. "There must be no more Powderhorn Creek disasters," he vowed.

All this was very disquieting, and Doc hoped young Rafe Chapman would soon get his feet on the ground, learn his way around Washington, and settle down to making the district a good steady congressman, as Sam Mitchell had done. But Doc's misgivings about the new congressman were soon forgotten in a flurry of worry about the 1967 governor's election.

Doc knew for certain that Jack Weston must not be allowed to capture the governor's office. The primary was a rerun of 1963, with coal and its allies supporting Bix Carlisle, now four years older and a good deal wiser. He was determined to take off the gloves in the campaign against Weston and to tell the people of the state just what the reformer's proposals would cost them. The Appalachian & Northern contacted coal men and reminded them of the catastrophic consequences if stripping were outlawed, a severance tax imposed and a stringent new safety code adopted. They met quietly at Doc's house one night and listened to the A & N's vice president, Jasper Myles. "If you want to see your investments turn worthless and your customers driven to companies in other states, just sit still and let this wild man become the next governor!"

Doc led off with the first pledge. He was generous because he wanted to set an example that would make the others generous also. Some of them blanched when Doc pledged $25,000 cash to be delivered when the collector passed through in a couple of weeks. There were thirty-three operators or representatives of mining and land companies present from all the state's mountainous coalfields, and the pledges came to $335,000. The railroad people were generous too, as were the bargeline companies, the utilities and the rural electric co-ops. All of them dealt in coal in one way or another and wanted no new taxes or regulations laid on it. Thus their candidate was able to begin his campaign with nearly a million dollars in cash.

Weston was a tireless campaigner but was almost penniless, and the little money he managed to pick up came almost always in the form of occasional five- or ten-dollar bills. The virtuous, he soon perceived, can spare little lucre for their political champions. He made hundreds of appearances and talked and shook hands until his voice was hoarse and his right hand was tender and swollen. He had a lot of enthusiastic supporters in labor unions and among the young and on the college campuses, but Bix Carlisle's pitch was to the older groups with a vested interest in the state and its future. The television brought him into every living room to describe the state's progress since World War II and to warn that Weston's pledge to build new schools, clean up rivers, provide hundreds of scholarships for poor but ambitious youths, make the coal mines safe and raise the salaries and qualifications of state workers would cost millions in new taxes. "A severance tax on coal won't begin to do the job," Carlisle intoned. "It will drive the coal industry out of the state and put its 25,000 employees out of work and on relief. Then you, Mr. Average Citizen, will pay and pay and pay for the most extravagant spending spree in our history!"

The ad agency filmed Bix surrounded by his lovely wife and three children. For a moment they strode along a crowded street, then created a mountain to look down at a fruitful plain and across to another mountain. There was a balladeer singing the praises of the candidate to the strumming of a guitar; then the camera shifted to scenes of men working, children filing happily into classrooms, cars gliding over a new stretch of interstate highway while an unctuous voice declared, "Bix Carlisle cares about you and your state—all of you and all parts of your state!"

That ad alone cost $50,000—and Doc, Jesse J., the Carson brothers, Bonham Coal and Timber, Mountain Movers, Inc., and a few others whom Doc personally solicited paid it all. Doc himself took the money to the campaign headquarters and delivered it to the candidate and his finance chairman so there would be no doubt about where it came from—or to whom credit should be given for its benefits.

Doc made another effort that paid off handsomely. He called dapper Sam Chaney in his office at the national head-quarters of the United Mine Workers in Washington and persuaded him to come down to the coalfields for a speaking tour. Nattily dressed as ever at seventy-one, a member of the union's international committee and for many years one of the UMW's top organizers and general troubleshooters, the old firebrand brought a message from Tony Boyle that the UMW had no quarrel with strip mining. "Strippers pay the scale," Chaney said from a dozen platforms, "and they provide jobs. Labor and industry stand together against a man who would tax both out of existence. Labor supports its friends, and in this race, its friend is Bix Carlisle."

And Bix Carlisle won—just barely. The margin was tiny, 3,713 for the entire state. The voting machines enabled all the other counties to report final results within four hours after the voting ended—and Weston was ahead by a margin of 2,347. Slaughter, at the head of Indian River and sprawling over hundreds of square miles of jagged, coal-rich mountain-ous country, could not report until the last of its paper ballots had been unfolded, stacked, and carefully counted by twenty-four sweating tabulators. The process was not finished until 8: 10 P.M. on Thursday. County Clerk Elam Free announced the official results: 7,792 for Carlisle, 1,732 for Weston. The victor promptly called to express his genuine and slightly alcoholic gratitude to Doc and the people of Slaughter County and to say that he would never forget either.

Virtually every eligible voter in the county from the merest eighteen to the most crotchety ninety and nine had marked his ballot. Doc, Jesse J., Tess, and their cohorts saw to that with a smooth efficiency born of long experience. A swarm of cars brought them to the polls and carried them back again, and the blind and illiterate were aided by accommodating election officials who quietly marked their ballots for them. Doc thought it the best-managed campaign since he first got interested in politics, and the fact that Weston garnered nearly a third of the votes in the face of implacable opposition by the Bonham machine was a measure of his audacity and appeal. Doc sighed his relief and went to Tess's house for a small victory party. His old bones ached with fatigue as he sipped from a tall frosted glass of Seven-up and Old Grand-Dad and rejoiced that so much had been saved.

CHAPTER

20

Autumn was coming in on Doc's seventy-eighth year, and there was a touch of coolness in the afternoon air. He had been through a busy day that included two lengthy telephone conversations with Governor Carlisle, another with State Democratic Party Chairman R. J. Parker, and one with Carl Rutherford in Washington. Doc had been chairman of the party in Slaughter County for more than thirty continuous years and sometimes calculated a bit ruefully that his telephone bill for political calls amounted to more money each month than most of the workingmen in the county were able to earn.

He put on a woolen sweater and buttoned it down the front of the paunch the years had given him despite his best efforts at dieting and a brisk walk of a mile or two each day. Ruby Madden carried a glass and a pitcher of ice water out to the porch and set them on the round redwood table Twinkles had ordered for their new home an age ago. Ruby had spruced up a lot since she came to live with Doc; he had paid a dentist to fix her teeth, and she went every week to Blacksville to have her hair washed and dressed. She was wearing a stylishly tight knit blouse and slacks, and her buttocks vibrated as she bent to put down the tray, revealing the outline of her panties beneath the clinging cloth. She had been a delight last night, Doc reflected, and he intended to try her again tonight. But he gloomed that his sessions with her were less frequent now, usually twice and sometimes only once a week. God, what he wouldn't gladly pay in the fast-deteriorating dollars of these troubled times for a real honest-to-goodness aphrodisiac.

Doc brought a fifth of Old Grand-Dad from his room and poured an inch of it into the glass, then put in ice and water and stirred them together. He sat down in the spacious walnut rocker Sollie Potter had carved out by hand and given him after Doc's all-out effort to aid the survivors of the Powderhorn Creek disaster. He gazed into the amber depths of the glass, sipped the cool and potent drink and relaxed.

The coal business was booming again, roused into life by talk of the worldwide "energy crisis." Japanese and Germans stayed regularly in the Hospitality House, a new motel Doc, Tess, Jesse J., and a few of their close friends had built just below Blacksville, and enjoyed its splendid view of Indian River Lake which Carl and Big Red had persuaded Congress to direct the Corps of Engineers to build. It had displaced 273 families—most of them Bonhams and Frees and their kith and kin—who were now comfortably resettled in a huge housing project Ferpy Jordon administered as a part of the Blacksville Municipal Housing Administration.

The Great Society had been good to Slaughter County, and the board of education had just completed the Irene Jackson Bonham School for Exceptional Children, a project the federal school people vowed would soon enable "backward, culturally deprived Slaughter County children to move into the mainstream of contemporary American society." Doc snorted his disdain of such foolishness, but shared Tess's pleasure with the project generally. It meant money for the community and new jobs for Tess—after due consultation with her father—to fill. And the Japanese and German coal buyers swimming in the pool at Hospitality House after a day of visiting coal mines, taking samples and analyses and haggling about prices were icing on the cake of Bonham power and achievement. After all, the county was dotted with new consolidated schools, a splendid new hospital and courthouse, and a fifty-nine-mile stretch of four-lane superhighway running through its middle. There was the vocational school under construction to teach livelihoods to four hundred young men and women annually.

Doc had sold the board the site for that building which would stand a mile below Noreco, and was intensely interested in it. All had been paid for with state and federal funds, with only trifling contributions by the county. The population was down to 33,000, and 51 percent of them were drawing relief checks and food stamps, while the surge of mining activity provided jobs for all the able-bodied who remained, and was drawing back again some who had moved away. In spite of the meddling tours of journalists and publicity-hungry senators, there was no hunger in Slaughter County. Everybody was being taken care of one way or the other, and all of it had been engineered by the Bonham organization. As Bix Carlisle had once phrased it, "The Bonhams win because the Bonhams care!"

Still and all, there were ingrates who despised the Bonhams, notwithstanding their tremendous contributions to the progress and well-being of the county. The Runyons and their bunch of dyed-in-the-wool obstructionists didn't amount to much anymore. For more than a generation, nearly all jobs had been barred to them and the frustrated young had left. The others farmed a little, mostly in tobacco, which they grew in the bottom land along Rockhouse and Dead Man Creeks. Doc had eased the pressure on some of the old ones who remained and gotten some of them on public assistance, and "made them into pretty good citizens" in the process because their dependency on the checks acted as a remarkable curb on their old-time virulence.

Even poor old Arthur Hall had been befriended and defanged. He came to Doc one day, down and out in every line of his frail, weary body, to say that he had reached sixty-five and was desperate for money. His application for Social Security had been turned down because he hadn't worked long enough as a "covered" employee. Doc took pity on the wretch and got him a job for a year weighing coal at the dock on Powderhorn Creek. Those four quarters of work made him eligible and he drew the checks to his last day. Doc called the food stamp office where his nieces and nephews dispensed the pieces of paper that had replaced the bags of grub J. Fred Bonham had handed out—and got Arthur a hundred dollars worth of free food every month. He and Doc got to be quite good friends after that, and sometimes when he or his rheumatic wife felt particularly bad they would come to Doc's little office for some pills or a prescription. No, it was not his old enemies that bothered Doc; it was the new ones—and some of them Bonhams at that.

That screwball Newt Deskins had talked so long about

the riches of Appalachia that a lot of the pampered young had pricked up their ears and gotten interested in his message. He told them that they and the land on which they lived were manipulated and exploited like checkers on a board, and that they should organize and take over the courthouse. In one of his scatterbrained speeches, he compared the Appalachian counties with Switzerland and said counties like Slaughter had gotten poor in a rich land, while Switzerland had gotten rich in a poor land. "You have been betrayed, are being betrayed and will be betrayed by Tom J. Bonham as long as you will stand for it! Wise up and wake up and stand up!" he shouted. Some high school students went on a rampage and waved banners saying "Freedom from the Bonham Dictatorship" and "Let the People Run Slaughter County."

Doc wanted to expel the lot of them. Tess cooled him down some, though, by saying it would all blow over and be forgotten, but still Doc didn't like it at all and got the names of all who were involved in the outrage and the names of their parents as well. And there were Bonhams and Frees on the list, and Earlys, Robertses, Potters and Gibbses—all of them related to the man they denounced as a dictator and whose parents Doc had often befriended in times of stress and peril. The new generation, he concluded, is growing up without either gratitude or discipline and will bring the whole country to grief. Besides, they know nothing about their own traditions as a people from backwoods to modern times, and how their forebears fought for this mountain country on battlefields, in courthouses and at polling places. Without such knowledge, Doc gloomed, they cannot understand the obstacles that have been overcome and the progress that has been made for their enjoyment. Parents and schools, he decided, must teach the young about the flesh-and-blood men and women who made—and are continuing to make—this country, and instill appreciation into them and gratitude. Otherwise, Old John-of-All and his descendants have settled this valley to no avail, and the bold and the foreseeing have toiled in vain.

Doc sipped slowly and watched trucks carrying coal to the tipple on the other side of the valley. Newt Deskins liked to point out that their thirty tons exceeded the legal limits by twelve tons. The big Macks had been challenged only once since they came into the county three years earlier, and after that disturbing occasion, someone passed the word to the state police commissioner that oversize and overweight coal trucks in Slaughter County were to be left strictly alone. Doc watched the trucks dump their immense cargoes, and clouds of black coal grit floated away toward the little four-room houses. One of the last things Ben Fleming did before he left the management of the company was to lay the town out in surveyed lots and sell the little rectangles and the houses at auction to the camp people. A house and lot had brought about a thousand dollars in 1952 and few had received a drop of paint since. In a few days, though, Doc noted with a little surge of satisfaction, a gang of "happy pappy" relief workers would start painting and repairing the old shacks under an OEO project.

All Office of Economic Opportunity efforts in the county were supervised by County Judge Woodrow Bonham's son, John, and by Tilford's grandson, Winston. They had master's degrees in the social sciences and were pushing a series of "programs" that were very beneficial and had brought them a glowing note of commendation from Sargent Shriver's office. Doc watched the dust settle over the thin walls the pauper workmen would paint and wondered how much of the "black lung" and emphysema he had diagnosed in nearly fifty years of practice had been contracted in the mines and how much from the dust clouds billowing from the shaker screens on the tipples and the acrid smoke emanating from the burning dumps. It was a sad situation, but, anyway, one could not accede to West Virginia Congressman Ken Hechler's crazy notion that the environment in the coal country ought to be cleaned up to fit some ideal standard. It would cost too much and hinder or destroy the industry that keeps the power plants burning. Coal is dangerous, Doc decided, and people who dig it and live in its shadow just have to make some sacrifices in health and in other important respects as well.

His eyes wandered to the decapitated hills on Finn's Fork. The spare, rock-capped, timber-cloaked ridges that T. Finn had discovered and on which he had hunted deer, elk, and bear had been reduced to flat-topped stumps. Nothing grew on the sinister yellow mesas, and here and there on their low dead tops, pools of sulfurous water reflected the slanting sun rays. The slopes were mounded beneath the rubble from the "top removal" that had recovered the Moose seam and the immense contour gashes and augering that had torn into the Gray Elk and Splint veins. Only near the ghastly, mudchoked stream where Finn's black bears had once lain in wait for unwary bass had any vegetation survived the clumps of weeds—an occasional willow or sycamore. The rest—the oaks, beeches, gums, hickories and tulip trees, the ferns, mosses, lichens and wild flowers—had been swept away and buried by a storm more ruinous than any that ever swept Flanders or Monte Cassino. Slides of dirt and huge yellow rocks had rolled into the yard around Fort Bonham so that the old cabin seemed to heave itself up out of an engulfing and primordial sink. Beyond the cabin on the little flat, deep layers of mud had crept down to the graveyard where so many of Doc's ancestors were buried, and he made a mental note to send a man to shovel it away and build a wall to prevent further encroachments.

It was an ugly sight and Doc wished it could have been avoided, but progress has to be paid for by somebody and something. This hill was dead, and Old John-of-All's place and the weed-grown campus of the abandoned institute choking beneath a layer of mud were doomed, too, but they had not died for nothing. Doc's stock portfolio bulged with GM Appalachian and Northern, Mountain Electric, Ohio and Southern Barge Lines, AT&T and several of the petroleum giants. He had two or three safe deposit boxes at the bank stuffed with state and municipal bonds. And without the accumulation of capital, there could be no progress for any society, he mused. Yes, this land and its people had been good to Doc, and he acknowledged it with humility.

In return he had given a lifetime of work to the people—he and his wife and both their children, as a matter of fact, had been sacrificed to their service. And his children were continuing that service and would do so to their last gasp. And most of the people—the solid, decent ones, at least—were grateful for that concern and labor, as demonstrated by the good people of Powderhorn Creek who, at Doc's request, had voted four to one for Bix Carlisle in last year's gubernatorial election. On the whole, he felt pretty good about things and relished the soft glow imparted by his glass.

The new situation in the coal market had made something of a giant out of Mountain Movers, Inc. Doc had chosen to keep his involvement in the corporation a secret known only to his own household and to the Carsons and the firm's accountants. What people didn't know couldn't hurt them, and a hell of a lot of resentment had grown up against the Canadians. After all, it had outgrown the Bonham lands, and the company had leased huge tracts of mineral from Northeast Coal and Iron and Indian River Minerals Corporation. The trouble lay in the fact that these companies owned the minerals under the old deeds William Bonham had denounced to his inquiring clients, while the grandchildren of those clients owned the surface—or thought they did. The industry and the Carson brothers in particular— thought otherwise, because they calculated that ownership of the minerals implied the right to mine them. Did not the yellowed documents declare the mineral owner could do anything "necessary or convenient" to get out the coal? And what of the waiver of damages "and all claims for damages?" Roy and Jay Carson and their lawyers asserted the right to strip-mine on their leaseholds, even if stripping totally ruined the land, and without having to pay the surface owner for his loss, either.

Of course, the farmers and small landowners along the creeks were aghast and raised a rumpus. They lined up Newt Deskins as their lawyer, and there were lawsuits. Jesse J. vacated the bench, claiming kinship with some of the agitated landowners—most of whom were Frees, Earlys, Bonhams and Gibbses. The chief justice consulted his colleague, Justice Daniel Boone Dickson, as to the appointment of a suitable special judge to try the cases. Daniel Boone consulted Doc, and Doc called Carl Rutherford. These deliberations brought Circuit Judge Elmer Jackson up from the counties of James, Croghan and Bonner to rule on the difficult issues raised by the clash of interests between mountaineers and mining companies. None of the plaintiffs suspected that the new judge was a second cousin to Jesse J., but, in any event, old William Bonham had foreseen the outcome more than sixty years before. Judge Jackson decided that the coal companies were proceeding within the powers granted by the old deeds and enjoined the "surface owners" from "hindering" the strippers or "molesting them in any way." In these legal battles, Doc won the everlasting gratitude of the companies and their lawyers by rummaging around somewhere and finding a copy of an age-yellowed legal opinion written by his father for some people who were thinking of selling their minerals. The document warned that the buyers would acquire legal authority to destroy the surface if they wanted to do so, and cited court cases so ruling. The lawyers said the opinion showed there was "a meeting of minds" on the matter when the deeds were signed and that Doc was descended from a most astute and discerning counselor.

Mountain Movers and five or six other companies had torn up twelve thousand acres since then. That lovely troublemaker Naomi Howard turned up again from someplace or other to agitate and raise hell about the operations, but nothing much came of her efforts. There was one thing sure—the country had to have coal or turn off the lights—so everybody who knew anything or was anybody backed the strippers. Still, there was a measure of justice in the claims of the other side, too, so the federal government answered Ferpy Jordon's plea for new housing. The municipal developments spread in clusters up and down Indian Valley and along the hill slopes, and the displaced people were gathered into the lookalike houses along the fresh asphalt. Heat and electricity costs were included in the low rents and the stripping had reduced most of the people to welfare, so they were well cared for after all. As stripping splashed its way across the county, the Bonham organization was able to take care of most of the displaced and in better houses than they had ever owned along the creeks. Ferpy's latest project was a new wrinkle, a park for fifty trailers or "mobile homes" near the mouth of Bonham's Branch for the old people of Rum Creek and Knob Fork, who were being routed out of their cabins and little shacks by Mountain Movers' immense new operation, Lazarus Mine No. 3.

Doc felt good about the new houses and trailers and the successful resettlement efforts he had pushed so hard. Yes, the people were a thousand times better off now, but still he was glad things had been handled so discreetly. A lot of people were against progress and wanted to cling to the old ways and to their isolated houses and gardens with their pigs, chickens, and cows. Such people hated the Carsons and frequently brought their sentiments to Doc's attention, but, of course, he could do nothing for them except sympathize. To such he pointed out that the TVA was burning the coal and the TVA was an arm of the U.S. Government—and even

Adolf Hitler and his master race had bowed before the U.S. Government. Still, things could be eased a little for everybody and Doc had done his best to help out. As the ice clinked in his glass, he wondered whether HEW could be persuaded to finance some rows of houses for the flattened trunks of mountains overlooking Fort Bonham. Perhaps trees could be planted and grass sowed. If so, there would be some more much-needed shelter for indigent persons and surely the land, even in its present sad state, would be worth at least a few thousand dollars to its owner if sold for such a benevolent purpose.

Amid all that had happened to him in the last few days, Doc had deeply and genuinely regretted the death of his old and cherished friend, Richard "Big Red" Brady. Doc had never asked the senator for anything he did not receive, and he had never disappointed the senator either. They had understood each other perfectly, and their long association had produced innumerable benefits and advantages for Slaughter County, and for themselves as well. Big Red recognized the rise of a new mood across America, a strange blending of rebellion and many old prejudices that television commentators sometimes called "the new populism," and he rejoiced in it. He accepted an invitation to discuss the phenomenon at Huey Long's old campus at Baton Rouge and used the occasion to extol the virtues of "the Kingfish" and his mighty contribution to American democracy.

He was just moving into high gear before a receptive audience of several thousands when the end came. His red hair had turned white, but the freckles and fair skin still burned through in all their Irish glory as he clenched his right hand into a fighter's fist and slammed it into his left palm. "For a lifetime my calling has been public service, and I urge you to join me in it! It is a calling that will set your feet on a hard and rocky road beset by burning suns and the lonely darkness and chill winds of long dreary nights. But at the end it will bring you a reward only the just and unselfish can know." Big Red paused, his hands dropped to his sides, and he pitched forward dead as a mackerel. The papers headlined the dramatic manner of his passing, but not until after Jane Bonham had called Doc to tell him that his friend and her own was no more.

Doc went to the funeral in the tiny lumber and cotton village of six hundred where Big Red had started his climb up out of the cotton rows. Dignitaries crowded nearly all the local people out of the little church, and Doc sat a few rows behind Bix Carlisle and the venerable Carl Rutherford and marveled that so many good things could be dreamed up and uttered about a man after he was dead. Then after the turf was back in place over the dead senator's grave and the last prayer had been read, the governor murmured that he hoped Doc could visit him at his office about 11 o'clock on the following day.

Doc went, taking a dozen splendid white, red and yellow roses for the receptionists and typists, and they received him as if he were royalty. "Miss Louise" Hardin, the governor's lovely personal secretary, planted a succulent kiss on his cheek and said, "We just can't ever do enough to show our appreciation to the wonderful, wonderful people of Slaughter County!"

Bix Carlisle sat behind the same huge red desk at which

Doc had first found Big Red back when the New Deal was spreading goodies across the land. R. J. Parker was there and the Carsons and some of the other businessmen whose generous support had made the governor's victory possible. There were enough of them that they crowded the executive office as the governor leaned back in his tall leather swivel chair with his hands clasped behind his head and talked to them and Doc about the appointment of a successor to Senator Brady—an appointment the governor was required to make for the thirteen months until a senator could be "duly elected and qualified."

It was, he said, a ticklish and difficult task. The state boasted dozens of men and women who could fill any office with honor and distinction. And there were dozens to whom the governor owed a heavy burden of gratitude. He could not appoint them all—only one could be chosen, and he hoped the others would feel neither anger nor disappointment. He had discussed the matter with his most trusted advisers, and they agreed with him that Dr. Thomas J. Bonham was in a position to render another great service to the state.

He turned to look at Doc, and Doc drew his own cards close against his chest. There was one other little matter, however, and at this point Jasper Myles of Appalachian and Northern took up the subject. "Doc," he said, "to put it bluntly, the way you have always thought and talked, we want you to go to Washington as senator for the next thirteen months. You deserve the honor and will make a damned fine senator. But we want you to join us next year and help us elect Governor Carlisle for the regular term." Then, after a pause and a smile, "You're like me, Doc. You'll be just too damn old after that anyway. You'll know how to do it, but you just won't be able to get going on it!"

Doc was all modesty and humility in accepting the honor and the office. He would seek the advice of his friends in discharging its duties and would be cautious and discreet in reaching decisions. He was grateful to all for their confidence and to the governor especially, and until Bix Carlisle arrived next November, he would stand firmly beside Carl Ruther-ford in his matchless service to the state and country. He was not wholly successful in preventing the escape of a tear as the good and loyal friends who had gathered at the governor's behest pressed about to shake his hand and offer their con-gratulations.

Doc told no one about the governor's decision, not even Jesse J. and Tess. Nor did he tell them about the sealed letter the governor had handed to him at the end of their meeting. They could learn of them like everyone else when the gov-ernor made his announcement and issued the official man-date. Doc would have to go back to the state capital on Monday of the coming week for a sort of introduction to the people of the state, and he mulled over the statement he would make to the press and television on that occasion. He wanted to sound liberal and progressive so as to impress and please the media, but without embarrassing the governor in conservative quarters or tying himself to liberal positions on specific issues. Carl had once summed up the proper credo for a congressman with, "Talk liberal and vote the way you want to!"

Doc poured more bourbon into his glass and felt so good that when Ruby came out onto the porch, he ran his hand around one of her legs and pulled her over to him. He stroked the knitted cloth as it hugged her thigh and wondered how he could sneak her into Washington and how the miner's widow from Noreco would take to the nation's capital. One thing was certain, he had no intention of going without her.

When she went back into the house, he hiccuped and took the governor's letter from his shirt pocket and reread it. It reiterated that Dr. Bonham was the governor's choice for the high office so tragically vacated by the death of Senator Brady. It expressed the governor's pleasure that the doctor shared his own thoughts about the future and the necessity of protecting and perpetuating the ideals and principles of government to which both so staunchly adhered. There was a strong conviction in the governor's mind that his appointee could and would bring new luster to their party, the party which had served so well and for so many generations the best interests of "the broad spectrum of the American people, from the poor to the rich and including all races, creeds and colors."

Doc savored with special pleasure the concluding paragraph:

"The Bonhams are a numerous and honored line in our mountain counties and have served the state and nation many times in peace and war, and in keeping with their long and distinguished tradition, you have labored for the people of your county through a lifetime, as physician, industrialist, employer, and spokesman. You have earned and enjoy their respect, confidence and esteem. I can think of no one so well prepared by background and temperament as yourself to advance the general welfare of the people of this state in the

United States Senate."

Doc knew that as a stalwart party warrior he had earned the year in Washington and felt up to its challenges. At his age and as an appointee, he would not set the place on fire, but he would do his duty, and his vote would equal Mike Mansfield's or Hugh Scott's on any roll call. He had learned a lot about the art of persuasion, and a quiet voice coming out of a lifetime of experience in politics, medicine, business and public service at the nethermost grass-roots might carry considerable weight with younger men. Certain it was that he would take some solid opinions to Washington.

Now there was that federal severance tax bill Senator Lee Metcalf of Montana was sponsoring, with a proviso that the money would come back to the states and counties. It would apply to all minerals taken out of the American earth and would raise a half billion dollars a year. It sounded logical enough to a lot of people, but Doc could point up weaknesses in the scheme. Here was something to strongly oppose for the next thirteen months.

The war in Vietnam was an issue on which the new senator wasted little sentiment. From the beginning, he had been against U.S. involvement, and all the ill effects he had foreseen had come to pass, including inflation, tumult and rioting in the cities, less money for domestic programs, and frustration on the battlefield. But he would support no settlement without honor! The nation's good name must be preserved even if it meant bombing Vietnam into a desert. Jesse J. had served his country in World War II, and this generation of young men had no right to complain of a year or two spent fighting its battles. He would give the grumblers and complainers little comfort, indeed.

He was going to be a law-and-order senator, too. Law officers would get his unstinting support for appropriations, and if some long-haired radical dissenters got shot down now and then, that would be all for the good in any event.

The federal education acts ought, by all odds, to be simplified so superintendents like Tess could get the money without a lot of strings attached for special purposes and programs. Local officials should spend the funds for general purposes, knowing from long and intimate experience with their needs and problems where and how best to spend them.

Doc sighed and frowned at the thought of Senator Edward Kennedy. The Massachusetts solon was a young whippersnapper with a lot of phony ideas about the country's medical needs. The old system was good enough, without a lot of complicated "special impact programs" leading straight to national socialized medicine. Doc was for a simple setup that would give eligible welfare people a card so stating, with federal funds funneled down through the states taking care of their bills as rendered by the doctor. The physicians could be trusted to see that their colleagues were honest and that the arrangement was not abused. A lot of meddling federal supervisors and snoopers were to be avoided at all costs. It was better to deal with state men anytime.

With nearly all the coal mined out of its hills, Doc hoped he could get a Corps of Engineers dam approved for the mouth of Powderhorn Creek. That would be the best thing to do with Rockhouse and the Camp Fork, too. The people could be resettled in projects, and the undesirables like most of the remaining Runyons could be eliminated by taking their old houses without setting them up in new ones. Building costs were so high that only a handful would collect enough from the government to provide roofs of their own. With a few such "reservoirs" the whole shape and character of Slaughter County could be recast for the future.

Doc pondered the possibility of promoting some kind of new industry for the county to hire the hundreds of young men and women Tess's schools were turning out, but he was suspicious of factories. He had observed that in other counties they brought in rebellious people who had a bad influence on local folks, and the managers were often uppity and uncooperative. The employees looked to the plant and its union and lost contact with their friends in the courthouse who had done so much for them and their parents in the past. Factories were eagerly sought because they brought jobs and money to backward counties, but they could bring upheavals, too, and the most pernicious disquiets.

There was one idea he would support wholeheartedly: federal fund-sharing with states, cities, towns, and counties. Doc agreed with Bix Carlisle that there should be no federal requirements or limits on the spending. If Slaughter County, for example, received a half million dollars, the elected officials should dispose of it for such roads, schools or other purposes as they deemed prudent. Take, for example, Slaughter County. Woodrow Bonham, Tess, Jesse J., and their friends knew the people's needs and could be trusted to act wisely in their behalf. "Unfettered funds" was the phrase that appealed to Doc. What, he mused, could not he and Twinkles have accomplished in their time with a few hundred thousand dollars a year from Washington?—free and unfettered and with dependable regularity!

Doc reread Bix Carlisle's letter. He was a bit wobbly as he poured himself another drink of the excellent bourbon, but not so wobbly that he disagreed at all with His Excellency's conclusion. The Senate, he glowed happily, was a fitting reward indeed for the years of service rendered to a poor and helpless people, just as Rose Quinlan had urged him to do back when life and the world were new.

BOOKS BY HARRY M. CAUDILL

Night Comes to the Cumberlands, 1963.

Dark Hills to Westward: The Saga of Jenny Wiley, 1969.

My Land Is Dying, 1971.

The Senator From Slaughter County, 1973.

The Watches of the Night, 1976.

A Darkness at Dawn, 1976.

The Mountain, the Miner and the Lord, and Other Tales from a Country Law Office, 1980.

Theirs Be the Power: The Moguls of Eastern Kentucky, 1983.

Lester's Progress, 1986.

Slender Is the Thread: Tales from a Country Law Office, 1987.